GET THE DAMN STORY

GET THE DAMN STORY

HOMER BIGART AND THE GREAT AGE OF AMERICAN NEWSPAPERS

Thomas W. Lippman

Georgetown University Press | Washington, DC

Library of Congress Cataloging-in-Publication Data

Names: Lippman, Thomas W., author.
Title: Get the damn story : Homer Bigart and the great age of
    American newspapers / Thomas W. Lippman.
Description: Washington, DC : Georgetown University Press, 2023. |
    Includes bibliographical references and index.
Identifiers: LCCN 2022005784 (print) | LCCN 2022005785 (ebook) |
    ISBN 9781647122973 (hardcover) | ISBN 9781647122980 (ebook)
Subjects: LCSH: Bigart, Homer, 1907–1991. | Reporters and
    reporting—United States—Biography. | War correspondents—
    United States—Biography.
Classification: LCC PN4874.B467 L56 2023 (print) | LCC
    PN4874.B467 (ebook) | DDC 070.4/333092 [B]—
    dc23/eng/20220721
LC record available at https://lccn.loc.gov/2022005784
LC ebook record available at https://lccn.loc.gov/2022005785

⊗ This paper meets the requirements of ANSI/NISO Z39.48-1992
(Permanence of Paper).

24 23   9 8 7 6 5 4 3 2   First printing

Printed in the United States of America

Cover design by Faceout Studio, Tim Green
Interior design by Classic City Composition

CONTENTS

A FEW WORDS OF GRATITUDE

Any writer of history or biography needs the help of professional archivists and research librarians to track down documents, letters, and other relevant material. Much of the research for this book was conducted during the COVID-19 pandemic of 2020–21, which made the archivists' work even more difficult than usual.

I am deeply grateful to the staffs at the Mississippi State University Library; the Wisconsin State Historical Society; the New York Public Library; the Historical Society of Wayne County, Pennsylvania; and the Library of Congress who went the extra mile to help me find what I needed.

I am also grateful to my agent, Janet Reid, and to my wife, Sidney, who read drafts of the manuscript and improved it. Any errors it may contain are my own.

Undated portrait of Homer Bigart. Photographer unknown.
Courtesy Wisconsin Historical Society.

INTRODUCTION

Upstairs, in a haze of cigarette smoke, men in shirtsleeves, collars unbuttoned, pecked at typewriters with their index fingers. Some had their heads cocked to hold telephone receivers on their shoulders as they listened while typing. The noise level swelled as deadline approached.

Below street level, men in overalls and square paper hats loaded thick rolls of paper onto giant printing presses. Soon the product of those operations would be bundled onto trucks for delivery around the city. The big room upstairs and the factory downstairs had put another day's newspaper on the streets. It was the community's information lifeline.

Before the advent of radio and television, and long before the rise of social media, that newspaper, printed on paper and sold at newsstands on street corners for a few cents, set the conversational agenda for the people of the United States. Through much of the twentieth century, most cities of any size had multiple daily papers; small communities might rely on a single weekly. Either way, the newspaper was the primary source of information about government, politics, crime, sports, business, schools, the economy, natural disasters, entertainment, and world affairs.

Reporters, the people who gathered the news that appeared in the paper, were prominent figures in popular culture, featured in plays such as *The Front Page* and movies such as *Foreign Correspondent* and *His Girl Friday*. Orson Welles's portrayal of a newspaper magnate in *Citizen Kane* became a cinema classic. Even Superman was a reporter, in the person of the mild-mannered Clark Kent of the *Daily Planet*. The newspaper people of these fictional versions may not always have been admirable, but they were always entertaining.

At real-life newspapers, reporters were mostly less colorful than those cinematic heroes, but their job by its nature often brought them drama and danger. The best of them, by acclamation of his peers, was a rumpled, hard-drinking war correspondent named Homer William Bigart.

1

He had more lives than a cat and came close to losing several of them on battlefields in Europe, on Pacific islands, in Korea, and in Vietnam. Two soldiers with whom he shared a foxhole were killed by a mortar shell, but he survived to write about it. On Iwo Jima he took shelter against incoming fire, only to discover that he was on the wrong side of his little barricade. On a dark night in Korea, he and other reporters were trapped on a hairpin turn while North Korean soldiers fired at them; the others were wounded but he emerged unscathed. Vietcong rifle fire shattered the cockpit of his helicopter over the Mekong Delta; he walked away to tell the tale. His accounts of courage and terror, of bold leadership and timorous folly, brought him accolades and awards that made him the most honored reporter of his generation. His was the best of print journalism at a time when print journalism was preeminent.

Even after broadcast news established its value during World War II, no radio or television outlet matched the scope and depth of information available in print. Newspaper reporters worked in every city hall, state capitol, school board office, police headquarters, courthouse, and sports arena and in most government agencies in Washington. Families treasured newspaper clippings about a child's achievement in a sport, a school play, a winning entry in a baking contest, and even a first Communion, and looked to newspapers for reports about sons and brothers serving in the military. The newspaper was where readers found the stock market tables and sports box scores.

During World War II, radio reporters delivered gripping accounts of the conflict in Europe, but otherwise radio and later television brought little beyond sports and entertainment. They were not a primary source of news about of most of life's events, and because networks aimed at national audiences, their news coverage gave little time to local and community developments.

By the early 1950s, according to the Federal Communications Commission, "stations that were owned and operated by networks began to add their own local news segments: New York's WNBC in 1954, followed by CBS's WTOP in Washington, D.C., WBBM in Chicago, and WCAU in Philadelphia. Initially, their coverage was limited to a 'man-on-camera' format—an anchor reading telegraph announcements." Most of the stations not owned by the networks were owned by newspapers.[1]

Until 1963 the evening news broadcasts on the three national television networks lasted only fifteen minutes, a good part of which was devoted to commercials. People were dependent on the papers for the information that shaped their lives. In those pre-cable, pre-internet days, not so many decades ago, the decisions Americans made about what to wear, what to buy, what to see, and whom to vote for were largely based on what they saw in their local papers and not just in the news columns but in the advertisements. What's at the movies? What's this week's special at Safeway or Kroger? Check the ad in the paper.

The most successful and most reliable newspapers were those whose owners and publishers were committed to spending the money to deliver a high-quality product and who hired hardworking, deep-digging reporters determined to go beyond the obvious and the official.

It is easy to dismiss reporters as witnesses to great events rather than participants, as bystanders free to point fingers and cast blame at no risk to themselves. But as the Founding Fathers recognized in the First Amendment, the work of reporters is fundamental to the development of an informed citizenry that can hold to account authority figures, public servants, and business executives.

Homer Bigart was one of the first to expose the effects of radiation sickness among survivors at Hiroshima in 1945. His classic series of articles on hunger in America revealed poverty and privation that few in the educated classes had known about. And he was the first correspondent to recognize the fallacy and self-delusion of the US intervention in Vietnam. His articles about the early days of that conflict and his tutelage of young colleagues there planted the seed of skepticism that came to characterize press coverage of America's lethal misadventure in Indochina and stoked popular opposition to it.

When I arrived in Vietnam in 1972 as a correspondent for the *Washington Post,* Bigart had been gone from Saigon ten years, but the war was still going on, with no victory in sight—just as he had foreseen. Nearly sixty thousand Americans had died in a conflict that Bigart had recognized from the beginning as futile. He would have preferred not to be vindicated at that cost.

Bigart was a college dropout from a small town in Pennsylvania who spoke with a stutter that worsened when he was angry—not a promising background for a reporter. But he was recognized throughout journalism as the best at what he did, the definitive foreign correspondent and war reporter. He was the model aspiring young reporters such as myself wanted to grow up to be. He won every major prize and award in journalism, some more than once.

New York Times editor A. M. "Abe" Rosenthal once wrote of him, "There are reporters, good reporters, very good reporters, superb reporters, and Homer Bigart."[2] His colleague Malcolm Browne reflected opinion in newsrooms everywhere when he wrote that Bigart was "the very model of a hard-bitten, hard-driving reporter—infuriatingly dogged, abrasive, honest, brave, unmoved by political rhetoric and surprisingly learned."[3]

Some people assumed from Bigart's stutter that he was slow-witted. Andy Rooney, one of Bigart's sidekicks in covering World War II and later the resident curmudgeon of *60 Minutes*, wrote of him, "When I first heard Homer interviewing someone, he sounded so dumb and uninformed about the subject that I thought he'd lose the interest of the person he was talking to."[4] Bigart often took advantage of people's sympathy by playing the simpleton so that those he was interviewing would explain things to him patiently and in detail. His friends in the press corps called it "Homer's all-American dummy act."

Keyes (pronounced *Kize*) Beech, a veteran foreign correspondent for the *Chicago Daily News*, once wrote that among other attributes "the ideal foreign correspondent would command all the tools of the linguist, sociologist, anthropologist, and economist" and would be "gay and witty at diplomatic functions, as fluent in French, the language of diplomacy, as in his native tongue."[5]

By those standards, Bigart didn't qualify. He studied French in college but always said he knew none, and on the job he spoke no language other than English. He had no training in economics and was contemptuous of diplomatic stuffed shirts. But he met Beech's other criteria: he was daring, resourceful, courageous, and willing to listen to the impoverished and powerless. Skeptical of authority, he was a relentless questioner, and he learned early in his career not to accept at face value the statements of generals or politicians.

Bigart had no political agenda and was not a crusader. He had no interest in celebrity or self-promotion, and he was largely indifferent to fashion. If a movie were made about him today, his role would be better suited to Jeff Bridges than Brad Pitt. But he knew instinctively that the official account of any major event is never the whole story or even the true story. There was always more to be learned, especially when the politicians and generals did not want him to learn it. The bigger the office, the more brass on the hat, the more they had their own interests to protect. Bigart's goal was to find the way around them, or through them, to get the full picture.

In twenty-six years at the *New York Herald Tribune* and seventeen more at the *New York Times*, Bigart chronicled and brought to life the events that defined the era: the wars in Europe, the Pacific, Korea, and Vietnam; the civil rights movement; the creation of Israel; the end of colonialism in Africa; and the Cuban Revolution. He visited Hiroshima two weeks after Japan surrendered and described the effects of the atomic bomb. He was the first correspondent to penetrate the Haganah, the militant Zionist underground in Palestine. He recounted the trial of Adolf Eichmann, the Army-McCarthy hearings, and the court-martial of William Calley Jr. A model of versatility, he also wrote with verve and compassion about strip mining in Kentucky, squalor on the Bowery, the murder of two young women in their apartment in Manhattan, and a tobacco-spitting contest in Mississippi.

He was good at listening to the disenfranchised and the otherwise unheard, and he had a gift for spotting small details that propelled his narrative.

Bigart's four-thousand-word dispatch "From a Foxhole in Korea," describing a rout of American forces, became a classic of war reporting. "A particularly grisly feature of the action," the third paragraph said, "was the shooting in cold blood of seven Americans who were captured by the Communists. The men, four of whom were driving jeeploads of ammunition forward in a last-gasp effort to keep the force supplied, surrendered to the hordes of North Koreans who were overrunning the roads. The Reds dragged them from their jeeps, tied their hands behind them and shot them in the face, ignoring their cries for mercy."[6] Of the three reporters who witnessed that engagement, he was the only one who survived it.

That paragraph reflected Bigart's just-the-facts style; he appreciated the wisdom of gruff old editors everywhere who preached that the better the story, the less you have to hoke it up. The details—"shot them in the face"—carried the narrative. When Bigart died in 1991, his obituary in the *Times* said that his news articles were "taut, witty and astringently understated, even when created under deadline pressure and the appalling conditions imposed by war and famine, even when they concerned mundane events that lesser reporters regarded as routine."[7]

The newspapers of Bigart's day were incubators of some of America's best and most prominent writers: H. L. Mencken, Ring Lardner Jr., Heywood Broun, Tom Wolfe, Nora Ephron, Pete Hamill, Gay Talese. Bigart did not aspire to join those ranks. Not for him the transition to books or to *The New Yorker*. Nor did he desire to become a columnist, opining on events reported by others. He wanted to tell one great story as best he could and move on to the next. He never wrote a memoir or any other book, and in letters to his family he was not much given to introspection. He relished what one of his first editors called the "sweet satisfactions" of the reporter's trade: the deadlines, the competition, the thrill of a big story, and the sheer fun of seeing something new every day and getting paid for it.

Bigart's closest friend and confidante at the *Times* was Betsy Wade, a copy editor who had worked for the *Herald Tribune* until she was fired for getting pregnant. (Wade was later the lead plaintiff in a lawsuit against the *Times* by female newsroom employees who complained—rightly—about gender discrimination in pay and assignments.)[8] When Wade said that she sometimes felt depressed because newspaper articles often seemed ephemeral and she "despaired of ever doing anything enduring," he replied, "As you say, the newspaper business is an inadequate vehicle, but it will take a profound psychological shock to make me ever want to rise above it. I have no burning message." As another colleague put it, "All he wanted was to get the damn story."[9]

Books about the *New York Times* written by senior editors of Bigart's time such as Max Frankel, Arthur Gelb, and Harrison Salisbury contain long accounts of rivalries and power struggles at the top of the newsroom hierarchy. Bigart never wanted to play in that arena; he had little use for editors of any rank. He often refused to read his own articles when they appeared in the paper because he didn't want to see what editors had done to his copy. When a burly fellow named Charlie McLendon was appointed city editor of the *Herald Tribune* in 1936, Bigart sneered, "If this were a bank, there'd be a r-r-run on it."[10] Later, at the *Times,* he threatened to quit at least twice when he thought the editors were not backing him up.

Despite all his renown, despite the two Pulitzer Prizes, the George Polk Award, the Overseas Press Club Award, and the other honors that he gathered, Bigart never made much money. Reporters were working stiffs; unlike television personalities, they did not have agents who referred to a client as "the talent." In 1961 when he had been at the *Times* for more than five years and was a star of the reporting staff, he received a pay raise from $326.05 per week to $360. "Please note on your records that this is a merit increase," Managing Editor Clifton Daniel, who as a reporter had been Bigart's competitor in the Middle East, wrote in a memo to the accounting department.[11] That was equivalent to about $3,100 a week in today's dollars–comfortable and more than most reporters made but hardly lavish. Bigart worried about money for much of his career because he was helping to support his parents and a sister in Pennsylvania, and he never seemed to have enough. But his profession gave him a life of exotic travel and perilous adventure that he could not have matched in business, the law, or even the military. His expense account gave him access to hotels and restaurants around the world that he could not have afforded on his own money. He appreciated the good life. A fine meal and a few well-mixed cocktails compensated for whatever danger and hardship the day had brought.

His success never went to his head, and he never put on airs about the work he did. "Gough's is indeed a low saloon," he said about a popular *Times* watering hole across Forty-Third Street, "but newspapering is a low profession."[12] He was never flamboyant, and he was generally indifferent to fashion. I had the privilege of watching him in action at the beginning of my career, when we both worked in the vast newsroom of the *New York Times.* He had stylistic quirks—he double- or triple-spaced between words when typing—but he was mostly unobtrusive when he wasn't arguing with editors. That only increased the esteem in which colleagues held him. Whether they also liked him personally is another matter; he was irascible and could be very difficult to work with.

The news business is much different now, of course, from what it was in Bigart's generation. Most news is delivered online, even by the major newspapers that still publish print editions; some members of their staffs have titles and job descriptions that Bigart would not have comprehended. The deadline is always now, not four or five hours from now. But regardless of the current clamor about supposedly "fake news," the basic principles of the reporting trade are unchanged:

find out what happened, gather all the facts, and tell the story in clear, interesting language. Bigart did that better than anyone else.

Some people who become journalists, including myself, are hooked from an early age, perhaps at the high school newspaper, and never want to do anything else. Probably more are like Homer Bigart, who originally wanted to become an architect; they get into the news business more or less by accident and find a home there. They can do that regardless of what they studied or how well they did in school because the business has no standard set of credentials. Pilots, doctors, plumbers, and hairdressers require licenses, but reporters do not. Some of the best never studied journalism at all; if they knew economics or chemistry or political science, they could learn reporting on the job.

President Donald J. Trump may have considered reporters to be "enemies of the people," and the news media's collective credibility may have diminished in the age of Twitter, but a career such as Bigart's demonstrates the value to a democratic society of a relentless, inquiring mind examining its institutions and the people who run them. The subject may be the local school board rather than the White House or the 101st Airborne Division, but the principle is the same: the truth matters. The reporter's job is to dig it out.

ONE

FROM SMALL TOWN
TO GOTHAM

At the Green Gates Cemetery outside Hawley, Pennsylvania, there is no gate-keeper, no custodian, and no posted guide to the headstones. Visitors looking for the grave of Homer Bigart or any other of the dearly departed have to go back into town, to Teeters' Furniture store and funeral home, which has stood at Main and Church Streets since 1845. Teeters' made the coffins for decades and still maintains a crumbling, hand-drawn chart showing who is buried where.

It is an oddly charming quirk for a town of about thirteen hundred residents tucked into the Pocono Mountains, far from any big city. Its small-town environment is enhanced by the absence of chain restaurants and auto parts stores; those are ten miles west, in Honesdale, the seat of Wayne County. All but a few of Hawley's residents are White, everyone seems to know everyone, and the same family names have appeared on businesses for generations. Hawley's principal commercial activity is tourism, centered on nearby Lake Wallenpaupack, but it was a coal town when Homer William Bigart was born there on October 25, 1907. The town is named for Irad Hawley, the first president of the Pennsylvania Coal Company. On its railway line and on barges on the Delaware and Hudson Canal, the town was a transportation hub for the shipment of anthracite coal to New York.

Homer Bigart's father, Homer S. Bigart, made his living in the area's other principal business, textiles. He ran a woolen knitting mill, Bigart & Kerl, whose long-defunct plant is now an office building. That enterprise began in a large red barn that still stands behind the family home at 824 Church Street, a modest clapboard house in a comfortable neighborhood. Bigart spent his boyhood there, although he may have been born next door in a house owned by his mother, Anna Schardt. He worked at the knitting mill after school. The family was insulated from World War I because Homer was too young to be drafted, his father too old.

Outside 824 is a faded plaque that summarizes the career of this renowned son of Hawley:

Formerly home of
Pulitzer Prize Journalist
Homer W. Bigart 1907–1991
World-wide and Wartime Correspondent
New York Herald Tribune 1929–1955 and
New York Times 1955–1972

In smaller type it lists many of his awards, including two Pulitzer Prizes, and some of his major reporting assignments, including World War II and the wars in Korea and Vietnam, and the trial of the Nazi war criminal Adolf Eichmann. It also summarizes his education: "Hawley Schools Carnegie Institute New York University."

As with any such monument, the information is accurate, but it tells little about the person described. It gives no clues about how a small-town boy with a bad stutter developed into a globe-trotting war correspondent who was the toast of his profession.

As a youth, he was a good enough student to gain admission to a selective college, despite his stutter, but there are no surviving records of his academic performance at tiny Hawley High School, from which he graduated in 1926. The school was too small to have a yearbook, and it ceased to exist decades ago when it was consolidated into a regional high school several miles away.

In Bigart's formative years, the country was experiencing what became known as "the Roaring Twenties," a prosperous postwar era of big industry, big bands, big bootleggers, and short skirts. "I was brought up in the 1920s when all kids thought like they do in the present generation," he told an interviewer many years later, "that they didn't have to really work, they were going to get richer and richer. I decided I would become an architect because it sounded so prestigious and easy. Especially easy."[1] One reason he thought architecture would be easy was that it required relatively little conversation, which was difficult for him because of his stutter.

Bigart's parents never left Hawley, even after his father's business failed during the Great Depression, nor did his sister Gladys, who lived there all her eighty-six years. Young Homer, however, was soon up and out, and would spend the next half century traveling the world. He was a big-city guy throughout his working life, and if the rolling countryside of the Poconos and Lake Wallenpaupack instilled in him any love of nature and the outdoors, there was little sign of it until after his retirement.

His first stop was Pittsburgh, at the other end of Pennsylvania, where he enrolled to study architecture at Carnegie Institute of Technology (now Carnegie Mellon University). He "quickly discovered that if you were going to be an architect you at least had to learn how to draw. But I couldn't even do that," he said. "The only passing grade I got was English, so I decided that about the only thing I could do was to become a newspaperman."[2]

Just like that, after showing no previous interest in the news business? In fact, the decision may have been made for him. After the debacle at Carnegie Tech, he needed someplace to go—other than back to Hawley—and something to do. "Luckily," he said, "a high school pal of mine had a copy boy's job on the *New York Herald Tribune* and he got me a job. I went to New York in 1927."

It was easier to break into frontline newspaper journalism in that era than it is today, because there were far more papers and less competition for jobs, given, as Bigart said, "that the pay was extremely low."[3]

New York was not the object of his boyhood ambitions; it was just the place where fate took him. "I felt as though I had to be pushed out in the world," he recalled. "That sounds pretty corny, doesn't it?"[4]

At the *Herald Tribune*, popularly known as the *Trib*, he reported for work as a part-time copyboy on the night shift and launched himself into the improbable life of adventure and accomplishment that would draw the admiration and envy of his colleagues and competitors.

His starting salary was twelve dollars a week. New York was a good place to live during the Great Depression, he recalled, because "everything was cheap." He got a room near Prospect Park in Brooklyn for three dollars a week; it wasn't much, but at least it was clean and had no bedbugs. He often took his meals at the Automat, a unique New York institution where a few coins opened a vending machine door to some item of food inside.[5]

Bigart interacted very little with New York's theaters, galleries, and upscale restaurants. If he had girlfriends, there is no trace of them, partly because he worked till midnight and partly because he was back in college and paying for it himself.[6] Beginning with the fall semester in 1927, he enrolled in a full slate of courses at New York University's journalism school. By his account, New York University (NYU) at the time "would take anybody, regardless of his grades," and its journalism school "was absolutely horrible."[7]

According to NYU records, he took three journalism courses in his first semester plus Economics 1, French 3, Law 1, Management 1, and Technology and Information 1. He took a similarly heavy program in each semester through the spring of 1930. In French, he got as far as French 6, which he could not have done without learning at least the basics, but throughout his professional life, he insisted to colleagues and editors that he knew no French and was handicapped by this lack in French-speaking lands such as Algeria and Indochina.

Asked on a personnel questionnaire that he filled out years later, "What, approximately, was your academic standing?" he replied, "Very poor." Asked what his major was and why he had selected it, he wrote, "Failed in architecture at Carnegie; took up journalism at NYU because only good grade at Carnegie was in English." He gave no response to questions about extracurricular activities, participation in sports, military service, summer jobs, or foreign languages.[8]

New York University declined to disclose his grades, but based on the personnel questionnaire, it is safe to say that he did not distinguish himself. He never received a degree, but journalism is one of the few white-collar occupations for which no degree is required. What matters is the ability to get the story and beat the competition. When Richard Kluger, the author of the definitive history of the *Herald Tribune*, asked Bigart to describe his philosophy of journalism, he replied, "I just wanted to get the goddam story written."[9]

With the onset of the Great Depression, his father's business faltered. Bigart, sending money home, did not have enough money to continue his studies, so he became a copyboy full time.[10] His salary went up to twenty-five dollars a week.

The New York News Scene

When Bigart entered the shabby newsroom of the *Herald Tribune*, he was entering the rough-and-tumble, competitive, colorful world of New York newspapers, a world that was about as far as he could get from small-town Hawley.

In this new, bigger world, daily newspapers were ubiquitous and fiercely competitive. They were as much a part of New York life as the subway. In the city's business districts, there was a newsstand on every corner, selling the latest editions as well as cigarettes and snacks.

In the endlessly restless city of Broadway and Greenwich Village and Wall Street, of high culture at the museums, and of honky-tonk at Coney Island, a newsstand stood upstairs from every subway station or downstairs from every elevated train station; many stations had newsstands on the waiting platforms.

"In those days a well-loaded newsstand was a fine sight, particularly around the noon hour, when the just arrived city editions of the afternoon papers would have been stacked in place," wrote Joel Sayre, who began a long New York newspaper career a few years before Bigart. "They really looked good and were a pleasure to handle, and you could take an armload of them to read at lunch, reading them against each other, tearing out stories and columns and editorials and cartoons that you liked."[11]

In those very early days of radio, and long before television, newspapers were the city's lifeblood of information, as they were for much of the country. Only in 1920 did radio station KDKA in Pittsburgh broadcast the first widely heard report on the results of a presidential election, and the information it put on the air was provided by a local newspaper, not obtained through its own reporting. The days of networks of broadcast correspondents were still in the future.

Many New York subway commuters read one newspaper on the way to work in the morning, another on the way home. It cost only a few cents to buy a paper, so almost everybody could afford to read one. The riders' choice of paper reflected who they were: the guy in overalls reading the *Daily Mirror* had little in common with the gentleman in the suit reading the *Herald Tribune,* except their mutual New Yorkness. They could both be New York Yankees fans or like their bagels untoasted, but they surely did not live in similar neighborhoods or send their children to the same schools.

As people moved about the city and through their day, the latest editions of the newspapers were to them what the cellphone is today. The essential information the papers conveyed lay not just in news articles but in voluminous charts and tables: stock market activity, ship arrivals at the port, Broadway theater listings, horse-racing results, baseball box scores, the weather. Virtually every merchant—automobile dealers, grocery stores, department stores—used advertisements in the local paper as the primary channel for delivering information about what was for sale. Classified ads filled page after page. All the information routinely available online today was then available only in newspapers.

Other cities had good newspapers, of course—there were about twenty-five hundred daily papers nationwide, twice as many as today—but none of those cities was as big or diverse as New York or had as many papers. New York's morning papers were especially influential in cultural matters. A review of a new Broadway play in one of the big New York dailies could determine its fate as no out-of-town paper could. In cities that developed in the automobile age, with little public transportation, such as Houston and Los Angeles, newspapers were important conduits of information but were consumed differently. People commuted in their cars, not on trains, so they read their newspapers at home—morning editions over breakfast, evening papers after work.

In some superficial ways, the proliferation of news outlets that readers can find today online, ranging across the full spectrum from political right to left, from serious to frivolous, from authoritative to dubious, is not much different from what readers had in the 1930s except that now the words and photos appear on a screen rather than the printed page.

But it's not the same. Newspapers in Bigart's day had a tactile, almost personal relationship with their readers and their communities. They occupied impressive buildings in the center of town. Passersby could watch their trucks roll away from the loading docks with the latest editions. Their reporters, photographers, printers, and advertising sales representatives lived among the readers. In many communities, local boys delivered the papers to subscribers, often by bicycle; that was the first paying job for millions of youngsters, including me. Advertisers were mostly local merchants and, in the classified pages, local people. None of those characteristics applies to the *Daily Beast* or *Vox,* or even to the online *New York Times.*

The papers competed not just on news and opinion content but also on the quality and verve of the writing. Many reporters and opinion columnists became well-known writers, including H. L. Mencken of the *Baltimore Sun*, Heywood Broun of the *New York World*, Ring Lardner of the *Chicago Tribune*, Damon Runyon of the Hearst Newspaper syndicate, and Ernest Hemingway, who went to Paris as a correspondent for the *Toronto Star* and later covered the Spanish Civil War. Jack London reported on the Russo-Japanese War for the *San Francisco Examiner*.

Sports news and writing provided a forum in which many journalists rose to writing prominence. Americans who were sports fans, and even many who were not, could quote Grantland Rice's purple-prose account, in the *Herald Tribune*, of a football game between Notre Dame and Army at New York's Polo Grounds in 1924:

> Outlined against a blue-gray October sky the Four Horsemen rode again. In dramatic lore they are known as famine, pestilence, destruction and death. These are only aliases. Their real names are: Stuhldreher, Miller, Crowley and Layden. They formed the crest of the South Bend cyclone before which another fighting Army team was swept over the precipice at the Polo Grounds this afternoon as 55,000 spectators peered down upon the bewildering panorama spread out upon the green plain below.

Rice's nationwide fame and the popularity of other sportswriters spurred the stodgy *Times* to create its Sports of the Times column in 1924.[12]

Beginning at about the time Bigart got into the business and for decades afterward, newspapers and newspapermen—they were almost all men—captured the popular imagination through plays and movies. They were sometimes depicted as raffish characters, as in the play *The Front Page*, and sometimes as well-dressed sophisticates. In the film *Northside 777*, James Stewart, as a crusading reporter trying to prove the innocence of a man accused of murder, wore a pinstripe suit and a fedora; he was the most elegant police reporter ever. One of Alfred Hitchcock's first Hollywood hits was *Foreign Correspondent*, featuring a trench-coated Joel McCrea as an American reporter sorting out intrigue in prewar England. Walter Winchell, an influential columnist for the Hearst newspaper chain, was the model for the vicious character played by Burt Lancaster in the movie *The Sweet Smell of Success*.

When the renowned newsman Pete Hamill reached his eighty-fourth birthday in 2019, a profile in the *New York Times* said he was "a star city columnist when such a thing was still possible . . . a living archetype of a dying breed, the celebrity newspaperman—famous enough that in 1977 Jimmy Breslin, his friend and fellow columnist at the New York Daily News, outed him for dating Jacqueline

Kennedy Onassis." HBO filmed a profile of Breslin and Hamill, portraying them as "two Irish outer-borough guys who became kings of the city back when New Yorkers still announced who they were by the newspapers they read."[13]

As Bigart began his career, New York had eleven daily papers of general circulation; some had hyphenated names, indicating that they were products of mergers in earlier years when the city had even more papers. Only the *Times,* the *Daily News,* and the *Post* are still in business, but in Bigart's day the whole crowded corral competed not only for readers but also for advertisers. The rates a paper could charge an advertiser depended on the number of its readers, just as the rates a television station can charge advertisers today depend on the size of the audience. The advertisers' choice of where to spend their money often reflected the demographics of the papers' readership: high-end department stores on Fifth Avenue advertised in the *Times* and *Herald Tribune*; the discount stores in other neighborhoods advertised mostly in the tabloids.

According to Frank Luther Mott's comprehensive history, the newspaper landscape of Bigart's early days had largely been shaped by World War I, the first great international conflict of the telegraph age in which the United States participated. Americans discovered international news, which was costly for newspapers to acquire because it involved sending reporters overseas, covering their expenses, and paying the fees for the cables they filed.[14] International cable companies charged by the word. Just as people today who have data limits on their phones may write "ICYMI" in texts instead of "in case you missed it" to save words and money, overseas reporters and diplomats of the twentieth century developed a peculiar pidgin of abbreviations and combined words to save cable costs. Conjunctions were often omitted; the pronoun "I" was written as "eye" to distinguish it from the number 1. In the absence of punctuation, the end of a sentence was marked by the word "stop," the end of a question by the word "query." Every international reporter knew the (probably apocryphal) story of a foreign correspondent who, scooped by a competitor, received a cabled message from his editor back home: "WHY WE UNHAVE QUERY NEED MATCHER SOONEST." Hemingway, furious at an editor who asked to see his paperwork before reimbursing his expenses, cabled, "SUGGEST YOU UPSTICK BOOKS ASSWARDS."[15]

During the Great War of 1914–18, many afternoon papers thrived because the time difference between Europe and the United States made it possible to publish news of developments earlier that same day. After Armistice Day, the United States was a world power, and foreign news retained its new importance with the unraveling of the Weimar Republic and the rise of Joseph Stalin. But the cost of obtaining international news—reporters' travel expenses, cable fees, and subscriptions to global news agencies such as the Associated Press (AP)—squeezed many publications. Smaller papers fell by the wayside, some merged to pool their resources, and many relied entirely on the AP and other news agencies for their reports from overseas.

Some papers raised their prices, but even a penny increase could drive readers away. If they had been buying two papers, they dropped the one that raised its price. Joseph Pulitzer's *New York World*, for example, failed when it raised its price from two cents to three while the *Times* and the *Herald Tribune* stayed at two. Advertisers, Mott wrote, "found it cheaper to buy space in one paper with general circulation, even at increased rates, rather than in two with overlapping coverage."[16] More mergers followed as publishers found it more efficient to put out a morning paper and an evening paper in the same printing plant, using the same circulation trucks. Newspapers that had been independent sold themselves to chains such as Hearst, which could supply all their papers with news from Washington or Berlin out of a single bureau. The consolidation and contraction of daily newspapers across America, a topic of frequent hand-wringing commentary in today's era of online news, was already under way even before Bigart joined the *Trib*.

By 1930, according to Mott, "eight cities of over 100,000 population were served either by one paper or by a morning and evening newspaper under the same ownership."[17] New York, even with eleven citywide papers, had far fewer than it had before the Great War; in the decade after Bigart went to work, the Great Depression would reduce the field even more. The number of papers declined, but the pressure to compete with those that remained did not.

Four of the papers that were publishing in New York when Bigart started were tabloids; the others, including the *Herald Tribune*, were full-size papers known as broadsheets. Every New Yorker who read a broadsheet on the subway knew how to fold it so that it could be read in the cramped spaces on crowded trains.

At the top of the list in status and authority was the august *New York Times*, the only one that did not have circulation-boosting features such as comic strips and a horoscope column. The *Herald Tribune* was a close second, unable to match the *Times* in depth and scope of coverage but often livelier and better written. Out-manned on big stories, Joel Sayre recalled, "we tried to beat them by outwriting them" and often succeeded.[18]

In the economic and educational levels of their readers, and correspondingly in their influence on public policy and on culture, the *Times* and the *Trib* stood above and apart from the others. At the bottom of the prestige ranks was the *Evening Graphic*, a scurrilous tabloid created in 1924 by the fitness guru Bernarr Macfadden. It never achieved much traction with the public and went out of business in 1932.

Each of the other papers had its own style and its own stars.

The *Daily News*, a morning tabloid, was founded shortly after World War I by the family that owned the *Chicago Tribune*. Purchased each day by more than a quarter of New York's people, it had the largest circulation of any general interest newspaper in the country; it was a paper for the masses. It won many honors for its serious reporting, but its foundation was a breezy combination of photos, gossip, crime news, garish headlines, and outstanding sports reporting. It billed itself as "New York's Picture Newspaper."

It was the *Daily News* that sent a reporter to a New York prison in 1928 to cover the execution of a woman named Ruth Snyder, convicted of murdering her husband. The reporter smuggled in a small camera under a trouser leg and shot a photo of her, strapped into the electric chair, at the moment of death. The next morning the photo took up the entire front page of the *News*, under the headline "Dead!" Years later, during New York's financial crisis of the 1970s, the *News* reported President Gerald R. Ford's refusal to provide assistance under the famous headline "Ford to City: Drop Dead."

The newspaper tycoon William Randolph Hearst created another morning tabloid, the *Daily Mirror*, in 1924 to compete with the *News*, and it did so energetically if not profitably. The paper featured bright young writers such as Ring Lardner Jr., and it published Walter Winchell's popular column. Winchell was in a class by himself: he set up shop every night in the Stork Club, the center of New York nightlife, looking for celebrity gossip, and then roamed the streets in the wee hours while listening to a police radio scanner, looking for crime. He had a punchy writing style—one woman, he wrote, "has been on more laps than a napkin"—and coined clever phrases, such as "Reno-vated" to describe a quickie Nevada divorce.[19] His column was widely popular and syndicated nationwide by the Hearst chain, but it was not enough to make the *Mirror* profitable. Hearst subsidized it with profits from the chain's other papers.

The *New York Post* was an afternoon tabloid, as it still is. Founded in 1801 by Alexander Hamilton, it claimed to be the oldest continuously published paper in the country. The paper has run such immortal headlines as "Headless Body in Topless Bar" and "Bezos Exposes Pecker," the latter on a story about Amazon founder Jeff Bezos's feud with David Pecker, the publisher of the *National Enquirer* gossip sheet. Under longtime publisher Dorothy Schiff, the *Post* was reliably liberal and featured such popular columnists as Murray Kempton, Pete Hamill, and Eleanor Roosevelt. It underwent a political reversal after Rupert Murdoch purchased it in 1976 and is now strongly right wing in its news coverage as well as its editorials. Its best-known feature is the gossip column known as Page Six.

The New York *World*, founded in 1860, was the paper that brought the publisher Joseph Pulitzer to New York from his base in St. Louis. He bought the paper in 1883 and introduced one innovation after another to back his circulation war with Hearst, catering in particular to immigrants. The paper was one of the first to appeal specifically to women, with articles about fashion, food, and etiquette. The

World also published the first color supplement. Nellie Bly made her reputation as an investigative reporter at the *World* by having herself committed to a mental hospital and exposing conditions there. Among its star writers were Heywood Broun and Westbrook Pegler.

Hearst published the broadsheets *New York Journal* and *New York American*, the *Journal* in the morning and the *American* in the afternoon. The *American* created the first full-page comics section in 1912. Ford Frick was a sportswriter for the *American* before becoming the president of baseball's National League and later the commissioner of Major League Baseball.[20] In the late nineteenth century, the *Journal* published a comic strip called "The Yellow Kid," as did Pulitzer's *World*. The term "yellow journalism" is believed to have originated as a description of their circulation war, which featured scandalous and sensational stories. Hearst merged his New York broadsheets into a single afternoon paper in 1937.

James Gordon Bennett founded the *New York Telegram*, an evening paper, in 1867. It merged with the *World*, becoming the *World-Telegram*, in 1931, a year before Bigart was promoted to reporter at the *Herald Tribune*.

The *Sun*, founded in 1833 and priced at one cent, was popular with working-class New Yorkers who found in it stories about crime and other matters of interest to them that appeared nowhere else. It was the first newspaper to print an account of a suicide. It is best remembered for its 1897 editorial assuring eight-year-old Virginia O'Hanlon that "yes, Virginia, there is a Santa Claus." The *Sun* merged with the *World-Telegram* in 1950.

These newspapers were circulated citywide and sought their circulation among the population at large, but they were by no means the city's only dailies. Each of the five boroughs had its own paper, such as the *Brooklyn Eagle* and the *Bronx Home News*. Specialized papers catered to specific segments of the economy: the *Wall Street Journal*, the *Journal of Commerce*, and *Women's Wear Daily*, which chronicled the city's garment industry. The *Amsterdam News*, founded in Harlem in 1909, devoted its pages to coverage of New York's Black community, which the mainstream press mostly ignored. The *Daily Racing Form*, which billed itself as "America's leading turf authority since 1894," offered comprehensive coverage of horse racing across the country. The Communist Party USA published its own paper in New York, the *Daily Worker*. And then there were the foreign-language papers serving immigrants whose primary language was Italian, German, Greek, Spanish, or Yiddish.

The Yiddish paper, the *Daily Forward*, was widely known as the "Daily Backward" because it was read from right to left, back to front. Everyone in the news business had heard the joke about the reporter for the *Forward* who ran into the newsroom with some big scoop yelling, "Hold the back page!"

Every reporter writing about news of the city was in two competitions—against all those other papers, to find something they did not have, and against his colleagues for space and display in his own paper.

Dramatic Changes in the Business

During Bigart's first decade in New York, the news business changed in dramatic ways. The Great Depression spurred the deaths of some papers and the consolidation of others. After an uproar over the Ruth Snyder execution photo prompted the *Daily News* to clean up its act, and after the demise of the *Graphic*, the blood-and-sex tabloid wars subsided. As more Americans went to the movies, they could see faraway events reported in newsreels, which were more vivid than words on paper. And the rapid growth of radio enabled Americans to consume their news in different ways. The Depression-era Rural Electrification Administration extended electricity service across the country, making radio accessible in remote hamlets and previously isolated farms. Whereas before the 1930s most Americans were limited to whatever news they could find in their local papers, with the spread of radio and its news networks, all Americans had access to the same news at the same time delivered in the same accent. As the historian Jill Lepore wrote, "With radio, more than with any other technology of communication, before or since, Americans gained a sense of their shared suffering and shared ideals: they listened to one another's voices."[21] Live sports broadcasting began in 1921, with the blow-by-blow call of a boxing match. The first major league baseball game was broadcast the same year, followed by the first live broadcast of a college football game.[22] By the mid-1930s, it was no longer sufficient for newspapers simply to report results and brief accounts of how they came about. Sports fans knew that information almost as soon as the games ended. They wanted their newspapers to give them less from the playing field and more from the locker room or interview session.

Bigart, beginning his career as a reporter and learning how to do the job, was oddly unaffected by these developments. The genteel *Herald Tribune* was largely uninterested in the excesses of the tabloids; its competition was the *Times*. Radio, no matter how fast it expanded, could not deliver to New Yorkers the sophisticated coverage of culture, politics, and commerce that the good newspapers offered. Bigart's job as a reporter was pretty much the same in 1940 as it had been at the beginning of the Depression. And he seems never to have gotten caught up in the show business appeal of the newspaper world or in the romance of New York. Little in his correspondence or in interviews he gave later shows his interest in New York's theater or jazz clubs or museums. He stayed home at night to read. He came to appreciate fine food and witty companions, but if he ever developed any interest in the art or the romance of city life, there is little trace of it. In an interview he gave to the writer Karen Rothmyer years later, he recounted the entire period between his arrival in New York in 1927 and the start of World War II in a single paragraph.

As he learned the newspaper business from the ground up at the *Herald Tribune*, Bigart would have benefited from the attention of a mentor, an elder statesman of the newsroom who would have imparted his wisdom and experience. That should have been Stanley Walker, the revered city editor, who understood news and the people who reported it, saw all their flaws and those of his organization, and yet appreciated what he called the "sweet satisfactions" of newspapering.

As the city editor from 1928 to 1935, Walker was not much concerned with the rise of fascism in Europe or the Japanese invasion of China or the politics of the New Deal. His territory was the New York metropolitan area, where Bigart worked for the first decade of his reporting career.

In his 1934 book titled simply *City Editor*, Walker wrote that the person in that job is usually not the "consistently brutal curmudgeon" of reporters' tales who tortures his staff, the "mythical agate-eyed Torquemada with the paste-pots and scissors." In reality, he "appears to be very much like other men. He suffers from migraine and buck fever. He has moments of fumbling and fright; he knows that no matter how good he is, he is not quite good enough."[23] Some city editors snarl and lose their tempers, some drink too much, and some "drive themselves without mercy" and expect their reporters to do the same. All have to deal with "the parade of freaks and fakers and mountebanks, the complaints and libel suits, the reporters who got drunk and couldn't write their stories, the campaign to get a $5 a week raise for a deserving reporter with a wife and too many children, the pictures with the wrong captions, the tense speed of election night [and] the patient drive to instill a few sensible 'don'ts' into the lives of young men."

Yet for all that grief, he wrote, "the city editor has one of the best jobs which journalism has to offer" because of his influence over the newspaper's content and the careers of his staff.[24]

In Bigart's case, that influence was not at all helpful. For some years, Walker was not interested in promoting Bigart to reporter because Bigart did not meet his standards of education or class background.

Walker believed that the era of the reporter of unsavory reputation, who "gets his greatest scoops while sleeping off a drunk in some boozy haven in the red-light district," was coming to an end. New times called for better-educated, more sophisticated practitioners. The new generation, he said, "often flabbergast elders with their erudition—a scholarly but lively sense of words, a sound background in history and economics, the ability to translate or even to speak two or three foreign languages, a comprehensive knowledge of literature, and sometimes a definite expertness in art and music."[25]

One of the beginners at the paper during Walker's tenure fit his criteria for the new era of journalism—the elegantly attired, patrician Joseph Alsop, Harvard class of 1932, a native of New York's posh Upper East Side. Another did not—Homer Bigart, a young man from a Pennsylvania coal town with a bad stutter and no college degree.

Alsop was an indolent slacker who had done nothing to distinguish himself at Harvard; he did not write for the Harvard *Crimson*. He could not type or drive a car. He got the job because his grandmother had been a friend of the Reid family, the *Trib*'s owners. All his life, even years later when he was an influential columnist, he affected an English accent and wore bow ties. Between reporting assignments, he ostentatiously read Proust in French in the newsroom. He even had a Japanese manservant.[26]

Bigart, on the other hand, was a hustler, doing the mundane work that copyboys do while also taking on writing assignments that full-fledged reporters disdained, such as covering Sunday sermons by prominent clergymen. "After a while," he recalled, "I started doing obits that people would phone in. The paper paid space rates then—you got paid according to how much you wrote. As a result, I wrote up many a humble person way beyond his worth."[27] Writing a simple obituary is normally not difficult, but for him, asking questions and obtaining information over the telephone was a challenge because of his stutter.

He stayed with it, he said, because he was "hungry." As Betsy Wade put it, he "just wanted to get the damned story."[28]

That determination showed even in the thankless job of writing obituaries, which he did with the enterprise and passion for accurate detail that became his trademarks. He once found in the *New York Times* a paid death notice of a prominent college president and wrote a news obit about it, beating the *Times* to the story.[29]

Five Years a Copyboy

The job of a copyboy is to move paper around the newsroom, from reporters to editors and from editors to reporters, and to keep the reporters and editors supplied with paper and pencils. It is also a traditional break-in job for young people hoping to learn the business and rise higher. Alsop never put in time as a copyboy; he was hired as a reporter despite his total lack of experience. Bigart, striving to work his way up, rose no higher than chief copyboy for five years.

Bigart summed up this contrast with one telling anecdote. An editor working on a story written by Alsop sent Bigart the copyboy to find a piece of wire service copy Alsop had left somewhere in his desk. What he discovered in his search was a stack of uncashed paychecks. Alsop didn't need the money and had apparently been waiting to cash them until they accumulated into a worthwhile amount.[30]

Even with his humble status, Bigart was not a passive figure in the newsroom. He was one of several people in the news department who resigned from the Newspaper Guild, the union that represented reporters and copy editors (and copyboys), because they found its leadership tainted by pro-communist politics and too sympathetic to Soviet dictator Stalin. And Bigart created an in-house newsletter called *The Copyboy's Call*, which sometimes needled the management.

In 1932, for example, as the Great Depression set in, the *Trib* cut salaries, first of those making more than thirty dollars a week, then of everyone—even the lowest paid—while owners Ogden Reid and Helen Rogers Reid were partying at their house in Palm Beach. "There is a responsibility every employer must consider," *The Call* said, "and that is his responsibility to pay his help a living wage. Even copyboys have a standard of living." Cutting salaries when workers were already struggling, this item said, "is an imposition, a social injustice, a direct attack on a fundamental necessity, food. Mild hunger is no incentive to increased efficiency nor to fond regard for our employers."[31]

Bigart was twenty-six years old when he became head copyboy. It was a promotion, but it was still a support job, not to be confused with journalism. His salary was still twenty-five dollars a week. Richard Kluger, who worked at the *Herald Tribune* and interviewed Bigart for his history of the paper, gave this description of Bigart in this new position:

> He served with a mustached distinction that would have been almost laughable in one more prepossessing. He wore a dark suit and vest all the time, even in summer heat that approached the unbearable in the *Tribune* and resembled nothing so much as a mortician-in-training. He would stand in the middle of the city room directing the other copyboys like a traffic cop. On errands himself, he moved with a swift, stiff-legged gait thought to be military in manner and therefore highly efficient. On the job, his charges thought of him as something of a tyrant; off it, they thought him almost a recluse. He often donned a crooked smile that was sometimes taken by its beholder as a sneer or sign of disapproval—a trait that did not measurably speed his advancement.[32]

Only in 1932 did Walker finally promote Bigart to reporter, but even in his new status he was an outsider and was excluded from Walker's circle of drinking buddies at a nearby saloon.

As a reporter, Bigart was not a natural. He was limited by his stutter. He was a slow writer and a poor typist whose copy was often marred by strikeovers where he had struggled to find the right word or phrase. And at least at the beginning of his career, he was not an outgoing or engaging personality, despite his dramatics as head copyboy. "I was pretty timid so it was awfully hard for me to cover politics, because I could never ask the necessarily rude questions," he said.[33]

He studied the literary style of the *New Yorker* and the columns of Walter Lippmann and Franklin P. Adams, working to polish his writing. Bigart was put off by the long, ponderous paragraphs that often began articles in the *Times*.[34]

He was not interested in the police beat, often a starting point for new reporters, because he disliked the cops, as he would dislike and mistrust authority figures throughout his career. Nor did he want to be a "legman," phoning in facts from the streets for someone else to write up in the newsroom. So he was categorized as "general assignment," meaning he would be assigned to cover whatever caught the attention of editors on a given day. It could be a major news development, but it could just as well be some trivial event.

The first article bearing his byline, published on May 2, 1934, was a seemingly endless, excruciatingly detailed account of the investiture of the Reverend Stephen J. Donohue as the auxiliary bishop of the Catholic archdiocese of New York.

At the age of forty, Donohue was one of the youngest members of the Catholic clergy elevated to the bishopric, so the well-attended ceremony at St. Patrick's Cathedral was certainly worthy of coverage, but Bigart's article went on and on, as if he were still being paid space rates for an obituary. How many readers were interested in the initials inscribed in the new bishop's coat of arms or the fact that the coat of arms decorated two small barrels of altar wine? Was it necessary to describe the supposed religious significance of every flower on the altar? Did the article need to identify by name every one of the new bishop's eight brothers and sisters who attended or to list the name and diocese of every one of the forty-six bishops from around the country who participated?

Details are important and sometimes critical in news stories, and Bigart's eye for detail served him well throughout his career, but this was excessive. He got away with it because it was a Sunday, without much other news competing for space. And because the ceremony took place in the morning, even at his ponderous writing pace he had no difficulty meeting the early evening deadline. In fact, he said deadlines helped him because of his passion for detail and his normally ponderous pace. "With me there had to be a deadline; otherwise it would never get done," he said.[35]

In his first few years, he wrote competently and sometimes adroitly about events big and small, people famous and unknown. He interviewed a lexicographer who deplored the use of the term "okie-dokie." He went to Princeton University to write about the Triangle Club's annual show. He also interviewed the novelist Thomas Wolfe, who, Bigart reported, was "fed up with being a legend." Later he said Wolfe was the most interesting person he ever interviewed. They talked about the novelist's *Look Homeward, Angel* and hometown of Asheville, North Carolina, although, Bigart said, "it was a little embarrassing" because Wolfe also had a speech impediment. "We got along very well," he said, even though Wolfe apparently "wasn't a very nice person."[36]

Bigart's first overnight assignment away from New York was to a Catholic conclave in Cleveland. Reporting on the aftermath of a coal mine disaster in Pottsville, Pennsylvania, he demonstrated an ability to capture the mood of a community: "Today's meeting served to emphasize the extent of local antagonism toward the coal companies. Not only the miners but most of the other residents seemed to be united in the belief that the operators have failed in their 'social responsibility' to the region, and that the bootleg situation was what they deserved."[37] (The term "bootleg" referred to unlicensed mines.)

He put his flair for detail to good use in a report on the opening of New York's first shelter for homeless women. "It was like visiting day at the old ladies' home. Party smiles brightened the sunken cheeks of the city's 150 guests," he wrote. "Saddest was a woman of perhaps thirty, who sat apart. She was smartly dressed in a black coat with fur collar and a hat which looked new. She was handsome in comparison with the others and stared intently at the floor." Dinner was ham, sauerkraut, mashed potatoes, stewed apricots, and coffee.[38]

Describing the Sanitation Department's annual picnic for its trash collectors at a suburban estate, he noted that "at the end of the afternoon thirty-five kegs of beer and 18,400 bottles had been consumed, as well as 6,000 frankfurters, forty gallons of soup, a ton of roasted meats and uncounted hamburgers."[39]

A. M. Rosenthal, who years later was Bigart's boss at the *New York Times*, poked fun at the relentless but halting interview style by which Bigart accumulated such a wealth of details: "Hello, I'm Homer Bigart, can you tell me about it? . . . I don't understand . . . I'm stupid . . . Explain it to me . . . Is this a coffee cup? . . . What's a coffee cup? . . . Why is it a coffee cup? . . . Explain it to me again."[40] It was Homer's all-American dummy act.

Life at the *Trib*

As the nineteen-forties began, the *Herald Tribune* was a serious, well-respected newspaper, but its newsroom was largely free of the intense self-importance that characterized the newsroom at the *Times*.

William K. Zinsser, a prominent writer and film critic who began his career at the *Trib*, gave this description of the working atmosphere:

Not to make friends in every cranny of the newsroom would have been impossible. We were a tribe in motion, meeting each other everywhere: going out on stories, getting clips from the morgue [the library of back copies], reading wire copy off a machine, stretching, smoking, visiting the water cooler, stopping at each other's desks, endlessly talking shop. The talk continued downstairs at the Artists and Writers Restaurant, known as Bleeck's and pronounced Blake's, a former speakeasy with a mile-long bar, just a few steps from the paper's back entrance on 40th Street, which was a second home—and often a first home—to almost everyone who worked at the *Herald Tribune*. Reporters and editors missing in midafternoon could reliably be found there and invited back up to work. [One regular denizen of Bleeck's was publisher Ogden Reid, who, having nothing to do after business hours, went downstairs to drink too much with his troops.[41]] . . . Every desk had an ancient typewriter in its sunken well, leaving only a small surface to hold the other necessities of the trade: a rotary telephone, a wire basket for copy, an ashtray, a cup of coffee, and a spike for impaling any piece of paper that a reporter might later regret throwing away. The spike was where old press releases went to die.[42]

Zinsser meant the word "spike" literally. Reporters and copy editors did not throw paper away. They had sharp-pointed metal spikes on little stands on which they impaled discarded drafts, unused wire service copy, and other notes that the copyboys collected after each night's final edition and stored in case some question arose.

Zinsser omitted from his upbeat depiction of life in the newsroom the fact that the staff was entirely White and almost entirely male. It showed in the paper: there was rarely any news from or about the city's African American neighborhoods, and women were routinely described by their physical attributes such as "plump" or "comely." The *Herald Tribune* was hardly the only paper of which that could be said; it was characteristic of the business at the time.

Bigart got a break with the appointment in 1939 of a new city editor. The formidable Lessing L. Engelking, the tallest man in the newsroom at six feet four, was a fire-breathing giant who demanded the best from his staff. He knew the paper could not compete with the *Times* in the scope and breadth of its coverage, but he believed it could compete on quality. One way he sought to achieve that was to work closely with reporters to ensure their accuracy and polish their writing.

One reporter he trained, Margaret Parton, described him as "my terrifying godlike teacher—he scared me to death and I loved him deeply." Robert J. Donovan, long a star reporter in the Washington bureau, said Engelking was "the greatest school of journalism ever invented." Peter Kihss, a longtime reporter in the *Trib*'s city room, described him as "exacting, competitive, and meticulous." Zinsser described him as "a choleric giant from Texas forever in pursuit of perfection."[43] Bigart said of Engelking that "if you made any mistakes that were due to carelessness, he would land on you heavily. But his praise was just as embarrassing, because he would bellow it out for the whole city room."[44]

Engelking encouraged Bigart, assigned him to more major stories, and allowed him to display a growing flair for colorful prose. Reporting on an exhibition of thousands of models of patented inventions, for example, Bigart said many of them were "masterpieces of uselessness."[45] Writing about a man whose job was to ride the subways all day sniffing for gas leaks, he observed playfully that "a cross-section of subway air is a symphony of smells—alliaceous, aromatic, ethereal, ambrosiac, empyreumatic and virulent."[46]

In 1940 Engelking chose Bigart to cover the city's annual St. Patrick's Day parade. Such an assignment is more difficult than it sounds because it is hard to find anything new to say, but Bigart was lucky because it snowed.

"With as bold a show of endurance as St. Patrick himself must have displayed the day he cast the snakes out of Ireland," his account began, "thousands of men, women and children trudged through the slush and swirling snow on Fifth Avenue yesterday in homage to the Irish apostle." The third paragraph, often cited by Bigart's admirers, said, "The snow lay an inch deep in the folds of the Mayor's large black felt hat by the time the County Kerry boys went by singing 'The Hat Me Dear Old Father Wore.'"[47]

After a year or so of working under Engelking, Bigart began to establish himself as a go-to reporter for major, complex news events. One of the first was a lethal stampede among thousands of patrons lined up on a Manhattan pier to board an excursion boat. They broke up and fled only when police arrived and began firing into the air. Three people died in the melee.

Bigart's account said,

> Three women were trampled to death and forty-two men, women and children were injured on the West 132d street pier yesterday morning in a wild, headlong stampede of 5,000 Negroes to board a Hudson River excursion steamer. The panic started when someone discovered that many of the Negroes were arriving with apparently spurious tickets. Immediately all but one of the four entrance gates were slammed shut in the passenger shanty near the pierhead. Negroes whirled in a turbulent flood. Hundreds tried to crowd through the single gate where each ticket was being turned over and laboriously inspected a dozen times by members of the excursion committee.[48]

Why were the people involved in this unfortunate event referred to by their race? It was clearly irrelevant to the nature of the disaster. But the whole tenor of the story suggested that this was some aberrant behavior that would not occur among nice White folk. The use of the word "Negroes" was not disturbing as it was the generic term in newspapers of the time, and African Americans used it themselves in the names of organizations such as the National Council of Negro Women and the United Negro College Fund. Whatever term was used, the issue was that the people's race was identified. The article listed the dead by name and address. All the addresses were in Harlem, which would have told readers what the victims' skin color was. Using the racial identifier at the top of the article, however, signaled that these people, dear readers, are not our people.

If any such considerations occurred to the editors of the *Trib*, there is no indication of it in the article, and Bigart's career surged ahead. He was the reporter the editors sent to Boston to report on the ghastly fire at the Coconut Grove night club in which 492 people died. Even now, eighty years later, reading his detailed descriptions of mounds of charred bodies, their clothes burned off and skin peeling, is difficult.[49] In August 1941, he was dispatched to a remote lodge in New Jersey to chronicle the annual convention of the American Sunbathing Association—that is, nudists. His account of that event was as lighthearted as his report on the fire was grim: he described a happy day of "bathing in the nude, tennis in the nude, and hiking in the nude." Despite the fun and games, however, he found the organization's leaders worried about the effects of a potential war on dedicated nudists: what would happen to them if they were drafted?[50]

Silly as that may have seemed, the possibility of conscription was real. After Germany invaded Poland in 1939, the threat of war and preparations for it were an increasing component of the news. Coverage of those developments gave Bigart his first exposure to military affairs. He learned fast.

TWO

HOMER BIGART GOES TO WAR

month after the invasion of Poland precipitated World War II, but still two
years before the United States entered the conflict after the attack on Pearl
Harbor, the War Department ordered extensive field training exercises for
some units of the New York National Guard that Bigart covered. It did not take
him long to find and describe flaws in the guard's plans and their execution, as he
would do in three wars, to the military's annoyance.

After the first day in the field, Bigart reported that "today's maneuver clearly
showed one deficiency common to most National Guard Field Artillery Units, a
lack of staff cars. The present appropriation of the National Guard makes no provision for automobiles for the regiment commanders and the battery commanders
who are evidently supposed to hitch-hike or use civilian vehicles to get about."[1]

How could he know that the staff car shortage was "common to most National
Guard Artillery Units"? He had not seen any others. The likely explanation is
that some senior officer told him so on the condition that he not be identified, but
readers were entitled to some explanation.

Bigart went to Camp Drum (now Fort Drum) in upstate New York to observe
large-scale maneuvers. He described the state's plans for a holiday that would
give workers time to register if a draft were adopted and young men required to
register. He recounted the training of civilians who would be air raid wardens,
scanning the sky for enemy bombers, if the United States entered the war. He
reported on military training at Fort Bragg, North Carolina, where he found racial conflict between White and Black soldiers, his first experience of writing
about race issues. At Fort Dix, New Jersey, he informed readers, "three thousand
recruits of the National Guard, completing their first full day in camp, were convinced tonight that Army life consisted chiefly of housekeeping chores and waiting for mess call."[2] He had discovered the "hurry up and wait" reality of life in
the army.

In November 1942, with the United States fully engaged in the war, he went to Puerto Rico to report on conditions among the island's impoverished residents, their poverty having been exacerbated when the war effort diverted food and medicine that the federal government had supplied in peacetime. For the first time, the *Herald Tribune* ran an advertisement promoting his forthcoming series: "Reporter Homer Bigart's revealing articles will paint the picture exactly as it is—no retouching, no word-mincing."[3]

He certainly did not pull punches. He found the island's people malnourished to the point of famine, the arable land used for the cultivation of sugar instead of food, and the administrators sent by Washington unable to deal with it. His articles demonstrated for the first time an ability to report incisively in an area where he did not speak the language, an essential component of any foreign correspondent's work.

"Years of malnutrition have produced an undersized and scrawny race," he wrote, "so lacking in stamina that by Works Progress Administration standards, it takes two Puerto Ricans to do one job. Hunger is accepted as a natural calamity, like hurricanes, hookworms, tuberculosis and malaria. So, after the first shock of seeing wasted, misshapen children playing in the ghastly slum of La Perla—a half-mile from the governor's palace—you are likely to forget about it." He found that the island's governor, President Franklin D. Roosevelt's "brain-truster and master planner" Rexford G. Tugwell, "seems unable or unwilling to grapple with the pressing day-to-day emergencies." It was not Tugwell's fault that cargo ships had been diverted to military traffic, Bigart observed, but the governor had taken office four months before Pearl Harbor, when officials on the island were already clamoring for the development of emergency stockpiles and had failed to act. He was still "neck-deep in blueprints."[4]

Two weeks after the Puerto Rico series came his reporting on the Cocoanut Grove fire. That was his last stateside article about a domestic news event for the duration of the war. It was time for him to devote himself to writing about the war full time from the war zone. In January 1943, he sailed with the troops aboard a ship bound for England.

Britain at War

When the *Herald Tribune* sent Bigart to London, he was thirty-five years old, single, childless, and healthy. In theory he was eligible to be drafted into the armed forces under the Selective Training and Service Act of 1940, which required all men aged twenty-one to forty-five to register for the first peacetime draft in US history. Bigart had registered as required when he was thirty-two years old; in realty few men his age were drafted. War brought him his first international experience, which he relished, but he was not in any armed service; throughout the war, the extent to which he was exposed to danger was largely a matter of his choice, not military orders. More often than not, he chose to risk death in pursuit of the story because he understood almost instinctively the validity of many a wise editor's instruction on how to cover developing news events: go there.

He wrote his first file even before he arrived in London, describing a voyage aboard a troopship that was "only a little more uncomfortable and not much more eventful than a trans-Atlantic voyage at the height of the prewar June tourist rush"[5]—not that he was familiar with transatlantic voyages or the "June tourist rush" in Britain, this being his first trip outside the United States. Everyone aboard began the crossing in fear of a German bombing attack or submarine strike, but "the days passed and nothing happened. Everyone relaxed."

London was the ideal place for him to ease his way into combat coverage. The Luftwaffe's nightly air attacks, known as the Blitz, had eased off after May 1941. Bomb rubble and fire damage were still visible all across London, bombs still fell when the Germans could spare enough planes from the eastern front, and people rushed for shelter in subway stations when air raid warning sirens sounded, but on most days there was little imminent danger. In fact, life for the young men of the American press corps could be almost pleasant. The story they were there to write about was the bombing of Germany by the Royal Air Force (RAF) and, soon, by the Americans. There was hardly any bombing or artillery fire anywhere near them.

Andy Rooney, a decade younger than Bigart, was a soldier on active duty when the army sent him to London to write for the military newspaper *Stars and Stripes*. He wrote in his memoir that "I loved London from the first day." He and a friend rented "a nice, big, one-room flat on Bayswater Road with a good bathroom (bathrooms were scarce because the British had not then and still have not really mastered plumbing)." He detested British cooking, but being in the army, he was able to obtain goods from the military post exchange that were rationed for the British, including food and cigarettes.[6]

Bigart's experience was similar. "I tell you, I'll never run down war," he said. "I got sent to London and those first few months were about the happiest I think I've ever spent in journalism. I liked the people and I liked the city. There was sort of a lull in the air raid war so you had all the excitement of being in a war area without any real danger."[7]

Bigart, a slow writer and slower typist, benefited from the time difference between London and New York. When the day's last briefing by American officers and last interview with American pilots were in his notebook, he still had several hours to compose his story and transmit it. Harrison Salisbury, a wartime correspondent in London for United Press and later Bigart's distinguished colleague at the *New York Times*, gave this description of Bigart at work:

> The first time I saw Homer Bigart he was the solitary figure in the windy acres of the Ministry of Information press room in Malet Street on the edge of Bloomsbury. We had just arrived in London, Homer on January 19, 1943, and myself on February 4. . . . The glimpse of Homer transmitted the essential characteristics of the man who would become *the* war correspondent of his time. He was alone, a slim, almost frail figure hunched over his Olivetti [typewriter], slowly punching with two or three fingers, often pausing, often X-ing out words, often consulting notes, often looking out into space before resuming. He gave no sign that he saw me nor the oak-stained walls of the University of London lecture hall that had been converted into a press working space. He was alone in the corridors of his mind.
>
> That late afternoon Bigart was the only reporter still writing his dispatch on the latest RAF raid over Germany. The care, the precision of his reporting, the extraordinary attention to detail, the slowness with which he constructed his stories, and the luminosity of his prose were already making him legendary.
>
> I watched him for a few minutes from the rear of the room. It was an image that would remain in my mind for fifty years. To anyone who observed Bigart it was plain that it was no accident that he emerged as a brilliant recorder of war, setting it down with an eye as precise as Goya's. Inevitably, he became a role model for successive waves of reporters in the age of wars that was to follow 1945.
>
> Bigart was a man who worked with the skill of a diamond cutter, dipping again and again into the cornucopia of information he had assembled before sitting at his typewriter. Long since, his colleagues had become accustomed to his tedious questioning, going over a point again and again, repeating and repeating, asking explanations of the obvious, never satisfied. It could be very boring. But when the answers mortised together into the plain but intricate structure of Homer's prose his edifice of words stood out like a tower on a treeless plain.[8]

That "boring" style of relentless questioning, as Salisbury called it, is the earliest recorded description by a colleague of "Homer's all-American dummy act."

Shortly after Bigart's arrival in England, the relative calm was shattered when the Germans bombed an elementary school, killing thirty children. Bigart's wrenching account of the mass burial provided an early example of the painstaking, detailed narrative style that Salisbury admired.

The parents walked together to the hillside cemetery. Bigart wrote,

> The mile-long march took the mothers and fathers past the scene they will never forget. Beyond the low board fence, not far from the church, were the gaping wings

of the school sliced neatly in half. The parents could see the hall, which a week ago echoed to the anticipation of children assembled there for a matinee performance of "A Midsummer Night's Dream." Tons of masonry had crashed into the assembly hall, killing most of the children. One wall remained. On it hung a tiny red coat.

On the faces of the parents, he wrote, "there was something more than grief."[9] The name of the play, the fact that it was a matinee, and, later in the article, the fact that the tiny coffins were made of plastic because of a shortage of lumber—these were the sort of details another reporter might have missed or omitted.

The primary assignment for Bigart and the other Americans was to attend military briefings describing the air war against Germany and to interview pilots and bombardiers as they returned from their dangerous missions, but as in any war there was much else to write about. Bigart described a country estate that the military had made available as a "rest home" for weary flight crews of the US Army's Eighth Air Force. He interviewed Capt. Clark Gable about the actor's work making training films for the army. Bigart also recounted "the oddest prisoner exchange thus far in the war": the British and Italian navies swapped captives, and Britain and Germany exchanged captive merchant seamen in "the squalid little Mediterranean seaport of Mersina" on the coast of Turkey.

"The unique feature of the exchange is that the Italians and Germans were not British prisoners," Bigart's account said. "They had escaped from Eritrea when Italy's African empire collapsed, crossing the Red Sea into neutral Saudi Arabia. For eighteen months they were interned at Jedda." It was not clear how the exchange came about, Bigart said, but he noted that Saudi Arabia in 1943 could not afford to feed 862 Italians and Germans. To get rid of them, King Abdul Aziz approached Turkey, which was also neutral, and the Turks approached Berlin, Rome, and London. "Through some miracle of diplomacy not yet revealed," his article said, "the belligerents reached an agreement unprecedented in this war."[10]

That was a fascinating footnote to history, but such stories, like the children's funeral and the interview with Gable, were not the same as reporting military action from the front. Given an opportunity to do that, Bigart signed up.

The Writing 69th

The commander of the US Eighth Air Force in Britain was Brig. Gen. Ira C. Eaker, a pioneer of aerial combat from World War I. In the Second World War, he built American participation in the European campaign virtually from scratch, starting in early 1942 with no aircraft and no US base. By the end of 1943, Eaker had assembled an air war machine of 185,000 men and four thousand planes.[11] One of his prominent subordinates was a cigar-chomping colonel named Curtis

LeMay, who later served as chief of staff of the air force and was the model for the rogue bomber in the film *Dr. Strangelove.*

The British flew most of their bombing missions at night, but Eaker was a strong advocate of daytime missions. He believed daytime bombing was more effective militarily, because pilots and bombardiers could see their targets, and more acceptable ethically, because there was less chance of civilian destruction near missed military targets.[12] Daytime flights were more dangerous and carried a higher risk of casualties because the planes were visible to antiaircraft gunners on the ground and to enemy fighters in the air, but Eaker believed the results were worth it.

Bigart and other correspondents in London filed their accounts of the bombing campaign based on information provided by military briefers. Good reporters are seldom satisfied with secondhand information, especially when it is delivered by sources who have an interest in the outcome. The correspondents wanted to accompany flight crews on missions so they could see the action for themselves. Eaker, a publicity seeker who wanted to raise his forces' profile at home, decided to accommodate them.

On February 11, 1943, Eaker's staff sent him a memorandum nominating thirteen newspaper, wire service, and newsreel reporters for "participation in operational missions." The memo said that "in accordance with the desire of the Commanding General," all of them had completed a three-day training course and passed an eye examination. The list included Bigart; Walter Cronkite, then with the United Press news service and later the avuncular anchor personality of CBS television news; Robert B. Post of the *New York Times*; and Andy Rooney, then a sergeant in uniform assigned to *Stars and Stripes.*[13] Only eight of the thirteen reporters ever flew on a real mission.

These unlikely flyboys soon came to be known as the "Writing 69th," a reference to a James Cagney movie of 1940 celebrating the performance of New York's Sixty-Ninth Infantry Regiment during World War I. The moniker was apparently dreamed up by a military public affairs official, not by the reporters— Rooney called it "a lot of hooey"[14]—but it stuck.

The reporters were taught how to distinguish one type of plane from another, to adjust to the cold temperatures and shortage of oxygen at flying altitudes, to fire a machine gun, to jump from a damaged plane in a parachute, and to escape in a dinghy from a plane that landed in water in a maneuver known as "ditching out."

"It was during Lieutenant Alex Hogan's 'ditching out' lecture that some of us felt like hopping the next train" back to London, Bigart wrote in an article describing the training. "The lieutenant is a pleasant lad from Starkville, Miss., but his discourse was a bit grim."[15]

The article reported that in instructing them about the hazards of oxygen shortage at high altitudes, the officer told them the symptoms to be alert for, beginning with "a slap-happy feeling of the type attributed to Dodger fans." (In those days, baseball's Dodgers were still in Brooklyn and thus a home team for *Herald Tribune* readers.)

Bigart's report said nothing about the weapons component of their training, but for some of the reporters, it raised uncomfortable issues. They were observers of the war, not participants in it, but they had to do what Eaker's team wanted so that they could go on flights.

The air force's plan soon became apparent. Cronkite wrote in his memoir,

> [It] intended to train us as fully qualified gun crews despite the Geneva Conventions which, laughingly, were supposed to provide rules for armies in combat. It stated that civilian correspondents should not carry arms on penalty of possible execution if captured by the enemy. Apparently the Air Force considered, rationally enough, that once you bailed out of an airplane, the enemy could scarcely know whether you had fired a gun or not. And they figured that we might as well be able to take the place of wounded gunners.

By the end of training, Conkrite continued, "we were reasonably adept at taking apart and reassembling a machine gun—blindfolded. This is not a talent I have found much use for since."[16]

Rooney had an additional complication: he was actually in the military; therefore, he could be ordered to carry a weapon as part of his duties. "As correspondents we were not supposed to be armed or fire weapons of any kind," he wrote. But if he were captured on a bombing mission, "I don't know whether I'd have been considered a correspondent or a soldier."[17]

Another issue facing the correspondents was whether they would be assigned to a mission flown by a B-17 Flying Fortress bomber or a B-24 Liberator. Both were four-engine aircraft designed for the same purpose, but the B-17, which had been in service before the war and was better known to the public, was widely regarded as safer because it was more maneuverable. Gen. H. H. (Hap) Arnold, the highest-ranking officer in the US Army Air Forces, objected to "this false public impression that the B-17 is a fighting airplane far superior to any other heavy bomber in the world, because of the briefness of B-24 battle combat experiences and lack of publicity for its success in battle."[18] Nevertheless, the press corps believed the B-17 was more reliable.

Six of the correspondents were designated to go airborne toward Germany on February 26, 1943, each on a separate plane. They all understood the danger that awaited them. Cronkite, writing for the United Press, quoted *Times* reporter Bob Post as predicting that one—most likely Bigart—would not return, given the casualty statistics among American aircraft. "It will probably be you, Homer, you're the Frank McHugh type, the silent amiable guy who always gets it in the end," Post said. (McHugh was an actor who appeared in the *Fighting 69th* movie.)

Maj. Bill Laidlaw, the public affairs officer organizing the mission, complained that the reporters all wanted to fly on B-17 Flying Fortresses. "Come on," he said, "one of you has to go with the B-24 Liberators. Those guys deserve some recognition, too." Some accounts say the reporters decided to draw a name out of a hat, but Cronkite in his memoir said Post volunteered because "the *Times* doesn't care about headlines."[19]

All the flights encountered heavy aircraft fire from the ground and were attacked by German fighter planes, but Post's was the only one that went down.

"The crews of other ships in his formation reported seeing his ship on the way to the ground near the target area," Cronkite reported that day. "It had one engine on fire, which the crew put out only to have the fire burst out in a second engine."[20]

"The six correspondents that went out that day were to meet after the raid at Molesworth, where facilities had been set up for us to write our stories and transmit them back to London," Rooney recalled. "Five of us straggled into the press room at intervals over a period of half an hour, and then came the word that we dreaded. There would never be more than five of us. Bob Post, the friendly and able young reporter for the New York Times, was missing."[21]

He never returned. His body and those of the crew on his flight were found months later.

The planned target of those first bombing runs for the reporters was the port at Bremen, but cloud cover forced a change after they were airborne. The new target was the heavily defended submarine base at Wilhelmshaven. The Eighth Air Force lost thirteen of the sixty-four bombers on that mission.[22]

"Our target was Wilhelmshaven," Bigart's first-person account in the *Herald Tribune* began. "We struck at Fuehrer Adolf Hitler's North Sea base from the southwest after stoogeing around over a particularly hot corner of the Third Reich for what seemed like a small eternity." He reported that his plane's load of five-hundred-pound bombs struck its designated target on the first run, but, "frankly, I wasn't so much interested in the target. What intrigued me was the action upstairs. Flak was bursting all around the squadron just ahead and to our left. The shells were exploding in nasty black puffs, leaving curious smoke trails of hourglass shape."

Although "enemy fighters were darting in all directions," no flak came closer than two hundred yards to Bigart's plane. He observed,

The worst moment came early in the attack. I saw a ship ahead of us go down in a dizzy spin, with two parachutes opening in its wake. For an instant I almost wished I was back in Brooklyn. Yet the whole trip was so theatrical that you forgot to be scared. The technicolor was excellent, the action fairly gripping and the casting superb. Only the scenario needed cutting. I got awfully tired of looking at the North Sea, a disagreeable piece of scenery in February.[23]

Cronkite's experience on that first run was quite different and no joking matter. "We were under constant attack for two and a half hours" by Luftwaffe interceptors, he recalled, and from the ground "the antiaircraft fire was intense, golden bursts of explosives all around us, dissolving into those great puffs of black smoke."

From his position in the nose of the plane, "I fired at every German fighter that came into the neighborhood. I don't think I hit any, but I like to think I scared a couple of those German pilots."

Back on the ground in England, Bigart asked Cronkite what the first paragraph, or "lede," of his story would say. They could share such information because they were not direct competitors. Cronkite was writing for a wire service that had newspaper and radio clients in every time zone in the world who wanted his copy right away. Bigart, writing for a newspaper in New York, had several hours before his deadline.

"I think I'm going to say," Cronkite told Bigart, "that I've just returned from an assignment to hell, a hell at 17,000 feet, a hell of bursting flak and screaming fighter planes, of burning Forts and hurtling bombs." Homer, "whose Pulitzer Prize–winning prose was never tinged with purple, looked at me for a moment and finally said: 'You—you—you wouldn't!' "[24]

But he did write that, and more: "American Flying Fortresses have just come back from an assignment to hell—a hell 26,000 feet above the earth, a hell of burning tracer bullets and bursting gunfire, of crippled Fortresses and burning German fighter planes, of parachuting men and others not so lucky. I have just returned with a Flying Fortress crew from Wilhelmshaven." The rest of his account was equally colorful and dramatic.

Many news outlets published Cronkite's story, including the *New York Times*, which ran it in the place where Bob Post's version would have been if he had survived to file it.[25] Cronkite became famous overnight. Bigart, however, poked fun at his story. He wrote,

True perspective is rather hard to maintain in the hours immediately after an assignment in which your own neck was directly involved. You are apt to feel you had a ringside seat at the most crucial engagement since Waterloo or that final Yankee-Cardinal game at the Stadium. This is known as the "I have just returned from a suburb of hell" reaction. To relieve this condition, it is necessary for the patient to hurl himself at the nearest typewriter, rap out a tingling yarn of a flak-filled heaven, of epic dog-fights and derring-do.

Part of the problem, he acknowledged, was that he did not have enough experience to understand fully what he was seeing. And part of it was that he and other reporters had unwittingly absorbed some of the chipper confidence and the "it was nothing, really," pose of the flight crews they had heard from in the briefing room. They whistled past the graveyard to bolster their own morale. In the crews' accounts after the Wilhelmshaven mission, "the enemy opposition was very sorry indeed. The German anti-aircraft [fire] was inaccurate, they relate, and the fighters untrained." As for the seven planes that were shot down, they "were lost simply because they drifted out of formation—they were asking for it." None of that was true, but it made the crews feel better to believe it.

Bigart's retrospective article said it would benefit the flight crews and the overall war effort if prominent civilians went on such missions so they would understand what the crews were dealing with, what they needed in equipment, and how their planes should be modified. He nominated Eleanor Roosevelt and Westbrook Pegler to "ride in the nose of the lead ship." All his readers would have understood the joke: Pegler and the First Lady could not stand each other, and everyone knew it.

He closed the article with this sheepish confession: "I must be crazy, but I should like to go again."[26] His tone was somewhat flippant for a life-or-death situation, and he soon regretted it. A week later, he reflected in the newspaper about the "drivel" he had written.

Unlike Cronkite, Bigart wrote nothing about firing any weapons, but he later acknowledged to Harrison Salisbury that he had done so. Like the others, he had only a few hours of training on the machine guns. "I used mine," he said. "I just hope I didn't shoot down one of our planes. I saw one of the B-24 Liberators go down. Wouldn't it be awful if it was one of us who shot down the B-24 with Bob Post in it?"[27]

Long afterward, Bigart said he probably owed his life to Bob Post: "This is a terrible thing to say, but I suppose one of the reasons I'm alive today is because the New York Times man was killed on the first raid, and the bad publicity that came out of that squashed that idea, that it was going to be a steady job, going on air raids. . . . None of us went on any more air raids."[28]

That was his recollection four decades after the raids, but it was not accurate. "In the short term," Jim Hamilton wrote in his history of the Writing 69th, "Post's death made editors rethink their decision to send correspondents into danger, but in the long run, most correspondents just went back to their dangerous occupation. They continued to fly with the bombers on occasion, and they accompanied troops on the front lines." Among those who flew after Post's death were Cronkite and Herbert L. Matthews of the *Times*, whom Bigart would encounter years later in another conflict in a different part of the world.[29]

Homer Bigart at work in a war zone, probably Italy, 1944.
Photographer: Rudolf Jonas. Courtesy Wisconsin Historical Society.

THREE

THE ITALIAN CAMPAIGN

After the German defeat at El-Alamein in Egypt, the Allies' amphibious landings in Morocco known as Operation Torch, and the Allies' seizure of Tunisia in 1943, North Africa was secure. Winston Churchill, Roosevelt, and their military chiefs met at Casablanca, Morocco, in January 1943 to decide where to go next. The discussions were sometimes difficult because the two leaders had different strategic visions; the talks lasted ten days. The decision that emerged was to take the war against the Axis to Italy, beginning with Sicily, rather than going directly into Nazi-occupied France.

A *Herald Tribune* correspondent named John "Tex" O'Reilly had covered the North Africa campaign. When the invasion of Sicily appeared imminent, he asked for reinforcements, prompting the editors to transfer Bigart from London to Allied headquarters in Algiers.

Through that spring of 1943, Bigart chronicled the campaign from Algiers, while O'Reilly was at the front. Then they switched assignments; by July 1943, Bigart was on the ground in Sicily, seeing the war up close. He stayed with the troops through the capture of Sicily and then all through their long, deadly march up the Italian boot. Bigart was now reporting on the war not from seventeen thousand feet but from the foxholes and ridgelines where the weapons were not bombs but grenades, bayonets, and M-1 rifles, and the face of the enemy was often visible a few yards away.

"The Tribune regarded me as humanly expendable, and they would send me off to all kinds of wars and brush fires," he said. His feelings about these life-threatening assignments were ambivalent and sometimes contradictory.

"I wasn't any crazy who wanted to go out and get shot up," he told an interviewer.[1] But he spent the better part of the next two decades on one front line after another, sometimes taking risks no editor would have assigned him to take, because he always wanted to see the action up close, beginning with that first assignment after London.

During the first month of the Sicily campaign, while O'Reilly was on the ground with the troops, Bigart did basically the same job he had been doing in London—describing the action based on briefings and conversations at headquarters. That form of war coverage is necessary, as it enables a reporter to write a composite account of all the day's events, across multiple fronts; but it is often dry and detached, and usually conveys only the information commanders want to give out. Bigart chafed at this one-way conduit of information. He said he "found being at headquarters such a rotten bore and the army personnel so awful that I just wanted to get away" from that tidy, sanitized reporting. "The job of the officers at headquarters was to give out propaganda but the ones in the field, the actual commanders, would tell the truth."[2]

Bigart knew that any competent news agency reporter could do the headquarters work and give readers the overall narrative of the war. He wanted to be out in the combat zone with the troops, hill to hill, foxhole to foxhole, village to village. Aside from the Wilhelmshaven raid, he had little direct experience in war zones, but he had seen war's impact on civilians at the funeral of those English schoolchildren. Doing close-up reporting would limit him to recounting only what he could see or hear, and it was often extremely dangerous, but it enabled him to put flesh and blood into his articles and convey the reality and humanity of war to readers at home. In July 1943, he got his wish. He was in Sicily with the US Seventh Army commanded by Lt. Gen. George S. Patton.

The renowned *Newsweek* correspondent Edward Behr put a cynical twist on this firsthand reporting of war and disaster in the title of his memoir, *Anybody Here Been Raped and Speaks English?*[3] But for Bigart such reporting added a whole new dimension to his career and enabled him to develop the flair for the compelling narrative, the revealing quotation, and the colorful detail that characterized his prize-winning work. He became not just a war correspondent but also a foreign correspondent. The jobs may overlap, but they are not the same.

A foreign correspondent's mission is to penetrate communities and societies of which he or she is not a member. That often means going to places where little English is spoken and where newspapers and street signs are in some foreign script. The task is to assess the political and social dynamics, the human impact of war or disaster, the economic conditions, and even the workings of art and culture. Bigart did that wherever the troops went. The questions that motivated him were not just who won or lost but what the troops were thinking and how the war affected civilians in its path.

In his new role in the field, Bigart wore combat fatigues and a helmet and often had a lighted cigarette dangling from his mouth. He was unarmed but otherwise looked pretty much like the soldiers he was writing about. In his reports he often referred to the American forces as "we."

His first article from the front was filed July 25, the same day that Italy's ruling council forced out Benito Mussolini, the fascist leader who had taken the country into the war on the side of the Germans. The Italian armed forces were already facing near-certain defeat; now the Germans assumed full responsibility for holding Italy as the Italians stood down. Bigart reported that the Seventh Army was fighting its way against stiff German resistance along the road leading to the Strait of Messina.

"In the early part of this engagement today, the Americans lost eighty men in dead and wounded," he reported. "There are fresh graves, blanketed with red geraniums, in the cemetery beside the limestone cliff of Cefalu."

Despite those casualties and a day of slow progress against German tanks and artillery, he observed, "it is hard to realize that this is a war and not just a summer maneuver. One reason is that our casualties in land fighting remain extremely small. Furthermore, war is associated with mud, foul weather and hostile civilians. There is none of that here. The weather has been perfect and the civilian conduct exemplary. In fact, the Sicilians are too friendly."[4]

A few days later, the Americans took the little seaside town of Castel di Tusa. Bigart described the military action, but his story focused on three hundred of the town's inhabitants who had "lived for six days in an abandoned railroad tunnel on meager rations of fodder beans and water" until the Americans arrived. With the ouster of Mussolini, the local fascist leaders had abandoned the populace, taking most of the food with them. The people had holed up in the cave as artillery fire pounded the town.

"It was cool in the tunnel, but the stench of accumulated filth made the place even less endurable than the sirocco outside," Bigart reported. "Spiders had made a continuous cobweb of the vaulted ceiling, and the walls oozed a greenish slime." The supply of beans was about to run out, and some of the cave dwellers were subsisting on grapes plucked from nearby hillsides during lulls in the bombardment. The troops hauled cases of army-issue canned meat, cheese, biscuits, cigarettes, and "the inevitable chewing gum" into the cave.[5]

Such details were not available in headquarters briefings.

Within two weeks after Bigart arrived in Sicily and demonstrated his ability to understand and describe the action, the *Herald Tribune*'s editors were giving him remarkable leeway to express his own views and assessments, without the customary attribution to officers or civilian officials. In one early example, he reported on the hardships facing Sicily's civilian population. As they cemented their hold on the island, the Allies created an administrative organization, the Allied Military Government of Occupied Territories (AMGOT), to administer public services and provide for the populace.

"By and large, it has done a good job against tremendous odds," Bigart said in the first paragraph of a front-page article. The work was aided by "the amazing receptiveness of the civilian population." But AMGOT was "keeping its fingers crossed" for that very reason. "Too many Sicilians are under the delusion that America and Great Britain intend to import great stocks of food and clothing for the civilian population of this island and that no effort of theirs is needed to solve the deplorable conditions in Sicily."[6]

It was easy to demonstrate objectively that conditions were "deplorable." Palermo, the biggest city, he reported, "smells of death. It is a city of flies and malarial mosquitoes and filth." Much of the city lay in ruins, shops were closed, and there was little food. But how many Sicilians had Bigart interviewed to support the assertion that too many of them were under some delusion about the Allies? Bigart was a keen observer and shrewd analyst, but even at the writer-friendly *Herald Tribune*, it was unusual for a news reporter to be allowed to offer his own views in that manner. The *Trib*'s editors let him do it for the rest of his years at the paper and often let him write in the first person. As his reputation grew, his opinions and analyses became a selling point for the newspaper, praised in editorials and promoted in advertisements.

His account of a battle to take control of a hill he called Mount Crioll began with this sentence: "Nagging thirst is one of the things I will remember of the stand of an American infantry battalion on the parched summit of Mt. Crioll." At the end of the day, the Americans prevailed, but "we were too tired for any sort of elation. I started down the hillside at 8 o'clock past the torn bodies of American and German dead." When the troops found some food in an empty house, "I ate the bread and cheese, found some water and bathed for the first time in two days."[7] It is questionable how many readers were interested in the state of a reporter's hygiene, but they were no doubt interested in how the troops were faring.

Except for a brief interval back at headquarters in Algiers in September 1943, Bigart stayed with the advancing Americans as they fought their way northward in week after week of devastating combat against determined, well-organized German resistance. At each town and village, when the shooting stopped, Bigart looked for human details that captured the impact of war beyond the casualty count.

In Naples he found that on their way out of the city, the Germans committed "an act of vicious and senseless vandalism." They set fire to Pompeian Hall, the library at the Palace of Capodimonte, destroying fifty thousand books, three paintings by the artist Francesco Solimena, and other relics.

Until two weeks earlier, Bigart reported, "the Germans in Naples had acted according to the accepted rules of war, limiting destruction to buildings and installations of value to the Allies." But after Italian partisans shot a German solider, the Germans "went suddenly berserk, breaking down the heavy doors of the university, dashing kerosine on the book-lined walls of the hall and burning the Pontaniana, a collection of philosophical works on the politics and morals of the ancients."[8]

In a separate story about that university, Bigart told New York readers about a company of military police, mostly young draftees from New York's colleges and universities, who were billeted inside the Chemistry Department. They were all homesick for Brooklyn or the Bronx—"We wouldn't trade a vacant lot in Greenpoint for the whole city of Naples," one said—but what really bothered them was the university itself because "it has no campus and no football stadium."

"I don't see how they lived," said Pvt. Wilbur Weisel.

"In an effort to bring some enlightenment to Naples," Bigart wrote, "the boys have dragged a laboratory blackboard out onto the piazza and chalked up the results of the first two World Series games."[9]

The next day he watched as the first fresh white bread Naples had seen in three years went on sale at a small bakery. "A hungry mob of women fought like beasts for the bread," he reported. Two American paratroopers who happened to be passing by—Pvt. Lloyd N. Coty of Lansing, Michigan, and Pvt. Mell S. Adkins, of Beckley, West Virginia—tried to help an elderly woman who was being pushed against a window. "They confronted a sea of disheveled, sweating women who were in no mood to listen to the few words of Italian that Coty had picked up."

That bakery was in a normally sedate, middle-class neighborhood, Bigart observed, but extended hunger "has stripped the neighborhood of all pretense of gentility and today's riotous breadline was a revelation of the depths of depravity to which Naples has sunk."[10]

In the scope of the war, the baseball scores on a blackboard and the scuffle over bread were trivial incidents, but Bigart's accounts of them were stories that had, as Ben Bradlee often said when he was editor of the *Washington Post*, "nothin' but readers." The names of hills taken and creeks crossed in distant war zones meant little to readers unfamiliar with the geography, but everyone could relate to bread and baseball.

Bigart's colorful accounts did not please the prominent *New Yorker* writer Janet Flanner, who complained about the bread-riot story in a letter to the editor of the *Herald Tribune*. If Bigart felt such antipathy to Italy and the Italians, she said, he should come home. "Judging by his vocabulary alone in his Oct. 16 white-bread riot piece, he seems not to like it there," she wrote. She said that in an earlier article he had referred to "the dirty, coarse voiced southern Italians," and now he said the women "fought like beasts." As for the "depravity to which Naples has sunk," she sniffed, hunger may make people desperate but not "depraved."

Beneath that letter the paper printed an editor's response, which defended Bigart and his colleague Tex O'Reilly, noting that it was the latter who had actually written the phrase about the "dirty" southern Italians. "Both of these correspondents have written ably and realistically of what they have seen in North Africa and in Italy. They would have failed in their duty had they glossed over the truth" to please the Italians, the editorial commentary said. Moreover, "depravity" was the appropriate word. "It was not so much hunger as a general demoralization, engendered by German occupation, that caused the clawing and the fighting," the editor wrote. In standing with their reporters, the editors were also indirectly defending their decisions to allow such language to appear in the paper.[11]

That was the first of many occasions over the next three decades on which some prominent or well-connected reader criticized Bigart's reporting or his language. Each time, his editors supported him.

Breaching the Gustav Line

The Allies' march northward was a long, tough slog across difficult terrain, made more difficult by the onset of winter. Italy officially withdrew from the war on September 8, but the Italians had already ceased to offer serious opposition. The defenders were German troops commanded by Field Marshal Albert Kesselring, a noted specialist in defensive warfare. His troops dug in along a string of fortifications south of Rome known as the Gustav Line, which the Allies struggled to penetrate.

One of the costliest engagements was an extended battle to drive the Germans out of the village of San Pietro. Arriving with elements of the Fifth Army after the shooting had subsided, Bigart filed one of his longest articles of the war, describing what they found: dead and dying American troops and others wounded, thirsty, and calling for help; streets and buildings mined by the retreating Germans; hungry local people huddled in ruined churches, where statues had been decapitated; a baseball glove, unexplained; dead and dying pigs and mules; wounded Germans who had to be cared for; and hysterical children.

Then the Germans staged "a final vicious counterattack." An American detachment led by Maj. David Frazior fought them off for five days. "Outstanding among Frazior's men," Bigart reported, "was Lieut. Rufus J. Cleghorn of Waco, Tex., a barrelchested football player from Baylor University. Exulting in battle, Cleghorn clambered to the highest rock of [Monte] Samucro's pinnacle and howled insults at the Germans, pausing now and then to toss grenades. For variety, Cleghorn occasionally put his weight against a huge boulder and sent it rolling down the slope. He roared with laughter" as he watched the Germans scramble to evade the rocks.[12]

The Allies' northward progress stalled in January 1944 when they were unable to break through Kesselring's Gustav Line. Their solution was to go around it, taking to the water for an amphibious landing behind German lines at Anzio on the coast of the Tyrrhenian Sea, south of Rome. The maneuver caught the Germans by surprise. The landing was unopposed, but the Allies squandered their advantage because of blunders by their commanders.

This useful summary of the battle at Anzio comes from the National World War II Museum in New Orleans:

The Allies held all the high cards: endless waves of men, tanks, guns, and aircraft, and absolute control of the sea. Nevertheless, the men and officers of the Wehrmacht endured grimly, clinging to every mountain, river, and ridge, and contesting every inch of ground. Perhaps if they held on long enough, they would find a way to return to the attack like the Prussians of old. Perhaps the Allies would get sloppy, make a false move, and provide them with an opening.

And then, one day in late January 1944, the Allies did just that. They landed a small amphibious force—too small, as it turned out—on the western shores of the Italian peninsula, between the small towns of Anzio and Nettuno. Operation Shingle was everything a military operation shouldn't be: badly planned, indifferently led, and uncertain of its own purpose. Even worse, the landing handed the Wehrmacht an opportunity to do what it did best: launch a full-scale offensive. In the subsequent fighting, German mechanized formations came perilously close to crumpling the Allied beachhead, closer than they would ever come again to a battlefield triumph in this war. Anzio was the Last Ride of the Prussians.

Shingle was an attempt to outflank the Gustav Line by landing at Anzio in the German rear, 30 miles south of Rome. It was ill-fated from the start, and historians have had a field day picking it apart. Problems started at the top. Winston Churchill, the king of the cigar-butt strategists, conceived it. General Mark Clark, the problem child of the Allied command, planned it; and General John Lucas of the VI Corps was the less-than-inspiring commander tabbed to lead it in the field. But the problems ran deeper than personality. A lack of landing craft kept the force small, just two divisions: British 1st Division (General W.R. C. Penney) and U.S. 3rd Infantry Division (General Lucian K. Truscott). The Normandy landing loomed just months away, and the Allies couldn't tie up too much precious equipment or too many troops on a sideshow. Prelanding exercises were a fiasco, with the men strewn about hither and yon and several landing craft sunk. Even Truscott, a tough guy who once summed up his battle philosophy in the pithy phrase, "No sonofabitch, no commander," wondered out loud if they were all embarking on a suicide mission.

Despite these problems, the landings on January 22nd went smoothly. German fire was practically absent, and 36,000 men came ashore by nightfall. And no wonder—the landing had taken the Germans completely by surprise. From the theater commander, Field Marshal Albert Kesselring, on down, no one had seen this coming.[13]

Bigart was with the American troops when they landed. His vivid first-person account reflected their amazement at the lack of German resistance.

"It is incredible," his report said. "For nearly three months the Germans have all but stalemated an Allied crossing through the mountains from Naples, and now Lieutenant General Mark W. Clark's army, at the cost of a few dozen men, lands on the front doorstep of Rome. Why hasn't it been done before?" His dispatch, he said, "was filed eleven hours after the first assault wave surged over the deserted beaches. Not one enemy artillery shell has been dropped within the rapidly broadening beachheads. On my beach not one soldier has fallen from enemy bullets so far, and casualties are trivial."[14]

The euphoria was misguided. With General Clark's approval, instead of ordering an advance northward toward Rome, General Lucas told the troops to dig in on the beach. A week later, they were still there.

Still, Bigart reported, "at no time have we lost the initiative." The Allies were adding troops and weapons to the force gathered on the beach in preparation for moving toward Rome. "The three great breaks that have made this operation so brilliant to date are: First, the attainment of complete surprise; second, the seizure of Anzio with port facilities intact; and third, a remarkably fine run of weather."[15]

While the Allied troops were enjoying that nice weather, Kesselring was redeploying his German forces to block them from advancing. The Germans took control of the surrounding hills, dug in, and pinned the landing force down with artillery. Three days after his upbeat dispatch about how well things were going, Bigart reported that the front "is fast being stabilized. A very considerable German force now confronts the Allies and the prospect of quick, easy success appears to have vanished."[16]

He was correct: the grim siege lasted till May, with high casualties on all sides. Except for a brief break in Naples in April, Bigart was there for all of it.

As the cakewalk of the first few days ended and the Germans held, the tone of press coverage naturally reflected the change. The Allied commander in Italy, Gen. Harold R. L. G. Alexander, did not appreciate it. He said the war correspondents at Anzio, by "blowing hot and cold," were giving comfort to the enemy and damaging public morale at home.

"I have received an urgent message that the press reports from this bridgehead are alarming people. I beg of you not to take that attitude," Alexander said. It was normal for any major military campaign to have setbacks as well as gains, and he was disappointed that reporters "should put out such rot." Finding the reporters guilty of an unwarranted switch from overoptimism to over-pessimism, he announced that he was revoking authorization to use a military radio link to file their stories, "and I'm not going to open it again until I am satisfied."

More than half of Bigart's subsequent article reporting Alexander's remarks was devoted to rebutting them. When the initial landing succeeded with surprising ease, the six correspondents who were there reported that, he wrote. When the Germans struck back and began to reverse the tide, they said so. Both were accurate when written, he pointed out. The real issue was not morale or battlefield security, Bigart said, but the fact that "there are still some military advisers who feel that the British and American public do not yet realize that war involves risks, that the breaks do not always go to the Allies. They are afraid that the public cannot stand the shock of bad news and that it must be broken to them gradually over long periods of time and preferably after some victory."[17]

Alexander backed down two days later and restored the radio link. That was the first time Bigart had a public dispute with the military brass over his coverage. It was hardly the last.

By mid-March, German artillery and air strikes still pinned down the Allied forces near the beachhead. The troops had been under fire there for so long that they were exhausted, filthy, and hungry, to the point that the US Army opened a rest camp in a section of the beach relatively sheltered from enemy fire. Bigart constructed his report about that camp in such a way as to bolster the morale of people at home, which Alexander had accused the press of undermining.

"There is nothing softly comfortable about this rest camp," he wrote. "The troops still sleep on the ground. But still it is a world removed from the frontline foxholes," where they had been fighting without a break for nineteen days.

> There was a doctor to treat mild cases of trench foot, a dentist, and barbers. There were showers and hot water, so that First Lieutenant Glenn D. Griek, commanding a machine-gun platoon, who was a pie baker at Modesto, Calif., had his first real bath in six weeks.
>
> Clean clothes are issued as soon as the men arrive. Rations, which are as varied as possible, are served hot. Some men had nearly forgotten the taste of hot food.
>
> The chief recreation, of course, is sleeping, but there are films four times daily and a radio blares last year's jazz. Breakfast is served as late as 9:30 a.m.

Bigart also named several soldiers who had received medals for their courage under fire.[18]

Taking Cassino

The most important German stronghold on the Gustav Line was the mountain town of Cassino, the site of a famous Benedictine abbey. Beginning in January, Allied warplanes bombed the abbey and much of the town, reducing it to deserted rubble by the time the Germans finally retreated on May 17.

As Raymond Moseley wrote in his book about war reporting, "The Allied Command was convinced the Germans, despite assurances to the contrary, had occupied the Benedictine abbey on Monte Cassino, giving them a magnificent observation post. Thus, in February the decision was made to bomb the abbey—a major mistake. The ruins provided the Germans an excellent defensive position for fending off attempts to capture the stronghold. . . . Allied infantry attacked and was beaten back with heavy losses."[19]

Cassino was an extremely dangerous environment until the Germans finally pulled back in mid-May. In one engagement, Bigart got caught in the open in a small boat and narrowly escaped the strafing fire from a German plane. When the Allies finally took the town, Bigart and Kenneth Dixon of the Associated Press were the first reporters to enter.

Bigart found it "a bleak, gray, smoking ruin which, with a little sulphur added, would be more grim than a Calvinist conception of hell." No civilians remained. Houses, shops, even olive orchards had been bombed into blackened rubble. Only one hotel had a "guest"—a German tank that had been driven into the lobby and abandoned. "Everywhere," Bigart found, "the Air Force had done a truly remarkable job of flattening Cassino."[20]

The Allied planes that carried out those bombings were commanded by Lt. Gen. Ira C. Eaker, the same officer who been in command in England during the Writing 69th's flights to Wilhelmshaven. As the Allies failed week after week to drive out the Germans, Bigart wrote an analysis that absolved Eaker of blame for the stalemate but argued that the Allied strategy of relying mostly on airpower was flawed.

The reason for the failure at Cassino, Bigart wrote two months into the bombardment, was that "the Allied air forces have been victims of too much ballyhoo. They have been overglamorized at the expense of the infantry until the public has been seized by the delusion that the defeat of Germany could be brought about by air power with a very slight expenditure of infantry. Too many times wishful thinking has colored our assessment of air-raid damage."

He had seen that reality when he talked to officers who had led troops into the supposedly deserted Cassino, "only to be stopped cold by German snipers and machine gunners hiding in buildings in the southwest portion, which was virtually untouched by the bombs." The Germans, far from bombed into flight, had fought bravely and well. As a result, "Rome is no closer than it was two months ago when the first all-out attack on Cassino was launched to coincide with the landings at Anzio. The Gustav line is unbroken."[21]

That was an early example of many such analyses he wrote during three major wars and several smaller ones. He had no formal military training, but as he spent more and more time in combat zones—more time than many officers—he became increasingly confident of his ability to assess tactics, strategy, and performance. His editors shared his confidence and gave his assessments prominent display, often including his name in the headlines on his articles.

Next Stop: Rome

Learning their lessons from Anzio, where they had not deployed enough troops, and Cassino, where they had relied too much on airpower, Allied commanders waited until they had assembled an overwhelming advantage in manpower to undertake a ground assault on the Gustav Line. Even so it took several days of heavy fighting. The Germans finally pulled out in mid-May, opening the way for an advance toward Rome.

On May 17, Bigart was with a group of American soldiers as they rode in Jeeps toward the town of Formia, passing guns, food, and personal effects the retreating Germans had left behind. His driver retrieved a German accordion. Streets were mined and booby-trapped. A sudden burst of shelling forced them to seek shelter in what had been a children's hospital, where they found small beds that had been stripped of their linen and piles of dirty socks. On a wall of the rubbish-filled basement was a "German pin-up girl, overdressed and quite unattractive by 'Esquire' standards."[22]

Bigart's competitor from the *New York Times* during this campaign was Milton Bracker, a reliable old-school newsman. (When I worked at the *Times* years later, he was the last reporter in the newsroom who wore a green eyeshade on the job.) *Times* correspondents had much more feedback from home and far less leeway in writing than those from the *Trib*, so Bracker was under constant pressure to beat Bigart or at least to keep up with him.

One night during the Cassino battle, they returned to camp late in the evening, famished. Bracker and an AP reporter persuaded a cook to fry up a platter of eggs, but Bigart would not take a break from working on his story to eat anything. Bracker, hungry but afraid of being beaten into print, took a plate to his workstation and grabbed bites while typing. Bigart waited until he had finished writing, after midnight, before taking a crust of bread, which was all that was left of the impromptu meal.

According to Richard Kluger, who interviewed both men, "The day Cassino fell, Bracker was off on a story in another part of the sector, and when he got back to camp weary at nightfall, discovered Bigart had been up at the monastery when the Americans finally seized it. To match Bigart's dateline, Bracker had to make his way up to the abbey through the dark, over still heavily mined fields; traversing the same fields by daylight the next morning, two British correspondents were killed by mines."[23]

After finally breaking through the Gustav Line, the Americans advanced quickly toward Rome. Bigart was with the Fifth Army as the troops entered the capital. The vivid, intensely personal account he filed on June 5 appeared under the headline "Nazi Guns Put Tragic End to Roman Holiday."

"The entry of Allied troops into the heart of the Eternal City at dusk last night," it began, "was a moment of such wildly primitive emotion that even now, 12 hours afterward, it is impossible to write soberly of the nightmarish scene along the Via Nazionale, where jubilation gave way to frozen panic and sudden death. The Nazis, attempting to save their army from annihilation, sent a flak wagon charging into the lead column of American troops."

A flak wagon was a tank or tracked vehicle on which was mounted a heavy antiaircraft gun aimed not at planes but at people on the ground. After their initial shot at the Allied troops, the Germans unleashed a fleet of them against Romans who were in the streets and at their windows celebrating the Allies' arrival.

"We were within a few hundred yards of the Forum of Trajan at the end of the Via Nazionale," Bigart wrote, "when a flak wagon careened around a bend in the Via 4th of November, its guns streaming red tracers into the throngs outside the Bank of Italy. I shall never forget that dreadful moment of panic." When Americans in a Sherman tank destroyed the flak wagon, "it lay like a helpless black beetle . . . two Nazis were killed outright and a third was dying. Three others were taken prisoner. The infantrymen had to fire their rifles into the air to save the captives from the infuriated throng."

That article appeared in the *Herald Tribune* on June 6, 1944—D-Day on the beaches of Normandy. Overnight the campaign in Italy, where the outcome was inevitable after the capture of Rome, became a sideshow to the main event. By late June, while intense combat continued as the Allies fought their way north-ward, Bigart focused a good bit of his attention on the fate of Italy's troves of irreplaceable art masterpieces.

When Perugia was captured, he reported on the fierce fighting, but he also sent a separate story noting that the Church of San Domenico and the art inside had survived both "Nazi vandalism" and British shellfire.

Accompanying French troops as they entered Siena, he described the delight of the citizenry that all its treasures, including the famous Piazza del Campo, had been spared. That report prompted an editorial celebration on Forty-First Street.

"Our correspondent, Homer Bigart, with his unerring instinct for the right time and place, arrived in Siena Monday with the French troops of the 5th Army," the commentary said. It noted that American tourists knew Siena mostly from the run-ning of the Palio, a horse-racing spectacle in the Piazza del Campo. Bigart did not see that race, "but he told of delighted citizens gathered in the famous Fountain of Gayety, and he commented on the rich banners of the seventeen wards tossed high in the morning sunshine."[24]

In Vatican City, he watched as a team from the army's Monuments, Fine Arts, and Archives unit, or "monuments men," opened a crate of masterpieces the Ger-mans had taken from the museum in Naples and the monastery at Cassino. Bigart always minimized his education, but he had learned enough to write knowledge-ably about works by Breughel, van Dyck, and other masters. All the works known to have been taken, including five Titians, were in the recovered crate except one— *The Blind Leading the Blind* by Pieter Breughel the Elder, completed in 1568.

"It should be noted," Bigart wrote after talking to Maj. Ernest DeWald, an art professor at Princeton who headed the recovery team, "that the Germans have been combing France and Belgium for paintings of the early Flemish school and that Adolf Hitler reportedly is building his own personal collection around Flemish primitives."[25]

Bigart stayed with the advancing troops in Italy until mid-August. One of his last big stories from that campaign reported that the Germans blew every bridge in Florence as they abandoned the city except the Ponte Vecchio, one of the most celebrated structures in Europe. By the third week of August, he was reporting from liberated southern France.

From a village near Marseille, he reported that the troops had outrun their ration trucks and were subsisting on melons and vegetables from gardens along their route. Fortunately, those were plentiful, and the French seemed happy to share. Then a French farmer and his family drove up with a large ham. The farmer cut it up, and his children offered slices of ham with chunks of brown bread to the grateful troops.

This entire account, as it appeared in the paper, was only four paragraphs long. The last paragraph said, "The sight of fresh ham proved so entrancing that hardly any attention was paid to papa's daughter, a plump, blonde mademoiselle wearing a tight lemon-colored sweater."[26]

On the final day of August, Bigart watched as the Americans wiped out a last pocket of German resistance near the town of Montélimar. This was basically mop-up duty. The big news that day was elsewhere, as reflected in the next morning's front-page headlines: "Americans in North Take Rheims," "Soviets Capture Ploesti and Its Oil Fields," "Bulgaria Asks for Surrender Terms."

The defeat of Nazi Germany was now inevitable, although the Battle of the Bulge and the fight for the Ludendorff Bridge at Remagen still lay ahead. It was time for Bigart to move to a new front, but on his way out he had some fun with a tale of female German troops who had stopped their retreat long enough to loot the fashion boutiques and lingerie departments of the department stores in the walled city of Louhans.

They grabbed "dresses, shoes and lacy unmentionables which could not be purchased in the fatherland for love or money," he reported. The "pillaging frauleins" left debris but little else. At one store, he found a merchant shoveling broken glass into the street. "All that remained of his stock were some odd scanties too small to encompass a Westphalian bottom."[27] Like the tight sweater on the French papa's daughter, this sort of locker-room towel snapping didn't disappear from American newspapers—even from the sober-minded, respectable journals such as the *Herald Tribune*—until many years later as more women entered the business, bringing new attitudes with them.

Bigart at home in Hawley, Pennsylvania, with his parents, 1944.
Photographer unknown. Courtesy Wisconsin Historical Society.

FOUR

THE PACIFIC AND THE BOMB

The war's outcome in Europe was no longer in doubt after the liberation of France, so the *Herald Tribune* transferred its star combat reporter again, this time to the Pacific theater to chronicle the campaign against Japan.

"I didn't want to leave Europe for the Pacific but the paper asked me to go so I did," Bigart told an interviewer, without explaining his reluctance.[1] After a vacation in New York and a visit with his parents in Hawley, he was with the troops in the Philippines by early November 1944.

The Japanese had occupied the Philippines since 1942. Now, two years later, Gen. Douglas MacArthur, the overall commander in the Pacific, could have bypassed the country and sent his forces directly toward Japan across the islands and atolls of the Western Pacific, but he had personal as well as strategic reasons for wanting to retake the Philippines. When he had been forced to evacuate as the Japanese invaded, he made a public pledge: "I shall return." As Bigart arrived, the Americans were driving across Leyte toward Corregidor and Manila.

The transfer from Europe turned out to be fortunate for Bigart's career because his dispatches from the Pacific theater brought him his first Pulitzer Prize. Over eight months, he produced one riveting account after another, rich in perception and detail, describing the combat and its devastating effects on people and places. Many of the most dramatic articles were written in the first person because he was there, facing the same dangers as the troops.

The Pacific campaign was in some ways less interesting to American readers because the region was unfamiliar to most of them, and it lacked the cultural and historic treasures of Italy. But in his interview with Richard Kluger some years later, Bigart said he came to prefer covering the Pacific because there was no frigid winter—"I'd rather be terrified in a warm place"—and because he could often survey the entire battlefield, on a single island, rather than a small segment of a much larger engagement.[2]

In the Philippines campaign, he found a different kind of combat from what he had experienced in Europe, as he noted in one of his first dispatches. "This correspondent, coming from the European fronts, has been impressed by the weakness of the Japanese artillery, and the failure of the enemy to employ mines with anything like the diabolical thoroughness of Field Marshal Albert Kesselring's army in Italy," he wrote from Leyte.

"Here you can drive right up to the front line in broad daylight without drawing a storm of artillery or getting blown sky high by Teller mines," he wrote. It created "a false sense of security"—until the entrenched Japanese opened fire.[3]

Again and again, he would see American troops hit the beaches of the islands and atolls not knowing how much Japanese resistance they would meet, only to find out the hard way.

A few days after that unobstructed landing on Leyte, he reported, a group of Japanese soldiers infiltrated the American lines. They set up a roadblock and started shooting at an American convoy. Bigart's account of that engagement showed his ability to combine the personal and the human with the grim and menacing reality of war.

"For twenty-eight hours I was on the wrong side of the Japanese roadblock," he wrote. "I had spent Sunday night in a foxhole fifty yards from the spot where the Japanese had come out of the woods. At 7 o'clock I hailed a passing truck and hitchhiked to the front. Our truck was the last to get through."

Once he reached the command post at Breakneck Ridge, he encountered "a slim, bespectacled lieutenant colonel, straight as a ramrod and smoking a long cigar." His name was Charles R. Meyer, "who will be remembered as 'Monk' Meyer, an all-American West Point football player. He inquired after Stanley Woodward," the *Trib*'s sports editor.

As his unit moved forward toward the blocked convoy, "Meyer looked down and found himself straddling a Japanese playing possum," Bigart wrote. Meyer pulled out his pistol and shot him.[4]

A few weeks later, Meyer wrote to Woodward about his encounter with Bigart, and Woodward printed the letter in his *Herald Tribune* sports column. Meyer said Bigart "looked like a drowned rat. It was raining then, as usual. He'd spent the night in a mud hole which incidentally was attacked by some of this force that we were to fight," and he was very hungry, having missed several meals. (As printed, the letter uses a then-common racist term for Japanese people.)

Wherever I went Homer Bigart was there getting facts and never in the way. We fought all that day and after we settled for the night Bigart went for another story during the lull. He never seemed to tire. I was pooped out. That night I offered him a spot in the C.P. [command post] but this was crowded and he disappeared. Later I found out that he'd slept with the men down by a kitchen. At dawn he followed me out. We made good progress, then we got stalled for awhile. I borrowed a half-track to move up to the tanks. Frankly I was a little scared. We'd gotten to a place where some vehicles were in the road—dead lying around—and beyond was the Nip. The vehicles had to be moved to get the tanks up. They were road-bound due to the weather. I dodged in and out of the vehicles, more than a little bit leery of the situation. At the farthest point I looked around and there was Bigart—unconcerned, getting his story, disregarding his own safety and still never in the way.

"I thought he was a damn fine correspondent," Meyer said.[5]

As the troops fought their way across Leyte, Bigart observed in one dispatch that "the slow, brutal slogging that must come in the face of the enemy's fire doesn't make exciting reading. There's nothing very dramatic about an attack that gains maybe 100 yards and liberates twenty desolate palm-thatched huts."[6] For readers with no experience of war, Bigart was delivering the old soldier's truth: war is the only circumstance where it's possible to be scared to death and bored to death at the same time.

After the bloody recapture of Leyte, Bigart then reported each battle and skirmish, town by ruined town, as the troops slogged their way across Luzon toward Manila.

At Corregidor

Bigart was with the troops when they landed at Corregidor, at the mouth of Manila Bay, once again seemingly encountering no Japanese defenders. A Philippine military outpost that had guarded the beachfront before the Japanese invasion was a deserted ruin.

"For the first 280 yards, as we made our way in a landing craft toward Corregidor," his account began, "everything went well. Emboldened, we began sticking our heads up over the side. Lieut. Col. Edward M. Postlethwaite of Chicago, commanding the Third Battalion of the 34th Infantry Regiment of the 24th Division, was sitting calmly on a truckload of ammunition."

Suddenly a hail of .40-caliber machine gun fire erupted from the mouth of a cave above them.

Our boat was the nearest [to] shore and we caught the first fusillade. Bullets bit into the armor. We groveled in the slimy bottom near the ramp, keeping as much distance as possible between ourselves and the ammunition truck. There we lay in a close huddle during the long minute the Japanese gunners gave us exclusive attention. On my right, a doughboy suddenly raised the bloody stump of his right hand. An instant later, a soldier squatting next to him toppled dead. A bullet had gone through his back and out through his chest. The horrible tearing power of machine gun bullets was brought home to us for the first time.

At one point, they could not tell which direction the Japanese fire was coming from. As he had already learned on Leyte, "there is nothing more futile," Bigart observed, "than lying on the wrong side of protective cover."

Then there was a "quick, slamming blast" that brought rubble and dust down on him and the soldiers in his group. "A mortar shell had burst 20 feet to my left and a jagged fragment sailing over my foxhole instantly killed a soldier lying immediately to the right. That was enough. I loped to a big shell crater and stayed there until things quieted."[7]

When they arrived at the town of Dagupan, they were startled when a sixty-five-year-old saloon keeper named Elton Smithers emerged to welcome them.

"Doughboys stared at the tall, gaunt Smithers as if he were an apparition," Bigart wrote. "'You speak very good English for a native,' said an infantry officer who found him waiting on the beach with three half-grown mestizo offspring. 'I should,' drawled Smithers. 'I'm an old corn farmer from Dunbrook, Virginia.'"

Bigart detailed at some length the tale of how Smithers, despite a Japanese proclamation that any Americans found in the area would be shot, had survived with the aid of the town's mayor, who buttered up the Japanese commander and convinced him that Smithers had abandoned all ties to his native country. It was a negligible incident in the overall drama of the war, but Bigart once again showed his skill at using the story of one individual or a small group to give readers a much larger picture to which they could relate.[8]

In much the same way, at Tarlac a week later he told the tale of four nuns—three Germans and an Austrian—who had stayed throughout the war to operate their Catholic school and saved it from burning by the Japanese. "We are Germans, but one can't help where he was born," the mother superior said.[9]

During a respite at Dagupan, Bigart had reported, "it may get a bit sticky later on but at the moment the green Luzon plain looks like the seventh heaven of the Pacific to doughboys who have spent two years in the jungles and swamps of New Guinea."

Some days actually passed without rain, so that the troops "for the first time since leaving home can wander cross-country without floundering in waist-deep mud. There are cornfields and orchards, peanut plantations, and even occasional watermelon patches." To their delight they found hot dog stands, a movie theater, and two open saloons. The local women were so friendly that the exhausted troops had to threaten to remove their trousers so that the women would go away and let them get some sleep.[10]

He found a much less benign picture when he interviewed American troops who had been captured by the Japanese as the Philippines fell at the start of the war. They had been held in horrifying squalor, beaten, and starved; they said others died of dysentery because they had no clean water and no sanitation facilities. Those who had tried to escape were summarily shot.

At a place called Paniqui, Bigart found two American soldiers who had escaped from Japanese custody after Bataan and joined Filipino resistance guerrillas. When the troops entered now to retake the place from the retreating Japanese, "they were met by guerrilla cavalry led by Sergeant Joseph Donahey, of Bataan and Clinton, Iowa, and his pistol-packing bride, Corajon Mangrovany, who is credited with killing a Japanese pilot who parachuted down near her home last November."[11]

That tale prompted an editorial in the *Herald Tribune* hailing Bigart's work:

Guerrillas with the best stories, such as the sergeant, seem to walk or ride out of the jungle right into the arms of Mr. Bigart, as if he were possessed of a magnetism which compelled them to head directly for his pencil and notepaper. It is fortunate that it is so, for Mr. Bigart has a good ear for a fine yarn and can write one even when wet and cold and tired and in danger. When the guerrillas tell their superb tales of adventure to him they are talking to the right man.[12]

In the last week of January 1945, Bigart informed readers that "this war with the Japanese is a slow, exhausting war of attrition, and despite the deceptive speed of the advance it is not going to be won in the next few weeks or the next few months." But he also reported that the advancing Americans had unlikely local allies, such as Sergeant Donahey's guerrillas and "pygmy tribesmen" known as Negritos, who were renowned for their skill with the bow and arrow.

"These strange, shy people," American officers found, "have fought the Japanese with both primitive weapons and a few American rifles saved from Bataan. No other group in the Philippines has aided the American cause with more courage and blind loyalty."[13]

Bigart was with the troops when they seized Camp O'Donnell, which had been the terminus of the infamous Bataan death march in the early months of the war. No prisoners were being held there, but not far away they found a barracks complex holding nearly two thousand Americans, Britons, and other Europeans, mostly civilians, who had been imprisoned by the Japanese.

Those people had to be moved for their own safety, Bigart reported, but one young lieutenant from New York encountered "a frail middle-aged woman who refused to leave without her Persian cat. 'She's been gone since Tuesday,' she wailed. 'I'm afraid they've eaten her.'" That was the sort of human detail that made the war comprehensible to readers at home—a Bigart trademark. It is surprising that he failed to include the cat's name.[14]

It was February 1945 when the Americans finally retook Manila. By the time they entered the capital, they encountered only scattered Japanese fire. The more critical problem was the absence of water.

"With its business and financial and theater district reduced to a blackened ruin and fires still burning in the port district," Bigart's report began, "Manila faced still another menace today through the partial failure of the water system." People with jugs and pitchers were lining up at the few functioning hydrants. At a prison where Americans had been held by the Japanese, army water trucks brought drinking water, "but Americans there were told they would have to forget about washing."[15]

Next Stop: Iwo Jima

There were still Japanese holdouts in the jungle outside Manila, but after most Japanese troops pulled out of the city, the Philippine campaign was essentially over. Bigart promptly moved on to the final phase of the war, the drive across the islands and atolls of the Pacific toward Japan itself. The Marines had already taken Saipan and Tinian; his first stop in the islands was Iwo Jima, which he found far better defended than Corregidor.

"Iwo was even nearer impregnable, its garrison, estimated at 20,000 men, being three times greater than that of Corregidor and having far superior fire power," he reported. Those Japanese defenders, he wrote, "were combat troops under skilled commanders who made very few mistakes." They were dug in, concealed in pillboxes and firebases of heavy timber and concrete, and they could not retreat because on that small island they had nowhere to retreat to.[16]

The Americans had to take Iwo Jima, Bigart told readers as the battle began, "and we will have to pay for it." It took eighteen days of "desperate fighting," which Bigart observed at the side of Maj. Gen. Graves B. Erskine, commander of the Third Marine Division.

The headline on one piece Bigart filed from Iwo gave the flavor of what happened there: "Iwo Hospital: War Rages outside but Its Staff Performs Miracles: Surgeons, Aided by Blood Flown from U.S., Do 20 Major Operations a Day; Men Become Inured to Shootings on the Premises." At that rudimentary field hospital, doctors treated grievously wounded combatants from both sides, Japanese as well as Americans. Doctors told Bigart that the Japanese were mostly peaceable and grateful for the care.[17]

The next major objective after Iwo Jima was Okinawa, which at 466 square miles was fifty-eight times as large as Iwo Jima and provided the defenders with ample room and varying terrain to maneuver. Okinawa was the gateway to the Japanese mainland; knowing they had to take it, the Americans committed more than 180,000 soldiers and Marines and the Navy's Fifth Fleet to the attack.[18]

On the first day, April 1, 1945, the Japanese again shocked the Americans by retreating from the coast instead of contesting the landing. The enemy, Bigart reported, "yielded two of the island's three airports, its finest beaches on the sheltered west coast less than a dozen miles above the capital city of Naha and a generous hunk of the Bisha River flats, now dry and hard and admirably suited for mobile warfare.

"It was unbelievable—this Easter parade of doughboys and marines across beaches that might have been as bloody as Iwo Jima's." The troops encountered only light resistance, if any. "Of the seven amphibious landings this correspondent has witnessed, this was the weirdest," he wrote. By late afternoon, the scene was "about as warlike as a Poughkeepsie regatta."

Still, Bigart reported, nobody was euphoric. "It was too good to be true. Everyone, from admiral and general down to doughboys digging in for the night on the chilly plain, knew that the Japanese would not surrender the keystone defense islands of Ryukyu without a bitter campaign."[19]

His warning was all too accurate. By the time the occupation of Okinawa was complete, ten weeks later, more than 100,000 Japanese soldiers had been killed, in addition to thousands of civilian casualties. The Americans reported 12,520 deaths and more than 36,000 wounded. The Fifth Fleet lost thirty-six ships, many to kamikaze attacks.[20]

As was by then his style, in addition to a big-picture article about the overall progress of the campaign, he wrote about individuals and groups whose actions helped readers understand the fear, the pain, and the heroism to be found in any war. He told of a Marine pilot from Oklahoma who, when the guns of his plane froze, used the spinning propeller to shear the tail off an enemy fighter, sending it spiraling down into the Pacific.

He wrote about a conscientious objector serving as an army medic who saved scores of lives while under heavy enemy fire. The medic, a Seventh-day Adventist, went into the combat zone even on a Saturday after a moment of prayer.

For Bigart's New York readers, he went out of his way to file a detailed account of a critical breakthrough by the Twenty-Seventh Infantry Division, composed of New Yorkers who had been in the state's national guard. After that action, the Twenty-Seventh was pulled back from the front line.

"Normally, relief of the division would attract little comment," Bigart observed, "but because the division's action on Saipan was clouded by unfortunate publicity, it is perhaps necessary to explain why the 27th was replaced today by the 1st Marine Division."

He did not specify what that "unfortunate publicity" was about, but he was referring to the fact that Lt. Gen. Holland "Howling Mad" Smith, the overall commander at Saipan, had relieved its previous commanding officer, Maj. Gen. Ralph Smith, of his command after accusing him of disregarding orders. (Ralph Smith was later exonerated and given a new command.)[21]

"The battle conduct of the 27th Division during the recent offensive [on Okinawa] was such as to remove any doubt of its combat efficiency," Bigart said, providing perhaps some small comfort to the families of the many New Yorkers who died in the action.[22]

During the critical Okinawa campaign, Bigart went well beyond the reporter's role as an observer and projected himself into a controversy over the military's tactics and leadership as if he were a high-ranking officer. He often referred to the US forces and their officers as "we." He wrote about what "we knew" and what "we had expected" and about how at one critical point "we were wrong" about what the Japanese would do. His editors let him get away with it because by that time he was a well-known personality. His name and his articles were featured prominently in many papers through the *Herald Tribune*'s syndicate, and his opinions were circulated like those of the country's most prominent columnists. Moreover, he had seen more combat than many of the officers had.

In its edition of May 29, the *Trib* used on page 1 an Associated Press dispatch about the day's fighting. An assessment by Bigart of the US forces' performance appeared inside the paper as a "shirttail" added to the end of the AP story. Its placement in the paper did not diminish its impact.

The early joyride in Okinawa "yielded only an insignificant kill," Bigart said, because the Japanese commander "kept his garrison intact by withdrawing inside the Shuri defense belt" around a town south of the landing beaches. There, "two Army divisions—the 7th and the 96th—quickly stalled against the powerful outer defenses of Shuri." Because the Twenty-Seventh Division was still engaged in heavy fighting elsewhere on the island, it was not available to join the action at Shuri. The question facing the American commanders was how to deploy the Marine III Amphibious Corps after its "speedy clean-up" of the landing beaches.

> It could be landed behind the Japanese lines in the south, or it could be employed on the existing front to add power to the frontal assault on the Shuri line. A landing on southern Okinawa would have hastened the encirclement of Shuri.
>
> Our tactics were ultra-conservative. Instead of an end run we persisted in frontal attacks. It was hey-diddle-diddle straight down the middle. Our intention to commit the entire force in a general assault was apparently so obvious that the Japanese quickly dispersed their troops in such a way as to most effectively block our advance.

Without fear of an amphibious landing on his rear, the Japanese commander apparently moved the bulk of his force from southern Okinawa into the Shuri defenses. Thereafter he could fight on terrain of his own choosing, always consolidating his forces on the narrow front.

The result was a prolonged siege, with heavy casualties.

After reading Bigart's analysis, David Lawrence, an influential syndicated columnist in Washington and later the founder of *U.S. News and World Report* magazine, wrote a strongly worded piece about what he called the "military fiasco at Okinawa . . . a worse example of military incompetence than Pearl Harbor." He blamed the heavy US losses, in ships and men, on the "bungling" that had prolonged the battle. He demanded to know why the "truth" was "being hushed up."[23] His column appeared most prominently in the *Washington Star*, then the most influential paper in the capital. In New York, it was published in the *Sun*.

Lawrence's piece was a classic example of the second-guessing by armchair critics far from the action that often follows military setbacks. Americans have experienced it time and again—after the Tet Offensive in Vietnam, for example, and after the disorderly withdrawal from Afghanistan in 2021. Although predictable, it prompted a furious response from Fleet Adm. Chester W. Nimitz, the commander of US forces in the Pacific.

Had Nimitz kept quiet, Lawrence's column, and the report by Bigart that had provoked it, would have been forgotten in a few days. Instead, the admiral held a news conference on Guam, projecting the argument onto front pages across the country. Bigart was among the reporters at the news conference, and he wrote the *Herald Tribune*'s story even though he was part of it.

The Okinawa campaign was neither "bungled" nor "a fiasco," Nimitz said. He said Lawrence was "so badly informed as to give the impression that he has been made use of for purposes which are not in the best interests of the United States."

According to Nimitz, "New landings would have had to be made over unsatisfactory beaches against an alerted enemy defense. They would have involved heavy casualties and would have created unacceptable supply problems." He said Lt. Gen. Simon Bolivar Buckner Jr., the commander of ground operations on Okinawa, decided not to deploy the Marines in a separate amphibious landing, and as Buckner's superior officer, he agreed with it.

After reporting what Nimitz said, Bigart added, "This correspondent still believes that a landing on the south coast of Okinawa would have been a better employment of the marines. But to call the campaign a 'fiasco' is absurd. This writer covered the Italian campaign during the Anzio and Cassino actions, and he knows what a fiasco is." At the end of that article, the *Herald Tribune* published the text of Nimitz's statement, an excerpt from Lawrence's critical column, and a statement by Lawrence disputing the admiral's remarks. He said he had relied on Bigart's report to make his judgment.[24]

That could have ended this argument, which no one could win and mattered little in the overall scope of the war. But the next day the *Trib* published a long editorial about it, criticizing both Lawrence and Nimitz.

> Neither Mr. Lawrence nor the admiral comes out too well from this exchange. The former still bases his defense on Mr. Bigart's report, which did not, on its face, warrant the conclusions Mr. Lawrence drew. Mr. Bigart has not changed his mind about the advisability of an "end run," but he states flatly that "to call the campaign 'a fiasco' is absurd." This would seem to leave Mr. Lawrence open to merited rebuke. The unsupported suggestion by Admiral Nimitz that the writer was "used," however, is an unworthy one and can only lead to more heat and less light in a discussion in which the American people are vitally concerned.[25]

Meanwhile, the lethal combat on Okinawa continued through June. General Buckner was killed on June 18, four days before the Japanese commander on the island and his chief of staff committed ritual suicide, effectively ending the battle.

After Okinawa, US forces faced the prospect of invading mainland Japan. To avoid the untold thousands of American casualties such an operation would surely entail, President Harry Truman instead ordered that the atomic bomb be dropped on Hiroshima and Nagasaki, major cities that were largely intact.

Japan surrendered on August 15, 1945, six days after the bombing of Nagasaki.

On the same day, just before Emperor Hirohito broadcast his message of surrender, Bigart embarked on a B-29 Superfortress for the last bombing raid of the war. His last combat dispatch bore the dateline "IN A B-29 OVER JAPAN, Wednesday, Aug. 15, 1945." The pilot was "First Lieut. Theodore J. Lamb, 28, of 103-21 Lefferts Boulevard, Richmond Hill, Queens"—the ultimate "local angle" on a faraway story, as reporters called it.

Their target was Kumagaya, which Bigart described as "a pathetically small city of little obvious importance"—so little that the crews wanted to know why such a dangerous mission was necessary, since it was clear that surrender was imminent. The flights had even delayed takeoff for half an hour in expectation of the announcement. "No one wants to die in the closing moments of a war," he observed.

"We've got 'em on the one-yard line. Let's push the ball over," the commanding officer, Col. Carl R. Storrie of Denton, Texas, exhorted them.

While in the air, "we caught every news broadcast, listening to hours of intolerable rot in the hope that the announcer would break the news that would send us home," Bigart reported. That did not happen, so they flew on to Kumagaya, dodging sporadic antiaircraft fire, and leveled much of the town. By the time they returned to Guam, the surrender was official.[26]

Japan Surrenders

Two weeks later, Bigart was on the deck of the USS *Missouri* when the Japanese formally signed the capitulation documents. He described the event in one of his most memorable articles, a model of powerful brevity.

> Japan, paying for her desperate throw of the dice at Pearl Harbor, passed from the ranks of the major powers at 9:05 A.M. today when Foreign Minister Mamoru Shigemitsu signed the documents of unconditional surrender.
>
> If memories of the bestialities of the Japanese prison camps were not so fresh in mind, one might have felt sorry for Shigemitsu as he hobbled on his wooden leg toward the green baize-covered table where the papers lay waiting. He leaned heavily on his cane and had difficulty seating himself. The cane, which rested against the table, dropped to the deck of the battleship as he signed.

Noting that fallen cane was a classic Bigart touch, like the missing Persian cat on Luzon. General MacArthur, Bigart noted, never said a word to Shigemitsu, nor did Shigemitsu—clad in "frock coat, striped pants, silk hat and yellow gloves"—say anything. The entire article was eight paragraphs long.[27] More words would have been superfluous.

After the surrender, Bigart had one last big story to write from the Pacific theater.

American air crews had dropped the atomic bomb on Hiroshima on August 6 and another on Nagasaki a few days later. On September 3, the day after the ceremony aboard the *Missouri*, Bigart was one of a small group of reporters whom the US Army transported to Hiroshima to see what remained of the city and its people. What he found was not what he expected—the devastation was so total that there was very little rubble.

Before leaving Okinawa, he had seen aerial photos of the destruction caused by the atom bomb. It was the first time he had seen a bombed, wrecked city with no bomb craters—the atom bomb exploded in the air over the target, not on impact—but as he noted, "The utter erasure of a city cannot be easily grasped by studying a picture."[28] Now he would see the wreckage up close.

He and his small group were not quite the first reporters to arrive. Some trains were still running, and Wilfred Burchett of the London *Daily Express*, traveling by himself, had ridden one to Hiroshima a few hours earlier. He sent his dispatch by telegraph to avoid military censorship. "I write this as a warning to the world," his article said. He described hospital wards filled with people with no visible injuries, who were dying from what he called "an atomic plague."[29]

MacArthur's occupying army promptly canceled Burchett's press credentials. He had unwittingly walked into a controversy about the ethics of using nuclear weapons that basically pitted the US military establishment against the medical and scientific establishment. It was one thing to deploy a weapon that killed indiscriminately on a mass scale; it was another to deploy a weapon that would continue to kill long afterward.

The War Department and the army took the position that those who died at Hiroshima were victims of the explosion and of the fires that followed and that there was virtually no residual radioactivity that would go on killing people indefinitely. The official line was that because the bomb had been detonated in the air, it had unleashed blast and fire but had not deposited poisonous radiation on the ground. Like Burchett, Bigart found otherwise.

"We walked today through Hiroshima, where survivors of the first atomic-bomb explosion four weeks ago are still dying at the rate of about 100 daily from burns and infections which the Japanese doctors seem unable to cure," his report began. He had been in a war zone ten thousand miles from Washington for months and knew little about the ethical controversy, and he did not dwell on it. He simply reported, in his customary sharp detail, what he had observed.

"In the part of town east of the river the destruction had looked no different from a typical bomb-torn city in Europe. Many buildings were only partially demolished, and the streets were still choked with debris. But across the river, there was only flat desolation, the starkness accentuated by bare, blackened tree trunks and the occasional shell of a reinforced concrete building," he wrote.

In what had been a commercial area, "we passed what had been a block of small shops. We could tell that because of office safes that lay at regular intervals on sites that retained little else except small bits of iron and tin. Sometimes the safes were blown in."

The stench of death was everywhere. The reporters encountered few people because many residents who had survived the blast had apparently left town, but, oddly, some streetcars were running.

The reporters talked to local doctors who told them that rescue workers and others who had spent only a short time in the city after the blast apparently suffered "no ill effects," but many who continued to live amid the ruins "developed infections that reacted on the blood cells as destructively as leukemia, except that the white blood corpuscles and not the red were consumed. Victims became completely bald; they lost all appetite, they vomited blood."[30]

Another reporter in the group, W. H. Lawrence of the *New York Times*, asserted flatly, "The atomic bomb still is killing Japanese at a rate of 100 daily in flattened, rubble-strewn Hiroshima." Neither article changed the official line in Washington about radiation, but the reports stirred up members of Congress, who began demanding the truth. This was almost a year before John Hersey's famous *New Yorker* article obliterated all doubt about the residual effects of the bomb.

Alex Wellerstein, a professor at the Stevens Institute of Technology in New Jersey, has written extensively about this issue. According to him,

> The scientists had told the War Department that radiation was unlikely to be a major casualty-producer mainly because of the altitude of the burst and because they figured anyone close enough to get a fatal radiation dose would be killed by other factors (blast, heat, fire) anyway. But the real world is more complicated than this, so there were probably 15% or so casualties from primarily radiation. The War Department denied the initial reports of this as sympathy-producing propaganda (they felt they were losing control of the "narrative"), but also sent over its own scientists to study the medical effects, and they found that the Japanese physicians and scientists were correct.[31]

Interviewed years later, Bigart said of his four-hour tour of the city,

> I don't know what I was expecting but it was visually an enormous letdown. None of us knew what Hiroshima had looked like before the bomb but I think we were expecting to see vast heaps of debris as in Hamburg or Dresden or Coventry or London. But apparently the bomb demolished everything. There were only a few shells of buildings left standing, those made of iron and steel. And of course most of Hiroshima had been made of wood and it was just consumed by fire.

He also said that "some Japanese officers kept warning us not to loiter but we were suspicious of their warnings. In fact they were doing the correct thing because if we had hung around very long we probably wouldn't be here today. I knew nothing about radiation at the time and I don't think most of the Americans knew any more, although the army certainly knew enough by then not to send troops in."

Historians and ethicists still argue about the morality of inflicting mass death and prolonged suffering on civilians, but Truman never wavered in his conviction that it was the right thing to do at the time. Neither did Bigart. After all, American planes had incinerated much of Tokyo with conventional ordnance. Why was this different?

"It's very easy to look back and express shock and horror but at the time we thought it was just a hell of a good raid, just another big bomb," he said. "We were still full of the war spirit and Japan was an all-out war. We felt we had to win it and that we had to practically exterminate the enemy. Hatred was something you lived with. I'm very suspicious of people's expressions of shock now. They've forgotten how they felt then."[32]

A few days later, Bigart tracked down a Dutch military physician, Capt. Jacob Vink, who had been among the Allied prisoners of war held at Nagasaki at the time the bomb was dropped there. He confirmed that deaths continued at the rate of ten to twenty a day because of radiation poisoning.

Describing the symptoms, Vink told Bigart, "At first I thought it was simple lockjaw. There was swelling in the back of the throat, light hemorrhages under the skin, fever, and a high pulse rate. Then I noted a rapid consumption of white blood corpuscles. In one case the white corpuscles count dropped from 70,000 to seventy or eighty a cubic centimeter. Finally, there was internal bleeding in the intestinal tract."[33]

These early accounts by Bigart, Lawrence, Burchett, and a few other reporters alarmed American officials hewing to the party line. On September 12, Bigart filed a detailed, straightforward account of a statement by Brig. Gen. Thomas Farrell, the chief of the atomic bomb team at the US occupation headquarters in Tokyo, reiterating the official assessment.

Farrell confirmed that "many bomb victims were affected by radiation, but insisted that all cases could be traced to exposure to gamma rays at the instant of the detonation," Bigart reported. "Any residual radiation such as has been reported by the Japanese was not in sufficient quantity to be dangerous."[34]

In Washington, this argument went on for months, spurred by Bigart's interview with Vink and a *New York Times* report that American prisoners of war had been among those killed by radiation poisoning in Nagasaki. By then, however, Bigart had moved on. His war, the shooting war, was over, and the political war was not in his portfolio.

In one of his last reports from Japan, he described what he saw in what was left of Tokyo. The damage there resulted not from an atomic weapon but from saturation bombing with conventional ordnance.

"The Japanese capital is no longer a city," he wrote. "The catastrophic fires kindled by the American Superfortresses have transformed greater Tokyo into widely scattered settlements separated by vast piles of ruin."

Little food was available. Two major industrial districts were "horribly scarred and desolate." Burned-out trucks and trolley cars littered the streets. The US Embassy had been badly damaged, but repairs were under way, and the building would soon become MacArthur's occupation headquarters.[35]

In the last week of September 1945, after a brief stop in Korea, Bigart toured the Dutch East Indies, where he found the indigenous people in a rebellious mood. Then he was in Saigon, evaluating the future of Indochina after the end of Japanese occupation.

Shortly after the war, Admiral Nimitz wrote that he was authorizing Bigart to wear the Asiatic-Pacific Theater Campaign Ribbon. "The high standard of performance of his journalistic duties contributed to the successful prosecution of the war in the Pacific Ocean Areas," the letter said. The following spring, Secretary of the Navy James Forrestal gave Bigart a certificate of commendation "for outstanding performance and service rendered to the United States at war, as an accredited Navy war correspondent."

Bigart donated the letter and certificate to the Hawley Public Library, where they are displayed in a glass-fronted case of Bigart memorabilia, but there is no way to tell what he felt about them. It is not a reporter's job to "contribute to the successful prosecution" of a war or to "render service" to a country at war, even his own. The reporter's job is to tell what happened, and defeat can be just as good a story as victory, failure just as interesting as success.

When he received his first Pulitzer Prize, the premier award in journalism, the following spring, the *Herald Tribune* honored him with a remarkable editorial tribute:

In the Pacific campaign on Leyte, Iwo, Okinawa and elsewhere, Mr. Bigart merely continued to display those qualities of honesty, unawed discernment, effective prose style and unshakable physical courage which had already made him something of a legendary figure in Sicily, Italy, and France. It was not considered too healthy to go out with Mr. Bigart on a story: he began to get really curious about the time most other correspondents would begin hunting a foxhole. But as readers of this newspaper know, the stories which came back were as stripped, incisive and free of egotism or bravado as only a first-rate reporter could make them.[36]

Bigart in Greek mountains with rebel leader Markos Vafiadis (*left*) and an interpreter.
Photographer: "Roussos." Courtesy Wisconsin Historical Society.

FIVE

COLD WAR, TOUGH CALLS

Most of the 1,646 American reporters and photographers who had been accredited to cover the war went home when it ended, minus the thirty-seven who had been killed.[1] For the relative handful who remained involved in overseas coverage, the nature of the job changed almost overnight. There was no longer a single focus; instead, reporters and their editors had to prioritize among multiple issues. These included the emergence of the Cold War in a divided Europe, the reconstruction of Europe and Japan, the disintegration of colonial rule in Asia and Africa, the development of new international organizations such as the United Nations (UN) and the North Atlantic Treaty Organization (NATO), and the struggle between Jews and Arabs over the future of Palestine. These complex developments often did not lend themselves to deadline coverage. The job of foreign correspondent had to be done in different ways.

In the war, there had been undisputed good guys and bad guys. Taking sides was acceptable, even expected. And combat stories were generally straightforward: the battalion took the town or it failed to do so; the bombs struck their targets or not. On the new global stories that did not involve combat, and that was most of them, reporters were expected to set aside their personal views of any issue and present only the facts as best they could determine them. That was not as easy in practice as it was in principle, and it did not last long.

These new stories were considerably softer around the edges; often there was no right answer. Were the Muslims of India justified in demanding a separate country when Britain granted independence in 1947? Should the United States accommodate the Soviets in occupied Berlin or confront them? Should Palestine be partitioned into Arab and Jewish entities? In theory, these questions were for the opinion columnists and editorial writers, not for reporters in the field. But reporters were people; like their readers, they formed opinions based on what they observed and facts they uncovered, especially in dealing with oppressive, cruel, or corrupt regimes.

Bigart encountered this new reality as he evaluated the political and economic landscape of postwar Europe.

As the Soviet Union tightened its grip on Eastern Europe, the puppet governments Moscow installed were odious to a profession committed to freedom of expression, of the press, and of movement. It was difficult not to let sentiment seep into the news coverage. Just the choice of what to write about could reflect a reporter's attitude about whatever country he or she was in.

Bigart was in Poland during the brief period when the Soviet Union was going through the motions of permitting the emergence of an independent, democratic state. He soon saw through Moscow's pretense and judged accordingly. He picked a side and said so openly in a remarkable dispatch to the *Herald Tribune*:

> A reporter cannot stay two weeks in the poisoned atmosphere of Warsaw without developing a bias which, perhaps unconsciously, is bound to color his reports, and there is no correspondent in Poland today who hasn't in his heart aligned himself with either the Communist-dominated government or the now open opposition of Vice-Premier Stanislaw Mikolajczyk's Peasant Party. It is important that the reader remember this, for although the reporter is obliged to "give both sides"—few newspapers would keep him very long if he didn't—the bias creeps in. Sometimes it's in the clever stressing of one side's arguments over the arguments of the other. Or perhaps in the sly omission of a damaging fact.

He said most of the Western correspondents were, "like the present writer, somewhat left of center." They were not intellectually opposed to the establishment of a communist government in a country that the Soviets had liberated from the Nazis. "If Poland wants Communism, that is no business of ours," he wrote.

But because the government treated reporters as enemies, lying to them as it lied to the Polish people, and shutting out any who had dealings with the opposition, it was inevitable that journalists would come to resent it. "There is no middle ground, no impartial witness," Bigart wrote. "Battle lines are drawn and everyone has chosen his side. It is a war over the definition of democracy—East versus West—and because you have been conditioned to Western concepts, you find yourself drawn irrevocably toward Mikolajczyk."[2]

The *Trib*'s foreign editor, Joseph Barnes, said that article was "an excellent description of the central problems of foreign reporting." He saluted Bigart for his "candor" in "admitting frankly that he felt no omniscience, no objectivity, and no compelling urge to shout 'Wake Up, America.'"[3]

Moscow did not wait long to put an end to Mikolajczyk's opposition. He lost a brazenly rigged election in 1947 and fled the country. The Iron Curtain fell in Poland, pretty much ending the need for Western news organizations to keep reporters there, and Bigart soon moved on. But the events he had observed in Poland, like those he had witnessed at Anzio, would shape his reporting for the rest of his career. He was generally sympathetic to the oppressed and have-nots of the world and suspicious of authority figures and the self-important whether in foreign capitals or at the Pentagon or in city hall. He knew when he was being lied to and resented those who did the lying. Those views showed through in much of his best peacetime reporting in articles about the poor, the oppressed, the disenfranchised, and the exploited.

While he was still in Poland, in a "bedbug-infested hotel" in Warsaw, he received word that he had won the Pulitzer Prize for his reporting from the Pacific. He had a "mixed reaction," he said, "because a lot of stumblebums had won it" before him.[4]

Bigart's antipathy to dictators and autocrats was not limited to those aligned with Moscow. It was on full display in his reporting from Spain in 1949.

The ruler of Spain was the pro-fascist Generalissimo Francisco Franco, who had seized power in the country's civil war a decade earlier. As the Cold War spread across Europe in the late 1940s, the United States and its allies confronted the question of how to deal with Spain. It was a dictatorship, but Franco was rigorously anti-communist. Could Spain be a useful, if distasteful, ally? Should it be admitted to NATO, the mutual defense alliance created in 1949? Should the United States provide financial aid?

Bigart examined the Spanish question in four articles in February 1949 as the North Atlantic Treaty was being negotiated. He found that Spain was a "basically Fascist," one-party police state. Freedom of assembly was nonexistent. Labor strikes were prohibited. Books, radio, and entertainment were censored. The government controlled the allocation of newsprint, withholding it from papers that strayed from the official line.[5] The political mindset of Franco and his associates "hasn't changed much from the days when they were praying out loud for Nazi victory and the triumph of the New Order."

The allies faced "the old conflict between expediency and political morality," Bigart wrote. "So long as there is strong fear of war with Soviet Russia, expediency would seem to dictate early restoration of full diplomatic relations plus economic aid. But idealism rejects this as an abject admission that moral principles professed during the late war are now invalid and bankrupt, and that full recognition of Franco as an ally against communism means endorsement of a Fascist system as abhorrent as communism."[6]

These were not political opinions, in the sense of Republican versus Democrat or this candidate versus that one. They were what might be called human opinions. The credible, the well motivated, and the honest had nothing to fear from Bigart, but beware, dictators and autocrats. These ingrained attitudes would manifest themselves most strongly, and most importantly, more than a decade later in Vietnam.

In principle, good newspapers professed to be "objective" in their news articles, leaving opinions to the editorial pages and signed columns, but it was not always possible. Bigart was honest with himself about this in a way that few reporters or editors are. He leveled with readers, enabling them to assess his factual reporting in the context of his views.

American newspapers had not always espoused "objectivity." Before the invention of the telegraph in the 1840s, the concept would have baffled most publishers. They saw their papers as forums for the expression of their own views on economic, political, and social matters. The telegraph made it possible in 1846 for a group of New York publishers to create the Associated Press, a cooperative news agency that served clients of divergent perspectives. The only way the AP could satisfy its clients was to deliver news that was straightforward enough to be acceptable to all of them.[7] That standard of neutrality and objectivity did not necessarily apply to content that individual papers or chains generated on their own, which was often loaded to promote the publisher's objectives. In one famous example, Hearst's *New York Journal* gave splashy display to inflammatory, circulation-building but often false stories about Spanish behavior in Cuba that helped to foment the Spanish-American War.

In Bigart's day, even the most scrupulous papers could not claim total objectivity, nor can they do so now. Editors make choices every day about what to cover, where to send reporters, how long each article should be, and where to position it in the newspaper. They also have to decide whether to publish comments from people whose activities the news articles recounted if they were clearly false or offensive and how to respond to criticism from readers who found an article inaccurate or unfair. All those decisions inevitably reflect the views of the people who make them.

Bigart, whose reporting could be aggressive and provocative, often found himself in the middle of such situations, as he did in Palestine in 1947, the year after his experience in Poland.

His assignment was to chronicle the painful and often violent transition of Palestine from British rule to partition by the United Nations and the emergence of a Zionist state. This was war reporting in a sense because bombings, shootings, and interceptions of vessels at sea were near-daily occurrences. But it was entirely different from war reporting in Italy and the Pacific because there was no clear right or wrong. For American reporters, there was no "we" among the combatants, and there was no clear-cut enemy.

The traumatized survivors of Europe's Jewish communities who needed someplace to resettle securely were worthy of sympathy, of course, but what happened in Europe was not the fault of the Palestinian Arabs. In Palestine, the British were governing legally, not as colonists or conquerors: Britain had received a mandate from the League of Nations to take control of Palestine after the breakup of the Ottoman Empire. The mandate, which the league issued on August 12, 1922, was unequivocal in giving Britain full control over Palestine, including Jerusalem and its holy places, until the permanent status of the territory was determined. But it was entirely equivocal in setting out how that future would be established, because it instructed Britain to carry out the terms of the famous Balfour Declaration. That could not be done.

In November 1917, when it was apparent that the Ottoman Turks would lose the Great War and forfeit much of their territory, British foreign secretary Arthur J. Balfour wrote a letter to Lord Walter Rothschild, a prominent British Zionist. In its key passage, Balfour said, "Her Majesty's Government view with favour the establishment in Palestine of a national home for the Jewish people, and will use their best endeavours to facilitate the achievement of this object, it being clearly understood that nothing shall be done which may prejudice the civil and religious rights of existing non-Jewish communities in Palestine, or the rights and political status enjoyed by Jews in any other country."[8]

That being the stated British policy, the League of Nations included it when designating Britain as the governing power in Palestine and instructed the British to carry it out.[9] But the two parts of the mandate—to establish a "national home for the Jewish people" while protecting "the civil and religious rights" of those who already lived there (namely, the Arabs)—could not be reconciled then any more than they can be today.

By the time Bigart arrived in December 1946, the British remained the duly constituted, internationally approved authority in the territory, but they were in an impossible position. The Jews in Palestine, their numbers swelled by Holocaust survivors from Europe, were clamoring for the "national home" they had been promised. Some of them had resorted to violence to drive the British out. The Arabs, with at least the nominal support of virtually every Arab country, were committed to resisting the creation of any Jewish state. Because they had broad economic and strategic interests around the Arab world, the British tried to impose tight limits on Jewish migration to Palestine.

The atmosphere was volatile. The headline on one of Bigart's first dispatches said: "4 Britons Kidnaped, Flogged by Jewish Guerrillas in Palestine / Major and 3 Soldiers Are Whipped in Retaliation for Court Sentence of Boy, 16 / Underground Battles Troops at Tel Aviv Road Block."[10]

A few weeks later, Bigart watched as 650 Jewish migrants from Eastern Europe reached the port of Haifa, only to be rounded up by the British and interned on Cyprus. Some went quietly, he reported, "but others fought, screamed and clung to railings until they were beaten and dragged down the gangplank."[11] That evoked sympathy for the Jews, of course, but as Bigart reported, British officials and troops were dying, too, as the Jewish underground resorted to kidnappings and blowing up trains.

In the absence of any clear-cut right or wrong party, of any unarguable aggressor or victim, Bigart filed vivid, detail-rich accounts about Jews trying to reach Palestine and British efforts to keep them out while giving no indication where his sympathies lay, if any. He described the Jewish groups that turned to violence, the Irgun and the so-called Stern Gang, as terrorists, which they were, but otherwise he stayed neutral. His letters to his family from that period dealt mostly with working conditions, travel, and food—not with the rights or wrongs of the conflict.

He managed to maintain his dispassionate tone even in a long account of the clandestine induction of Jewish youths into the Haganah, the Zionist militia. He was the first foreign correspondent to witness such a ceremony; blindfolded, he was driven to a place he could not identify and was prohibited from naming any of the participants. His long article described the recruits and their commander, who was "tall, dark, gray-featured, and wore no signature of rank, being clad like the rest in a khaki shirt and shorts, with a black leather pistol belt and black shoes." He reported all the details of the ceremony, including a reading from Deuteronomy. At the end of it, he wrote, the cadets "had taken an irrevocable step, one that might lead to their death in the Galilean hills or on the beaches of Sharon." There was no hint of approval or disapproval of what they were doing or of the organization they had joined.[12]

Bigart stayed in Palestine as the conflict escalated through the summer of 1947, when he departed for a vacation at home. In October he was staying with his parents in Hawley when his editors unexpectedly asked him to report on a different kind of conflict—a college football game between Penn State and West Virginia University. In a news article announcing that Bigart would be covering the game, the *Trib* reported that "Bigart at first attempted to get out of the assignment on the ground he had never covered a football game. The sports editor's counter was: 'You never covered a war either, did you, until the last one started?'"[13]

The sports editor was right. He knew that a good reporter could cover pretty much any kind of story. Bigart's perfectly competent account appeared on October 26. Penn State, led by its "great Negro back," Wally Triplett, won 21–14 in "a thrilling and vicious game."

The article announcing that Bigart would cover the game also said that the *Trib*'s editors had come to regard him as a marketable star, like the lead actor in a movie. Over the years, he would be featured in many of the paper's advertisements for itself, and his name showed up in headlines: "Bigart Reports from . . ." or "Bigart Finds That . . ." This one told readers Bigart was at home "resting before undertaking another foreign assignment." By Christmastime he was in Italy, reporting on the state of its government and politics. In early January 1948, he arrived in Athens.

Civil War in Greece

The scrupulous neutrality Bigart had demonstrated in Palestine was harder to maintain in another conflict of the postwar era—the civil war in Greece. There, he made his views clear and unwittingly became part of the story.

The Greek Civil War of 1944–49 was rooted in bitter divisions among the Greeks that arose during the years of Nazi occupation, but by the time Homer Bigart arrived in Athens in January 1948, it had evolved into the first serious armed conflict of the Cold War, aside from the long-running civil war in China. For Bigart, the Greek war was an eerie preview of what he would experience in Saigon fourteen years later.

The conflict, marked by atrocities and brutality on all sides, ebbed and flowed, beyond the control of the British, who administered Greece after the Germans withdrew, and then of the Americans, who assumed responsibility for the country's fate when Britain was no longer able to support it. There were multiple Greek factions, but in essence the war matched pro-communist insurrectionists, based in the northern mountains, against a far-right royalist government that was backed by Washington even though it was oppressive and incompetent. The rebels were commanded by Markos Vafiadis, a reclusive founder of the Greek Communist Party who was known as "General Markos." The rebels were ideologically attuned to Moscow but received most of their direct military support from the communist government of Marshal Josip Broz Tito in neighboring Yugoslavia.[14]

President Truman committed the United States to support the royal Greek government in an address to Congress on March 12, 1947, in which he proclaimed what came to be known as the "Truman Doctrine": the United States would come to the aid of countries or peoples threatened by Soviet aggression or communist uprising. Greece and Turkey were the first countries on his list.

"The United States has received from the Greek Government an urgent appeal for financial and economic assistance," Truman said. "Preliminary reports from the American Economic Mission now in Greece and reports from the American Ambassador in Greece corroborate the statement of the Greek Government that assistance is imperative if Greece is to survive as a free nation. I do not believe that the American people and the Congress wish to turn a deaf ear to the appeal of the Greek Government."

He said Greece, a nation of about seven million people, was "industrious and peace-loving" but lacked the resources to deal with "the terrorist activities of several thousand armed men, led by Communists, who defy the government's authority at a number of points, particularly along the northern boundaries." At the time of its liberation from the Nazis, Truman said, Greece was utterly destitute and three years later was still struggling to recover. "When forces of liberation entered Greece," Truman said, "they found that the retreating Germans had destroyed virtually all the railways, roads, port facilities, communications, and merchant marine. More than a thousand villages had been burned. Eighty-five per cent of the children were tubercular. Livestock, poultry, and draft animals had almost disappeared. Inflation had wiped out practically all savings."

The president acknowledged that the Greek government is "not perfect" and "has made mistakes," but he said it deserved American support because "it represents eighty-five per cent of the members of the Greek Parliament who were chosen in an election last year" that appeared to be fair and open. He asked Congress to finance technical, economic, and military assistance, which the lawmakers agreed to do.[15]

The choice may have seemed clear-cut to Truman, but most of the American reporters who went to Greece found the picture considerably murkier. They described a Greek government that enforced its rule through restrictions on free expression, arbitrary arrests, exile of dissidents to remote islands, and mass executions in the prisons. They saw a Greek army unwilling to fight. Greek military leaders insisted that the armed forces lacked sufficient weapons and equipment to mount an effective campaign, so they declined to take the military initiative.

In a war where diplomatic and military headquarters are stationary in one city, as was the case in Greece, the international press corps tends to gather in one downtown hotel. The bar becomes an informal information center, where reporters congregate in the evenings to share their experiences and greet newcomers. In Athens it was the Hotel Grande Bretagne, on Constitution Square in the heart of town, still one of the city's best. Bigart checked in and was soon getting an earful from such colleagues as Phil Potter of the *Baltimore Sun* and George Polk of CBS.

From them and from his conversations around the capital with Greek journalists, diplomats, and whatever Greek and American government officials were willing to talk to him, he quickly discerned the state of play. Less than a week after arriving, he filed an article reporting that Maj. Gen. William G. Livesay, the chief of the US Army support mission, said the Greek army was capable of defeating the guerrillas if it had enough of the right equipment. Therefore, the general said, the United States would soon provide heavy artillery, machine guns, and officers with experience in mountain warfare to advise the Greeks, with more to follow.

This announcement, Bigart wrote, "represents complete surrender to Greek demands." The type of weaponry the Greeks had, he wrote, was of "trivial importance beside the implications" of the deployment of American advisers. "With American officers assisting Greek field staffs in the spring drive the 'war' suddenly becomes personal. Military as well as diplomatic prestige will be at stake, and should the Markos junta in the mountains receive recognition from Russian satellites it is difficult to see how another major war can be avoided."[16]

In general, serious news outlets prohibit reporters from making such statements on their own; reporters, who are not opinion columnists, are required to find academic analysts, credible opposition politicians, or diplomatic observers whose assessments can be quoted. Bigart had learned from his experience in Poland that a straightforward account of facts does not always give readers a full picture of the situation, and the editors at the *Herald Tribune* had decided he knew what he was talking about, so they turned him loose. He was just getting started.

Later that month, he sent a "situationer," an analytical article longer than a straight news piece that attempts to give a comprehensive overview of what is going on. His editors liked it so much that they ran an advertisement promoting it and displayed the article prominently at the top of the front page.

"Whether the American aid mission to Greece succeeds or fails depends heavily on the promised spring offensive of the Greek army," Bigart's article began. "Unless the army achieves final victory over the guerrillas, Americans will be forced to conclude that there is a basic and perhaps incurable rottenness in Greek civil and military administration, and that the Balkan phase of our attempt to contain Communism is a losing gamble."

If the Soviet Union intervened directly, "Greece would be untenable," the article said. "Among the Americans here there is a growing conviction that we should tell the Greeks quite frankly that we will not send combat troops into another Bataan." The Greeks had to understand that it was up to them to fight their own war.

The American aid mission was laboring to supply the Greeks with the aid they needed to shore up the civilian economy, Bigart's report said, but the government was doing a poor job of distributing it. Machine tools were piling up in warehouses, for example, "because there is no particular controlling authority to get them out."

Yet it was not entirely the fault of the Greeks, his report acknowledged. "A lot of stuff stays in warehouses because as the French say it is inutile." The useless material provided by the United States included "20,000 pairs of horse collars much too big for the scrawny Greek animals and heavy plows completely useless in a country where farmers use a walking plow. A fugitive decimal caused [the US aid mission] to ship enough strychnine to kill everybody in the Balkans."[17]

His next report said the American aid mission was pressing the Greeks to decentralize the government because Athens had become "a fantastic bureaucracy employing more than 80,000 civil servants in seventeen jealous, uncooperative ministries which often maintain duplicate bureaus and departments. Consequently, ministers spend most of their time squabbling over jurisdiction." Absent radical restructuring, Bigart wrote, "Greece will remain a bottomless rathole into which millions of American dollars are poured without visibly improving the condition of the Greek masses."[18]

When American military advisers went to the front in early February, Bigart went with them. His report ran on the front page of February 7, 1948, under this headline: "Reporter at Front Finds Greeks Need Initiative More Than Guns."

He filed his article from an outpost near the Albanian border, where "a handful of American officers are engaged in probably the weirdest assignment ever handed on by the War Department." They were there, he wrote, to persuade the Greek army to abandon static defense and "get out in the mountains and fight the guerrilla rebel forces of General Markos." But the Americans were required to be tactful about it because "the Greek is free, independent and excessively mulish" and didn't respond well to orders. The Americans' only leverage was a threat to withhold weapons and money, but "the Greeks, who are fairly smart people, know a bluff when they see one. Hasn't President Truman told the world that Greece is indispensable?"

He wrote that the right-wing Greek press parroted the military line: the army was poorly equipped, and the rebels were better armed. "This defeatist attitude," his report said, "is not solely for the consumption of foreigners and millionaire Greeks of Kolonaki Square who are squirreling away their gold in Switzerland and New York. Political officers have been heard preaching it to the troops."

Bigart reported in several dispatches that when the army did go into action, its tactics were often questionable: the troops bunched up when they should have scattered, fired indiscriminately at illusory targets, and retreated after minimal casualties. When they gained an advantage, they tended to squander it with dilatory maneuvers.

When General Livesay was reassigned out of Greece in mid-February, Bigart said it was because he was "an outspoken and completely candid soldier" who angered the Greeks by telling them that "their carping demand for more and more artillery was a lot of twaddle and that they could very well lick the guerrillas with what they had."[19]

In late February, the public affairs office of the US Embassy, responding to criticism of the Greek government's efforts to control the press, issued a statement saying that "there is no country in Europe where a greater degree of press freedom can be found than in Greece." Bigart, unpersuaded, did not make that the lead paragraph of his report. Instead, he led with the arrest the same day of two newspaper editors whose paper had criticized the mass executions of prisoners from the opposition. He called the issuance of the embassy's statement a "sorry coincidence."

He said the embassy's press office had "probably" issued its statement "to offset the flood of undesirable publicity Greece has been getting in the American press." American and other foreign reporters were indeed free to move around and report as they wished, he said, "but to say that the Greek press was free was stretching the truth."[20]

Bigart's reporting naturally distressed the US Embassy and the US aid mission, and it infuriated the Greek government, eliciting the same type of reactions he would elicit in Vietnam. It did not take long for him to become a target of the right-wing Greek newspapers, which denounced him as a tool of the communists. He was hardly the only one.

At the instigation of Constantine Tsaldaris, one of the most powerful politicians in Greece, the right-wing papers kept up a steady barrage of verbal fire against George Polk, Raymond Daniell of the *New York Times*, and other foreign reporters, mostly Americans. Some were accused of being not only communist sympathizers but also drunks or adulterers. Bigart was soon one of the most prominent targets.

"My case is mild compared with the attacks being made against other outspoken reporters on the scene," Polk wrote in a report to CBS News headquarters. "At the moment, being a newcomer in Greece, Bigart is getting the 'treatment' that others of us already have had. In particular, he is being denounced by name as a Communist; he is ridiculed for 'looking at things upside down'; he is being refused interviews by persons he needs to see for news purposes," including Tsaldaris. The Greeks did nothing so crude as expelling reporters who were out of favor or censoring their outgoing copy, Polk wrote. "Instead there is a clever plan of making work as difficult as possible for critical correspondents."[21]

Polk and Bigart were obvious targets of the government and the right-wing press. Both represented major American news outlets and took a dim view of the Athens scene. Both were iconoclasts and skeptics, and despite their very different backgrounds, they had shared professional experience: Polk also had begun his journalistic career at the *Herald Tribune*. And both had worked for George Cornish, who became the paper's editor in 1941.[22] Shortly before Bigart's arrival, Polk had published a scathing article in *Harper's Magazine* exposing corruption and incompetence in the government, citing Tsaldaris by name, and his views were reflected in much of what Bigart wrote. They were, in the government's eyes, two of a kind.

Summoned to a Lecture

Bigart had been in Greece only a few weeks when Karl Rankin, chargé d'affaires at the US Embassy, summoned him for a lecture—a summons issued at the request of Tsaldaris, who in Bigart's reports was depicted as promoting a fascist-style autocracy.

Rankin was soft-spoken and well educated, but he was known as an anti-communist zealot who for that reason supported Tsaldaris and the royalist government regardless of their failings. He objected to Bigart's descriptions of Tsaldaris, who was now vice-premier in a government headed by a more liberal rival, Themistocles Sophoulis.

"Isn't there a danger in this appellation, Mr. Bigart," Rankin asked, "coming from a reporter as well-known as yourself, in one of our country's leading newspapers? Might it not be construed as representing American opinion in Athens? Your inference that Mr. Tsaldaris is trying to set up a 'rightist police state' and to get rid of Sophoulis could also harm the chance of further aid to Greece, could it not?"

Bigart said he was not trying to halt aid to Greece, but Rankin wasn't finished.

"I hold no brief for Tsaldaris," he said. "He can be a difficult man. But, Mr. Bigart, he happens to be the undisputed leader of by far the largest party in Greece. . . . And so far as setting up a rightist police state, well, I've heard nothing to suggest that Tsaldaris favored such a step. Democracy is a tender plant under the conditions that obtain in Greece today," he went on, as if Bigart could not figure that out for himself.

"On the one hand we Americans are driven by military and economic necessity to urge upon the Greeks drastic measures, many of which only a dictatorship could fully implement," Rankin continued. "On the other hand, we must press them constantly to observe democratic forms and to maintain a maximum of freedom and tolerance. We cannot push them too far or the whole thing could collapse. In view of this delicate situation, I'm sure you will understand the danger of your sort of reporting."[23]

Bigart was undeterred. This, for example, was the first sentence of one article about Greek political affairs: "The Congress of the Greek General Confederation of Labor, by which Americans set great store as the show window for democracy in the Balkans, has degenerated into a sorry farce."[24]

By the time he wrote that, he and George Polk had become, in the words of author Kati Marton, "two of the monarchy's most hated critics." The *New York Times* largely escaped the wrath of the government and the embassy, Marton said, because its resident correspondent in Athens, A. C. Sedgwick, was a compliant conduit for the official positions, although the tone of the *Times*'s coverage was different when Raymond Daniell was reporting on Greece.[25]

Aside from standing up for Greek reporters he respected, Bigart tried to avoid personal involvement in Greek affairs, but it could be difficult. In a letter to his parents on April 5, 1948, he wrote that "an hour ago a delegation of Greek women whose sons are in jail awaiting execution came into the lobby of the hotel and gave me a petition. They all wept and kissed my hand and it was very embarrassing. Of course I can do nothing to help them. I'm trying to help a Greek newspaper man named Vokos who was arrested after talking with me two weeks ago."

He had appealed to Constantine Rentis, the minister of public order, on Vokos's behalf. "Probably Vokos is a Communist as Vokos claims," he wrote, "but I don't want to have him shot or given a long prison term because of work I asked him to do."

In the letter, he wrote that he was "being attacked very bitterly by the Athens press" and that a Greek delegate to the United Nations had denounced him in a letter to the Reids, the owners of his newspaper. "It doesn't bother me. I'm used to it by now."

He was "used to it," but by the time he wrote that letter, he had had enough of it. He was leaving Greece for Yugoslavia, where Tito, although a communist, had broken away from Moscow.

Yugoslavia bordered Greece, but getting from Athens to Belgrade was no simple journey because of the war in northern Greece. Bigart gave his parents this forecast of what the journey would entail:

> At Salonika I will get in touch with the Yugoslav consul general who will see that I get automobile transportation to the Yugoslav frontier. The frontier is virtually closed, and there is no train or bus service, but the Yugoslav consul will telephone to the nearest Yugoslav town, Devedlija, where a car will come and fetch me to the railway station. Then I take a six hour train ride to the Serbian city of Skoplje (I guess that's how it's spelled) arriving at 7 p.m. in time to catch the overnight express to Belgrade.

The Death of George Polk

Once Bigart crossed the Yugoslav border, he thought he had left Greece behind, but the story there did not let him go so easily.

On May 16, while Bigart was in Belgrade, the body of his friend and colleague George Polk was found in the water off Salonika (now Thessaloniki). He had been shot in the head, and his hands and feet were bound. He had gone north from Athens to find and interview the reclusive General Markos. His murder has been the subject of investigation and controversy ever since. Bigart would later join a group of his colleagues to investigate what had happened, but in the meantime, he had another issue to deal with.

On May 2, 1948, after Bigart had left Greece and before Polk's death, the Opinion of the Week column on the *Herald Tribune*'s letters and opinions page was a piece titled "Reporting and Interpreting the News in Greece" by Dwight Griswold, the chief of the American Mission for Aid to Greece. Griswold was a conservative Republican, a former governor of Nebraska, and a future US senator. Polk once described him as "an unmitigated jerk."[26]

Griswold wrote,

> Mr. Bigart does not confine himself to factual reporting. He admits that his articles are interpretive. His interpretation is then interpreted editorially not only by the Herald Tribune but by other American newspapers influenced by the original dispatches. This process of interpretation and re-interpretation has, regrettably, led to the publication in the Herald Tribune and other American newspapers and magazines which are, to put it plainly, untrue.
>
> Mr. Bigart states that in his judgment Greece is a police state. I can find no other American newspaper man in Greece who agrees with this finding, and there are some very capable reporters here. [What Bigart had actually written was that "from almost any angle the Greek government is pretty awful, but it cannot truthfully be said that the present Coalition cabinet is either Fascist minded or particularly repressive."[27]]
>
> In his story from Athens of March 16, your correspondent writes, "Meanwhile the mass execution of leftists continued." A considerable amount of distortion is packed into those seven words. Death sentences were being carried out not because the accused were Leftists but because they were murderers. They were duly tried and convicted under a judicial system which, as far as I know, has never been criticized by any of the several foreign missions which have worked in Greece nor, for that matter, by any of the foreign correspondents. In the case of former E.L.A.S. [Ellinikós Laïkós Apeleftherotikós Stratós, or Greek People's Liberation Army] members, they were found guilty of killing fellow Greeks in cold blood, not of crimes committed against the German and Italian occupation forces. [The *Trib* had also made that point in an editorial on March 6.]

Griswold also said he based his assessment on full data on all those put to death from the liberation of Greece in October 1944 up to March 13, 1948:

> It is a document of gruesome detail. The names, dates and places are all there. The crimes are in most cases brutal murder, frequently on a mass scale, of men and women—local officials, police, political opponents of the Communists, and in

many cases Greek hostages captured by E.L.A.S. during the Communist uprising of December 1944.

He further objected to Bigart's March 26 account of a speech he had given defending the Greek government and disputing reports of mass arrests. In that article, Bigart had written that Griswold's comments "must be dismissed as eyewash" and that "Mr. Griswold did not tell the whole story. . . . He did not mention the 10,000–12,000 officers and soldiers suspected of Leftist tendencies who are confined." The truth, Griswold wrote, was that those prisoners were draft dodgers who refused to serve or military men who "have affiliations which cast grave doubt on their loyalty to the state." He maintained they were "well-treated" and "receiving indoctrination courses" aimed at turning them into loyal soldiers.

"As one who believes that the American press is the best and freest in the world—and the Herald Tribune is one of our finest papers—I regret to report that you have presented a distorted picture of Greece to your readers," Griswold wrote. He said that while police states "are the rule in the Balkans . . . Greece, happily is the exception." He said he wished Bigart's editors could see the ordinary people going into government buildings to get their problems and issues resolved or challenging government officials at public gatherings.

"I feel that the people and public officials of Greece merit our support and good will. After nearly eight years of almost continuous war, occupation and internal strife, they certainly deserve our sympathy." The real news, he said, was that "Greece is not a police state."

Griswold went on: "In all fairness, I must say that Mr. Bigart's reports have had some constructive effect. Many of his dispatches have been factual and stimulating and have helped to keep us all on our toes. Unfortunately they also have had the effect of giving an uncertain over-all picture at a time when American public opinion should be positively informed on the subject."

Griswold's column was promptly reprinted in several Greek newspapers.

On May 30, the *Trib* took the extraordinary step of publishing a reply by Bigart in the form a letter to the editor that ran even longer than Griswold's column.

Yugoslavia, where he was at the moment, was a communist country, Bigart said, but it looked good by comparison with Greece. He said that a visitor who arrived in Yugoslavia from Poland or Hungary, both of which were still relatively free, might find the atmosphere oppressive and restrictive. But a visitor who arrived in Belgrade from Greece "can hardly avoid being favorably struck. He cannot deny that the people's morale is vastly superior to morale in Athens. The Greek capital is mired in hopelessness and hate while in Belgrade there is an atmosphere of optimism and hope. And there are fewer executions."

There may well be "widespread discontent" in Yugoslavia because of the economic hardship imposed by the government's five-year plan, Bigart wrote, but "there is no underground of any consequence," as there surely would be "if the regime were hated as implacably as the government in Athens is hated by a considerable portion of the Greek population."

He said American officials in Athens wanted news correspondents to focus exclusively on the threat of communism, "which they apparently believe is a fate worse than fascism. We are expected to avert our eyes from the suppression of basic liberties, from the mass arrests and mass executions of 'bandits,' the closing of the 'bandit' press, the arrest of 'bandit' newsmen, and finally the shipping of whole boatloads of 'bandits' to exile in the islands."

In their last conversation, he said, Griswold "chided me for what he believed was an exaggerated concern over the activity of the firing squads. He did not like the phrase 'mass executions.'"

Bigart's problem, Griswold had told him, was that he was a "perfectionist." Griswold had observed that even in the United States there were sometimes unfortunate developments such as the mass internment of Japanese Americans during the war.

"I told him," Bigart's letter said, "that he apparently missed the whole point—that in a war of ideologies we did not dare for the sake of expediency to compromise the basic democratic ideals. Because a Negro is lynched in Mississippi we do not have to tolerate and support police terror in Athens. I reminded him that as chief of the American aid mission, which literally runs Greece, he could not avoid some degree of moral responsibility for the executions that were going on." He noted that Griswold had told another reporter he saw no problems with the Greek judicial system on "the same day that Greek firing squads dispatched 152 persons."

Noting that Griswold had not delivered his criticisms in person but waited till after Bigart had left the country, Bigart said he "should have given me a chance to answer his grave charges while I was still in Greece. Unfortunately such niceties have long since gone by the board. Athens is a jungle of intrigue, hatred [and] spiteful pettiness where the art of character assassination has acquired a certain Levantine finesse. An American correspondent who deviates from the official line immediately receives a barrage of abuse from the Athens press and frigid treatment from the American embassy."

Bigart had engaged the services of a Greek reporter named Costas Hadjiargyris, who also worked closely with Polk. In his response to Griswold, Bigart wrote that other reporters warned him that "doors will close to you" unless he got rid of Hadjiargyris, a stepson of Premier Sophoulis, who was suspected by the hardline rightists of communist sympathies. "As a radical he was slightly to the left of

Senator [Robert] Taft," Bigart wrote, referring to an Ohio Republican who was a prominent conservative. "Yet all during the time he was in my employ, Royalist papers harped that he was a Red," and Griswold's press office excluded him from the chief's weekly backgrounder.

"Just when Mr. Griswold decided I was laying on too heavily I do not know. But one day his publicity chief called me in for a frank talk. Congress was about to vote on Greek aid and the boys were worried. Greece was getting too much publicity. He asked me to write something nice and I said sure, I would if I could find something nice to write about."

Bigart added, "Mr. Griswold says he knows no other American correspondent who charges Greece with being a police state, but long before I came to Athens the late George Polk, who was murdered a few weeks ago, was writing eloquently about the nature of the regime we have created there."

This letter was followed by an "Editor's Note": "We are pleased to publish this reply by our correspondent, Mr. Homer Bigart, to the letter from Mr. Dwight Griswold printed on this page May 2, 1948. This letter was written in Jugoslavia [*sic*] where Mr. Bigart has been making an extensive study of conditions. We take this opportunity to express our complete confidence in Mr. Bigart's accuracy of observation and fidelity to the truth. He will shortly return to Greece to resume his reports of the Greek situation."

He did return to Greece, briefly, but not in a fashion anyone would have envisioned.

Finding Markos

On the evening of June 13, as Bigart returned to his hotel in Belgrade, he heard from the night clerk that a stranger had called looking for him and left word that he would return at 11 p.m. His caller turned out to be a young man who addressed him as "comrade," apparently believing from the exchange with Griswold that Bigart was sympathetic to the Left.

"Comrade, you had planned to return to Athens via Rome. Instead you will go via Free Greece and interview General Markos. Is that agreeable?"

Hesitantly, knowing what had happened to Polk, Bigart said yes.

That late-night conversation in Belgrade initiated an epic three-week adventure that not only brought Bigart a major journalistic coup but also featured elements of comic opera and ignited a furious argument with his editors.

On July 22, the *Herald Tribune* published a prominent advertisement under the heading "First Interview with General Markos."

"Weeks ago," it said, "famous foreign correspondent Homer Bigart received a mysterious phone call in his Belgrade hotel. That call eventually led to his 'going underground' and, deviously, across the forbidden Yugoslav-Greek frontier zone where partisans of the 'Macedonian People's Republic' brought him to their leader, General Markos. Bigart's account of his 200-mile secret trip and his interview will be reported in a series of four articles, the first to appear in the Main News Section of Sunday's New York Herald Tribune."

What the advertisement did not say was that the interview had produced little news because Markos spoke no English and had no competent interpreters in his entourage, that the series was therefore more about the logistics and mystery of getting there, and that the editors had held up publication of Bigart's reports for some time out of fear that the newspaper would be perceived as leftist for writing about Markos without condemning him.

Bigart gave this account to a writer who interviewed him years later:

> The Greeks made an appointment to meet me at night on a street corner. They took me down to the railroad yards and put me into a blacked-out coach that was later hitched onto a train that was going to the capital of Macedonia. When we got there I was kept in this compartment until all the other passengers had left. Then I was taken out and put in a truck with the canvas down and given a tire to sit on. The road from there to the border of Greece was pretty rough and we were several hours on the road. I was mystified by all the secrecy when we got down to the border because I didn't know at that time that Tito had broken with Moscow. The result of that was that Markos and the Greek communists didn't know where they stood in relationship to Yugoslavia. From the truck we switched to horses and after two days of riding on a trail we got to Markos's camp.[28]

Bigart told his parents that he had "gotten one of the biggest exclusive stories in Europe today, the story George Polk was murdered trying to get, and it should cause quite a sensation."[29] Later, however, he acknowledged,

> In fact the interview was a disappointment because we couldn't find an interpreter that was any good and because it was all propaganda. But what made it a story was the getting there. Afterward I got across the Greek lines into royalist territory and went down to Athens. The Greek Prime Minister called me in and questioned me about the route I had taken. I told him and he said, "That can't be right because our troops hold the surrounding area." And I said, "Not all the time."
>
> But then, after I'd written my story and sent it to New York, thinking that this was a real feat, nothing happened. It wasn't until later that I heard part of the story. It seems there was a difference of opinion among the top brass. Some thought it too leftist. Remember, the Red Scare was on. Westbrook Pegler was calling the Trib the "Uptown Daily Worker." McCarthy hadn't become terribly well known then but

Pegler was leading the cry. [Bigart was referring to Sen. Joseph McCarthy of Wisconsin, a bombastic demagogue who alleged that the US government had been infiltrated by communists.] The story was held for a week until the chief editorial writer told the owners that they just had to run it, and they did. I understand that some remarks of mine that were thought to be "Commie" were extracted from it. I've never seen how it appeared because I was too pissed off to read it.[30]

When it was finally published, beginning on July 25, the headline on the first article was "Homer Bigart's Perilous Trip to See Markos." The articles, written in the first person, cast aside what had been a fundamental rule at serious newspapers: the reporter should tell the story, not be the story. As Ben Bradlee, the executive editor of the *Washington Post*, put it in that paper's manual for reporters and editors, "A reporter should make every effort to remain in the audience, to be the stagehand rather than the star, to report the news, not to make the news."[31] But in foreign conflicts, when a reporter is at the scene, a first-person narrative is sometimes necessary to convey the full picture, as Bigart had demonstrated in Italy and the Pacific during the war and would do again in Korea. In describing the horseback portion of the arduous journey to find Markos, for example, he wrote, "I did not ride happily. I am over 40 and gone soft and suffered an intolerable aching from a wooden saddle that seemed designed as an instrument of torture." Any reader could wince in sympathy.

In another segment, he described the field hospital where a Greek army nurse who had joined the rebels was performing amputations and other surgeries without administering anesthesia, and he recorded his fear that he would be injured and face such treatment himself. He also reported that his physical discomfort during the journey was magnified by his lack of suitable shoes and the absence of alcoholic beverages.

Such details proved more interesting than anything Markos had to say, partly because of the interpretation problem and partly because Markos was an ideologue. What he did say that was comprehensible was mostly party-line platitudes: "Athens rejected our peace overtures. They thought they saw in it evidence of weakness. Well, they wanted a fight and now they are getting it." The rebel leader filled in details of his personal history but conveyed almost nothing of substance about the war, his sources of support, or what would happen if his forces prevailed. He offered estimates of the number of casualties his troops had inflicted on the Greek army, but those numbers were no more credible than those of military leaders anywhere.

Before setting out with the rebels, Bigart had dashed off a letter to George Polk's brother, William, saying he was "hoping to get the story your brother went after and to find out if the guerrillas can shed any light on the murder. If I have any luck I hope that the stories I send will be regarded as a sort of personal memorial to George, who never forgot there were two sides to every story and who gave his life trying to get 'the other side.'"[32] But neither Markos nor anyone in his entourage gave Bigart any useful information about the Polk affair.

A year after Polk's death, Long Island University established an award in his honor to recognize distinguished, groundbreaking journalism not just in newspapers but in any medium. After the Pulitzer Prize, the George Polk Award is the most prestigious honor in the field. The winner of the first George Polk Award for foreign reporting was Homer Bigart.

An article about the award in *Editor & Publisher* magazine, the industry's trade journal, began, "Homer Bigart, winner of the George Polk Memorial Award, probably stirs up more controversy per square inch of copy than any foreign correspondent this side of Lanny Budd," the central character in Upton Sinclair's eleven novels about intrigue in Europe. "In all, Bigart's career reads like the script of a Hollywood adventure, but the hero of the tale is hardly the dashing, cocked-hat type. He's 41, a bachelor, somewhat on the plump side, graying, and even-tempered."[33] That may have been the only time Bigart was described as "even-tempered."

The Polk Award included a cash prize of $500. At the Overseas Press Club dinner where Bigart received it, he had to wear a tuxedo, so he bought his first one, for $150. "I figure I'm losing money on this award," he told George Cornish. "Between the tux and the taxes, I'll be in the red." Richard Crandell, the *Trib*'s picture editor, said a photo of Bigart in his tuxedo showed "Homer in disguise."[34]

At the initiative of the New York chapter of the Newspaper Guild, the reporters' union, a Newsmen's Commission to Investigate the Murder of George Polk was established in 1948. Bigart was a member. In her definitive account of the Polk case, Kati Marton describes how the group's efforts to obtain the truth were stymied by the US government's determination to defend the Greek regime and how a separate group of elite, establishment journalists chaired by Walter Lippmann bought the line that the Greek communists probably did it.[35]

The Greek government found a scapegoat in the person of a journalist of pliable political convictions, Grigoris Staktopoulos. Tortured into confessing, he spent twelve years in prison. It is fair to say that no one who has looked into the Polk affair at any depth believes that Staktopoulos had anything to do with it. As for Markos, his rebellion failed, and he went into exile in Moscow. He returned to Greece under an amnesty in 1983 and was elected to parliament.[36]

SIX

TWO WARS IN KOREA

The United States and its war correspondents were still recovering from World War II when North Korea invaded the south on June 25, 1950. Within two weeks, many of those same war reporters were back on the battlefront, including Homer Bigart. He and many of his press corps colleagues had seen more combat, and more death, than most of the troops they were now writing about, but this was a different kind of war. As David Halberstam wrote, "The Korea venture was ill-starred from the beginning. It was a war Truman did not want, in a country he did not care much about, conducted by a commander whom he didn't like and who didn't respect him"—namely, the vainglorious Douglas MacArthur.[1]

The United States had not been attacked, and the American people had little stake in the conflict. But combat was combat, and American troops were doing most of the fighting, so reporters went to report about it.

In Korea, as in most wars, there were two groups of correspondents: those who generally stayed near headquarters and command posts, reporting what they could learn about the far-flung, fast-moving events from interviews and briefings, and the ones who went to the battlefields to see the action and talk to the troops. Bigart, of course, was in the second category. He knew that going out with this platoon or that company limited his view of the developments of the war as a whole, but he also knew that reporters for news services such as the Associated Press were capable of covering the headquarters briefings, which were held in Tokyo, and writing the daily surveys. He wanted to report from the hilltops and foxholes.

For him and his colleagues in the field, the war was difficult to cover and very dangerous. The mortality rate among journalists was higher in Korea than in any other American war.[2] Tank and artillery fire was all around them, conditions were harsh, filing their copy was difficult, and many American officers were suspicious and unfriendly. Bigart had an additional problem: he was dealing with two wars at once—one on the battlefield and one against his *Herald Tribune* colleague Marguerite "Maggie" Higgins.

Their feud quickly became the stuff of legend among the press corps. It was a topic of gossip and mirth, comic relief from the war itself.

It was also, as Bigart would acknowledge years later, one of the few episodes in his career in which his behavior was less than honorable. His churlish treatment of Maggie Higgins was unworthy of him.

Higgins was young, attractive, vivacious, fearless, and aggressive as a reporter. Most of her male colleagues and competitors detested her, and because she was a woman, they subjected her to snide innuendo about how she obtained such good information from male sources.

"Higgins was not admired by her colleagues, to put it mildly," Ben Bradlee wrote of her, "especially by her male colleagues, and more especially by the great—and popular—Homer Bigart." They believed, or said they believed, that "she got more than her share of exclusive stories in ways not available to them."[3]

Richard Kluger said flatly that the rumors about her were mostly true. In Berlin, where she was based before Korea, "her notoriety grew with her continued practice of taking useful lovers, among them a leading member of a competing Berlin bureau and an ample selection of ranking American army officers—preferably the kind with stars on their shoulders."[4]

Higgins came from a cosmopolitan background in every way that Bigart did not. She was born in Hong Kong in 1920 to an Irish father and a French mother who had met in Paris during World War I, and she lived outside the United States through most of her girlhood. She learned Chinese from her amah and French from her parents and two aunts in France. When she graduated from the University of California at Berkeley, her class adopted a slogan that was appropriate for her: "They knew what they wanted."

She was a very junior member of the *Herald Tribune* staff when she talked its editors into sending her to Europe just before D-Day. There, as one account put it, she "soon acquired a reputation as a hard-nosed reporter whose aggressive manner offended some of her colleagues."[5] She saw little combat but wrote dramatic accounts of the liberation of the concentration camps at Buchenwald and Dachau.

According to her biographer, she was initially skeptical of the horror stories she heard about what happened in those camps. When she arrived at Buchenwald, she saw how wrong she had been: "Sick with shame, she realized how insensitive she had been to the first prisoners she interviewed. She saw rigid bodies of thousands murdered in the last days."[6]

In the frigid winter after the war ended, she was based in occupied, divided Berlin, where she provided the *Trib* with first-rate coverage of the Soviet blockade and the Allied airlift even as her style and her methods alienated her colleagues and competitors. One colleague of that time told her biographer, "The Herald Tribune was a team exercise and Maggie was not a team player. She was alienating everyone and running herself ragged with that dogged sense of competition. We'd all have been better off if she was there covering fashion."[7]

Higgins wasn't interested in fashion or in any other subject found in the women's pages. She wanted to be where the action was, where she could demonstrate that she could do anything her male colleagues could do. After the end of the Berlin Airlift, the *Trib* sent her to be its correspondent in East Asia, based in Tokyo—an assignment she accepted reluctantly because there did not seem to be much news emanating from that part of the world. It was true that postwar Tokyo was less newsworthy than postwar Berlin, and East Asia was less interesting than Cold War Europe, but her colleagues in the Tokyo press corps resented it when she let it be known that she thought the assignment was beneath her.

Her reputation for obtaining information by what might be called unorthodox methods preceded her to Asia. By the time she got to Tokyo, she had been the very recognizable subject of a roman à clef titled *Shriek with Pleasure*, which described a man-eating, blonde, female reporter in Berlin with an Irish name who used men's beds as reporting tools. That the book was written by a woman did not diminish its unfortunate impact on Higgins.

The relative tranquility of the East Asia beat would soon end. As regional correspondents, most Tokyo-based reporters were responsible for covering several countries, including Korea. When communist North Korea invaded South Korea, they became war correspondents almost overnight.

In Tokyo the *Herald Tribune* shared office space with the *Chicago Daily News*, whose correspondent was an experienced Asia hand named Keyes Beech. He found the "girl reporter," as he called her, to be a nosy nuisance who eavesdropped on his telephone calls, and he soon moved out. But when the war broke out in Korea, they were thrown together, hurrying to Seoul with a handful of colleagues. Just getting to Korea was dangerous, but for the regional correspondents, there was no question about making the journey. It was their job, and for Higgins, it was an essential challenge.

She wrote,

For me getting to Korea was more than just a story. It was a personal crusade. I felt that my position as a correspondent was at stake. Here I represented one of the world's most noted newspapers as its correspondent in that area. I could not let the fact that I was a woman jeopardize my newspaper's coverage of the war. Failure to reach the front would undermine all my arguments that I was entitled to the same assignment breaks as any man. It would prove that a woman correspondent was a handicap to the New York *Herald Tribune*.[8]

When the shooting started, Beech, Higgins, and a few other reporters hustled to the airport and caught the only commercial flight, which was going to Korea to evacuate US citizens. When that plane was turned back by artillery fire as it approached Seoul, it took them three days to find seats on one of the last military flights bound for Korea to evacuate the personnel of the US Embassy. In addition to Beech and Higgins, that plane carried Frank Gibney of *TIME* and Burton Crane of the *New York Times*.

When the reporters disembarked at Seoul's airport, they found it cluttered with luggage, household goods, and vehicles abandoned by Americans and Europeans desperate to get out of the country. Some of the vehicles had ignition keys in them, and the reporters helped themselves. The owners would not be needing them. Beech commandeered a Jeep, and Higgins hopped in with him.

"One of the things that happened to me as a result of the Korean War was Marguerite Higgins," Beech wrote in a memoir. "If I hadn't shared an office with the New York Herald Tribune in Tokyo prior to Miss Higgins' arrival, if Miss Higgins hadn't worked for the Herald Tribune, if she hadn't been aboard the same plane as I flew into Korea at the beginning of the war, and if I hadn't driven a Jeep out of one end of Seoul as the communists were coming in the other—well, life would have been more serene but less interesting."

Reporters who did not have their own vehicles were dependent on the military for transportation. Higgins attached herself to Beech, he said, because "I had a Jeep, Miss Higgins did not have a Jeep, and Miss Higgins valued her transportation."[9] Over the next several months, Beech's animosity fell away as they covered the war together, sharing the danger, the mud, the fear, and, by some accounts, a sleeping bag.

Higgins seemed to relish the danger. "She was reckless because what mattered more to her than life was winning," one chronicler wrote.[10]

James A. Michener, in an introduction to Beech's memoir, wrote that "Maggie Higgins could outsmart almost anyone in getting her story filed first" and that while some of her male competitors, including Bigart, were courageous and resourceful, "some of them were incredible bums" who were drunk half the time.[11]

Since the nineteenth century, from the US Civil War to Crimea to the trenches of World War I, combat had been the arena in which ambitious young journalists made their reputations, as Bigart had done in Italy. Higgins knew that and saw Korea was an opportunity; she threw herself into the assignment. One of her first major reports, about the rout of South Korean forces as they abandoned the capital, ran on the *Herald Tribune*'s front page under the headline "Seoul's Fall, by a Reporter Who Escaped." She had been trapped with some American troops on the north side of the Han River when fleeing South Korean soldiers blew the bridge, stranding thousands of their own troops. Her predicament was compounded by the fact that she was wearing a skirt and a flowered blouse. She never made that mistake again. The cover photo of her war memoir shows her in military fatigues.

She was the correspondent of a major American newspaper, covering the biggest story in the world and holding her own with the competition. Difficult and dangerous as it was, she reveled in it. But her editors in New York wanted a more experienced hand. A week into the war, Homer Bigart arrived and announced that he was taking over. He ordered Higgins to go back to Tokyo and said she would be fired if she refused.

"As a war correspondent of considerable experience," he explained, "I felt I should cover the action and that Miss Higgins should get back to Tokyo and cover MacArthur's headquarters." When she refused to leave Korea, "Tokyo went uncovered" because the *Trib* had no other reporters in the region.[12]

Beech observed,

> Homer may be the greatest war correspondent in the world, but he was a damned poor judge of how to get rid of Higgins. A comparatively unknown girl reporter, she was frightened by Homer's prestige. But the Higgins competitive instinct, a quality hardened and sharpened by childhood circumstance, was a fearsome thing to combat . . . Higgins had jumped astride the story at the start and was riding it for all it was worth. Korea, a thankless assignment, had been part of her beat before the war. Now that it had become a page-one story, she was being asked to surrender it to a more distinguished colleague.[13]

Nobody at the *Herald Tribune* had bothered to tell Higgins that Bigart was coming. She thought it was unfair and refused to follow his dismissive order. Encouraged by Beech and *LIFE* photographer Carl Mydans, she left the press center early the next morning—with Beech, in the Jeep—and headed for the front. When they arrived, they found inexperienced, poorly trained American troops, surrounded by farm animals, facing combat for the first time. Most of them were not combat troops: on occupation duty in Japan, they had been clerks, cooks, laundry workers, and even bartenders.

Higgins, Beech, Mydans, and Tom Lambert of the Associated Press were the first American reporters to see American troops die in their initial combat of the war. Higgins's dramatic first-person account was published on the front page.

Higgins asked for no special treatment as a woman and in fact turned down occasional offers from the military of extra protection or a more comfortable billet. For that she earned some sympathy in the press corps, even among reporters who disliked her, but Bigart was unmoved. He told her she had no friends in the press corps.

At first, she thought Bigart was right, but she got good advice from Mydans and from Jimmy Cannon, a renowned *New York Post* sportswriter who was covering the war. They told her to forget the criticism and focus on doing her job.

"If the *Racing Form* sent a race horse to cover the war, he wouldn't be any more of an oddity than you are," Cannon said. "That horse's activities would be the subject of all sorts of stories, and nobody would care how true they were so long as they were good stories. You're in the same fix and you'd better just quit worrying about what you hear."[14]

Mydans later wrote a sympathetic article about her for *LIFE*, describing her as "alarmingly brave, extraordinarily durable, and pretty even in her fighting clothes." It said she was "winning the battle of the sexes on the Korean front."[15]

Whatever Higgins's reputation, she had never done anything to Bigart. If he had been gracious, he might have seen her as an asset, a potentially valuable partner in covering the fast-moving story. Instead, he refused to talk to her. Correspondents for the same newspaper, even if not friends, almost always communicate regularly with each other if only to avoid duplication and to make sure that one of them—not both—is covering some important development for the paper. According to Beech, who tried to stay on good terms with both, they did not talk to each other for two and a half months.[16]

"We wrote our stories at the end of the day with total disregard for what the other was filing," Bigart said.[17]

One day they both showed up to cover the same battle. When Higgins saw that a competitor from the *New York Times* was going back to the press center to send his story, one of the two reporters for the *Herald Tribune* would have to do the same. Would it be Bigart or Higgins?

Beech suggested that she ask Bigart what he was going to do. "No," she said, "if I speak to him he'll just ignore me or bawl me out." Beech went to Bigart and asked him to talk to Higgins. He pondered for a moment, then said, "I don't see why not." They met in the middle of a road and conversed briefly. "There should be a plaque saying 'Homer and Maggie spoke here,'" Beech wrote.[18]

Beech was caught in the middle, but for the other correspondents, the feud was an amusing sideshow, a welcome diversion from the grim news of the war.

"In the press club bar in Tokyo, in the press billet in Taegu, wherever correspondents gathered, Higgins threatened to replace the war as the chief topic of conversation," Beech wrote. "Songs were composed celebrating the Bigart-Higgins feud." Bill Lawrence of the *New York Times* scored a big hit with the reporters when he coached a group of Korean children to stand outside the Taegu press center and chant, "Homer loves Maggie, Homer loves Maggie."[19]

Bill Prochnau, peerless chronicler of the American press corps, wrote that when Bigart arrived in Korea, he was already a "superstar," but "Higgins would make him even better, and he never forgave her for it." Prochnau said, "Higgins had a penchant for the sensational, for overwriting, and for injecting herself into the story, all of which rankled Bigart . . . but she held her own with Bigart every inch of the way through one of the most miserable and dangerous wars America ever fought."[20]

Back in New York, the *Herald Tribune*'s editors were not worried about relations between their two reporters. They loved the product they were getting. Kluger wrote,

> New York ruled that Bigart was the prime correspondent but, given the developing gravity of the war, Higgins could stay and file whatever color or sidebar pieces she could find. Bigart protested no more; he just turned his back on Higgins and pretended she was not there. But she was, and he knew it and she had Beech's Jeep at her disposal, and he had no Jeep, so he covered the U.S. army as he had in World War II, at the cannon's mouth or as near as he could get or just standing out there in the middle of some road seeming dumb and helpless with his jack-o-lantern grin and disarming stutter as younger reporters who admired him fed him their stuff.[21]

In her slender memoir of the war, Higgins never mentioned Bigart by name. She referred to him only as "my colleague" and devoted only six paragraphs to the episode.[22]

Despite the feud, or because of it, Bigart and Higgins filed one dramatic, hard-hitting story after another. On some days, stories by both appeared side by side on the front page. In those early days of television, the impact of their articles was amplified by the absence of combat coverage from the small screen. The *Herald Tribune* operated a syndicate that distributed its content to subscribing newspapers all across the country, so articles by Bigart and Higgins were read nationwide.

Three weeks after Bigart's arrival—three weeks of fear, mud, and incoming shells—Higgins had forgotten his threat to have her fired, but then she was suddenly ordered by the US military command to leave Korea immediately. Bigart had nothing to do with that development. The order was issued by Lt. Gen. Walton Walker, the commander of US forces in Korea, who simply did not want women there. Higgins could not just ignore the order because the army controlled the only channel of communication, a radio link that reporters were allowed to use for a few hours between midnight and dawn that was the only way they could file their stories. Without access to that, Higgins could not function.

Her editors of course objected to the expulsion order, but Walker ordered military police to take her to the airport, where they marched her onto a plane bound for Tokyo.

Walker's order was just common sense, another officer wrote. "Maggie Higgins wrote well, but she and the very few other women writers were distinctly out of place in a battle zone conditioned to the convenience and violence of the male. Open-air urinals of the funnel-on-a-pipe variety, uncovered latrine boxes, and communal sleeping and bathing facilities of an embattled army in the field were not designed to accommodate . . . the aggressively infiltrating female. Miss Higgins, her talents notwithstanding, was inevitably a nuisance."[23]

In Tokyo she went to see MacArthur, who had already heard from the imperious Helen Rogers Reid, the president of the *Herald Tribune*. Higgins told MacArthur that she was fully qualified to report from the war zone: she had seen combat in Europe, had used field latrines, and had heard plenty of coarse language. MacArthur countermanded Walker's order. "Marguerite Higgins held in highest esteem by everyone," he cabled to Helen Reid.[24]

Her competition with Bigart resumed, to the benefit of *Herald Tribune* readers. From the shifting front lines, Bigart was sending detailed, dramatic dispatches. One of the best, a four-thousand-word epic headlined "From a Foxhole in Korea" that described how American troops were overrun by the North Koreans, became a classic of war reporting.

The first paragraph reported that the Americans' unit "suffered severe casualties and was forced to leave all its heavy equipment behind." The second said, "This correspondent was one of three reporters who saw the action, and was the only newsman to get out alive. The others, Ray Richards of International News Service and Corp. Ernie Peeler of Stars and Stripes, were killed by enemy fire."

He had seen Richards and Peeler the night before, his long report said. They had planned to spend the night at the scene and hitchhike on a military vehicle back to headquarters to file their stories but did not survive the attack. His account did not make clear why he was not with them at the time of their deaths.

This was the celebrated story recounting the "gruesome atrocity," the shooting in the face of American soldiers begging for mercy. "It was not an encounter anyone will remember," Bigart advised readers, "except those who were there, and the outcome will have no bearing on the ultimate results. It is worth telling only as an example of what happens when men are thrown into action without adequate preparation."

His article included a timed chronicle of the battle, beginning with this: "5:55 a.m.—We hear the enemy jabbering over on the left, but can't see 50 feet through the fog. The show starts any minute now." By 11:50 a.m. the Americans were facing the oncoming enemy but were also being pummeled by misdirected shelling from their own artillery units. "This can't go on," Bigart's chronicle said.[25]

He was right: at 12:05 p.m., the commanding officer ordered a retreat. Bigart had been under fire in his foxhole more than seven hours.

Praise from Liebling

A. J. Liebling, the longtime writer of the Wayward Press column in the *New Yorker*, was generally critical of the reporting coming from Korea, but he made an exception for Bigart.

"It is my considered opinion," he wrote, "that a small group of correspondents, of whom Homer Bigart, of the Herald Tribune, appears to me the most effective, have done much to save the lot of us by pointing out our specific, and remediable, deficiencies in combat." He cited a Bigart article describing an engagement in which a US unit "lost all their artillery" including five 105mm pieces. The interesting part of Bigart's account, Liebling said, was not that the Americans lost their guns but that they were using 105s, obsolete weapons that had not been effective against German tanks in World War II. The Americans fired these outdated guns, but the North Korean tanks rolled ahead. "It was a clean, undramatic pictorial story that included everything but the smell of the rice paddies through which the defeated Americans ran," Liebling said, while the *Times*, reporting on this same engagement from a headquarters briefing, had described it as a success. The difference, Liebling said, illustrated "something I have always believed about war reporting—it is better done from where the war is."

He also cited the dispatch about the fight in which Bigart was the only one of three reporters to survive when the Americans were routed. Bigart followed "his magnificent description" of the skirmish with an attempt to set down what was the matter: the ill-trained troops had never heard artillery shells overhead and so were frightened by their own.

Liebling noted,

When the First Cavalry Division made its unopposed landing at Pohang on July 19th, Bigart reported that it was the first cheerful news he had heard since the beginning of the long retreat. It is too bad he could not have been reading headlines in the United States, which presented the country with victories at least every other day. But three days after the landing, he was reporting the hardest knock of all, the "costly" and "humiliating" defeat of the Twenty-fourth Division at Taejon, where it traded too much blood for too little time. I think his brief, unemotional account of the unarticulated effort—communications failed, and in consequence the troops assigned to cover the retreat never moved into position—will be remembered by several hundred thousand people who were not there. I shall not soon forget Bigart's report of his last glimpse of General Dean, the defeated commander, "sitting upon the porch of his command post, the picture of dejection."[26]

Maj. Gen. William Dean was taken captive and held as a prisoner in North Korea for the duration of the war. Bigart did not blame Dean for the debacle. "This brave and conscientious officer," he wrote, "was confronted with an assignment little short of suicidal. He was given the sorry task of conducting a series of delaying actions pitting green troops against a skillful, fanatic and numerically superior enemy." Because the ill-trained American troops "required constant reassurance," and some threw down their weapons, officers felt compelled to stay out in front of them. The result was a high casualty rate among majors and lieutenant colonels.[27]

In one long report, Bigart gave a detailed, almost minute-by-minute account of an endless night of death, desperation, and confusion in dense fog near the town of Chonoui.

"We passed an uneasy night on the hill," Bigart wrote. "At intervals our artillery banged away at possible enemy assembly points in the flats of Chonoui. 'Outgoing mail' screeched close overhead, but the hullabaloo failed to disperse swarms of mosquitoes that made things miserable until the horrors of the morning caused us to forget our lesser woes."

After that engagement, Bigart told his editors that, like his endless night in that foxhole, it was an unimportant skirmish in the overall picture of that war. It would not become part of the language, like Gettysburg or Iwo Jima; nobody who was not a participant would remember it. His editors disagreed. "Mr. Bigart's dispatch, it seems to us," they said in an editorial commentary, "not only was a singularly fine job of reporting but it also caught the real meaning of this war to the men who are fighting it." In the words of a lieutenant quoted in the article, "It's going to be tough."[28]

Bigart wrote favorably about the troops when they fought well—in one piece he called them "gallant" and said they "performed magnificently"[29]—but his forthrightness about the confusion of combat, the ill-considered orders, and the questionable performance of some troops did not endear him to the military brass.

After one disorderly retreat by American soldiers, General Walker issued what came to be known as his "stand or die" order: "There will be no more retreating, withdrawal, adjustment of the lines or any other term you choose. . . . We must fight until the end."[30]

About this, Bigart wrote that the "order against yielding another inch would make little sense if taken literally. . . . What General Walker meant was that there must be no more of the withdrawals in which some American units have run like rabbits, without inflicting much damage on the enemy."[31] The army took "run like rabbits" as a cheap shot. Hanson Baldwin, the military analyst for the *Times*, had said much the same thing but in more judicious language.

More than a year later, after Truman had fired MacArthur, MacArthur's former intelligence chief, Maj. Gen. Charles A. Willoughby, said his boss had been undermined by "biased, prejudiced, and inaccurate" press coverage. He named Bigart, Joe Alsop, and Hal Boyle of the Associated Press among the culprits (but not Higgins). Alsop wrote in his column that "men like Homer Bigart and Hal Boyle who were frontline correspondents right through the war knew a damn sight more of what was going on than General Willoughby, so far as I was able to observe."[32]

Higgins wrote her own distinguished copy and proved to be as adroit as Bigart in finding ways around military restrictions to get the stories to New York. She scored her biggest hit when she went ashore with the US Marines in their high-risk amphibious landing behind enemy lines at Inchon, perhaps MacArthur's greatest gamble and his most important maneuver in the war. Her opening paragraph described it as "one of the most technically difficult amphibious landings in history," and she was certainly right.

Bigart had beaten everyone with an article saying the landing was under way, published before the military announced it, but he was not at the scene as the landing unfolded. He was aboard a command ship to report the Marines' progress afterward. Higgins was on the water with the Marines and went ashore with them when they hit the beach. His coverage was detailed and vivid, but her magazine-length account of the landing was memorable.

Under heavy fire, in surging tides, the Marines went ashore in waves. She was in the fifth group, crouching with the men in the turbulent water, bullets and artillery shells flying overhead, while "as dusk settled the glare of burning buildings all around lit the sky."

Unexpectedly, she reported, they faced a greater danger, not from the enemy but from their side.

A sudden rush of water came up into a dip in the wall and we saw a huge LST (Landing ship, Tank) rushing at us with the great plank door half down. Six more yards and the ship would have crushed twenty men. Warning shots sent everyone speeding from the sea wall, searching for escape from the LST and cover from the gunfire. The LST's huge bulk sent a rush of water pouring over the sea wall as it crunched in, soaking most of us. The Marines ducked and zigzagged as they raced across the open but enemy bullets caught a good many in the semi-darkness.[33]

She survived to see the Marines secure the beachhead and to describe the landing of tanks, bulldozers, trucks, and Jeeps that followed.

Bigart nursed his grudge against Higgins for years. His wisecrack upon learning that she was pregnant became a permanent fixture of Bigart lore: "Wonderful! Wh-wh-who's the mother?" Higgins died of leishmaniasis in 1966 at the age of forty-five. Years later, Bigart acknowledged to Richard Kluger that there was "no way I can make my behavior toward her appear in a favorable light.

"I didn't behave well," he wrote, "and I sure as hell wasn't chivalrous."[34]

He told Kluger and other interviewers that he resented Higgins because in her recklessness she took foolish chances that obliged him to do the same. "She was a very brave person, foolishly brave," he told Karen Rothmyer. "As a result I felt as though I had to go out and get shot at occasionally myself. So I resented that."[35]

His explanation did not hold up for two reasons: First, he was hostile to Higgins from the moment he arrived in Korea, before he could see her in action and understand what kind of risks she was taking. Second, as he had demonstrated at Anzio, he was every bit as willing as she to embrace danger.

In his memoir of the war, Beech said that other correspondents shared Bigart's view that they were forced to take chances it made no sense to take just because a woman did so. But, he said, "the truth is that Bigart and I took no more risks than perhaps a dozen other correspondents and not as many as some photographers." Her real problem, he said, was that "Higgins had a genius for bad public relations. This, plus male envy of her success, made her cordially disliked by many of her colleagues. Higgins couldn't have cared less . . . she was too busy to care."

Yet Beech paid her the ultimate compliment: "In her quest for fame Higgins was appallingly single-minded, almost frightening in her determination to overcome all obstacles. But so far as her trade was concerned, she had more guts, more staying power, and more resourcefulness than 90 percent of her detractors. She was a good newspaperman."[36]

China Enters the War

Once China entered the conflict on the side of the North Koreans in late October, the early victories of the UN forces were swiftly reversed. The Americans—inexperienced, poorly trained, and underequipped—faced a disciplined, well-armed enemy, many of whose soldiers were familiar with the terrain. Increasingly alarmed words—"retreat," "rout," even "slaughter"—appeared in reports from the front.

For Bigart, who camped in foxholes near the front lines, "the brushes with death became almost mystical," Bill Prochnau wrote. "On one frigid night that winter, Bigart slept with two GIs in a foxhole so far advanced that they could hear the chatter of the Chinese who, by then, had entered the war. At dawn Bigart crept out to look around. Moments later he returned and both his companions were dead, killed in their sleep by an incoming mortar."[37]

In early September, Bigart and four other reporters were in a combat zone east of Yongsan to observe "the attempt by the First Marine Division to reduce the Communist beachhead east of the Naktong River," he reported. At dusk, drenched by rain, they "faced the dismal prospect of a night-long ride over a mountain road to Pusan."

They thought they were out of danger, but on a narrow ridge, dark but for their Jeep's headlights, they were ambushed by local guerrillas sympathetic to the invaders. At a hairpin turn, a bullet fired from somewhere on the road ahead of them pierced the windshield.

"Another gun opened fire from our rear and scored at least two hits on the Jeep," he reported in his article. "The firing continued until we stopped the Jeep and turned off the lights. This was a terrible moment of decision. There was a single carbine in the Jeep but it was solely for morale purposes. It wouldn't shoot. We had our choice of abandoning the Jeep and lying down in a ditch or proceeding down the road with headlights ablaze—an easy target for the sniper ahead."

They chose to press on through rounds of fire from automatic weapons. Phil Potter of the *Baltimore Sun* and Jean de Premonville of Agence France-Presse took bullet wounds in their legs but survived. Bigart was unhurt.[38]

Bigart did not write that story to glorify himself or to make himself the focus of attention. He did it to give readers a feel for what was happening on the ground in a faraway country. He and other journalists had discovered in Italy and the Pacific islands that in war zones, the usual rules of reporting—beginning with the principle that the reporter's job was to tell the story, not to be the story—did not apply. In peacetime, editors frowned on articles written in the first person. But in wartime, first-person articles were often welcomed because they could convey the drama of the battlefield as no dispassionate third-person narrative could.

A few days later, Bigart went to Tokyo for a much-needed break.

"Got here at 2 a.m. so exhausted I could hardly walk," he wrote to his sister Gladys. "Joe Alsop got me a room at the Ambassador and gave me a sleeping pill and today I feel okay. But it's been the roughest nastiest ten weeks I've ever experienced." The ambush, he told Gladys, "was a very nasty moment and we were all incredibly lucky."

About the larger questions of the war itself, he said only that "I wish they would get rid of Louis Johnson," the secretary of defense. Johnson, a zealous cutter of the military budget, was every bit as much a self-promoter as MacArthur. Truman forced him out a few days later. Other than that, Bigart told Gladys nothing about what he had been through. Most of the letter was about family matters—his parents' poor health and the money to pay for whatever care they needed. He added a postscript about what was really bothering him—the pennant race in baseball's National League: "Got an awful scare when I got back and heard the Phillies had lost six in a row. But feel better today hearing that they beat the Dodgers 4 to 3 with [Russ] Meyer pitching. Maybe the crisis is over."

It was. The Phillies beat the Dodgers again on the last day of the season to win the pennant.[39]

Blaming MacArthur

Homer Bigart then went back to Korea, where he was an anguished witness to what he called "the worst licking American arms have suffered since Bataan." In a long analysis published on December 6, Bigart laid the blame squarely on the officers who made the decisions leading up to it, beginning with MacArthur.

"The most questionable decision of the last few weeks was General of the Army Douglas MacArthur's abortive offensive, which the enemy quickly turned into a defeat," his front-page article said. "To fan out a small force along the rugged fastness of a 700-mile frontier with Red China and the Soviet Union simply made no sense. It was an invitation to disaster."

MacArthur's chief of intelligence, General Willoughby, had said publicly that there were ten Chinese army corps either inside Korea or just across the Yalu River. In that case, Bigart asked, "why was Maj. Gen. Edward M. Almond's 10th Corps given the green light to go traipsing up into the far reaches of northeastern Korea, leaving behind an attractive vacuum between it and Lt. Gen. Walton H. Walker's 8th Army on the other side of the peninsula? . . . It did not require any deep thinking by the Chinese communist commanders to strike their heaviest blow down the center of the peninsula."

His conclusion was unequivocal: "The overall strategic picture is even more depressing. Two-thirds of the existing trained professional troops of the United States army are pinned down in a part of the world where little damage can be inflicted on the arch-enemy—the Soviet Union. This is not a place where the West can achieve victory."[40]

As that article suggested, the war lapsed into stalemate. When it became apparent that no end was in sight, the *Trib* pulled Bigart out of Korea at the end of 1950. Once back home, he really let MacArthur have it in a celebrated article in *LOOK* magazine titled "Why We Got Licked."

"MacArthur grossly miscalculated the intentions, strength and capabilities of the forces against him, and no nation in the spot we are now in can string along with a leader whose ill-considered decision to launch the offensive of Nov. 24 precipitated and magnified the disaster," he wrote. The UN forces should have halted after taking Pyongyang and secured defensive positions, the article said, rather than rushing northward to be routed. As a result, "the harsh, unassailable fact is that a fine American army, powerfully supported by the Air Force and Navy, was defeated by an enemy that had no navy, virtually no air force, and scarcely any armor or artillery."[41]

News articles reporting what Bigart had written appeared in major newspapers nationwide, including the *Herald Tribune*, and even in Jerusalem and Hong Kong.

Asked by a radio commentator to reply, MacArthur accused Bigart of "biased and inaccurate reporting." He said that throughout the conflict, Bigart had waged an "irresponsible propaganda campaign" that "held up to universal contempt the courage and fighting qualities of the gallant American soldier and the leadership of his officers"—which was not true—and had served the interests of the Soviet Union. The general said his tactics had "probably saved the 8th Army from destruction and certainly from much heavier losses." He did not address how the Eighth Army had been placed in so precarious a position in the first place.[42]

Not all of MacArthur's colleagues agreed with him. Lt. Col. Melvin Voorhees wrote a book that was mostly quite critical of the press corps in Korea, but he made an exception for Bigart. "Generally conceded by his press colleagues and the military to be the best of the correspondents was Homer Bigart of the New York Herald Tribune," he said. "He was the hardest-working reporter and a splendid newswriter. After he had gone home and advocated the removal of General MacArthur as Korean commander, the General publicly branded him an inaccurate reporter. It was one of the General's most poorly advised statements."[43] Voorhees was later court-martialed, on charges of printing material not authorized to be made public, and dismissed from the army.

Four months after MacArthur's blast at Bigart, on April 11, 1951, Truman fired MacArthur, not for mismanaging the war but for insubordination.

When Bigart returned to New York in January 1951, *Newsweek* wrote that "by the almost unanimous agreement of colleagues there and of many Stateside readers, Bigart left the Korean battlefront as the best war correspondent of an embattled generation." In this remarkable tribute, the magazine said that "the way Bigart goes after his stories is enough to discourage most competition. Often, while other weary correspondents rushed to mess hall or bunks after a roughing-up on the front, Bigart would write, slowly and carefully," even when he was exhausted to the point that "his usually well-concealed stutter" reappeared. Bigart's weight dropped from 189 pounds to 160 in Korea, *Newsweek* reported, and because he was often too busy to change his clothes, he suffered "his only battle scar"—a case of ringworm.

The same article observed, "In the matter of Stateside publicity, however, another Herald Trib correspondent, Marguerite Higgins, took most of the laurels away from Bigart. As the only woman to stick it out at the front, the 30-year-old Miss Higgins rubbed her nose in the mud of the hottest actions and told her readers about it in some of the best personal-adventure stories of the fighting."[44]

Newsweek reported that *Herald Tribune* editors were planning to nominate both Bigart and Higgins for the Pulitzer Prize, and they did. In May the Pulitzer board at Columbia University gave its highest honor for "Distinguished Reporting on International Affairs" to an unprecedented six correspondents for their work in Korea. Bigart, Higgins, and Beech were among them. In its citation to Higgins, the jury said, "She is entitled to special consideration by reason of being a woman, since she had to work under unusual dangers."[45]

SEVEN

THE RED MENACE AT HOME AND ABROAD

In the spring of 1949, a year before the war began in Korea, the *Herald Tribune* had assigned Bigart to its bureau in Washington to write about US foreign policy.

Major newspapers have often moved foreign correspondents to Washington and the international affairs beat after their tours abroad. It seems logical because these reporters are already familiar with many foreign policy issues and with many diplomats, military officers, and elected officials in the foreign policy community, but it does not work for everyone. By its nature, the beat involves a relatively small universe of people that usually lacks dramatic events. In the absence of combat, hardship, troops far from home, liberated villages, desperate refugees, coups d'état, and exotic landscapes—the raw material of war correspondence and foreign reporting—the Washington beat can seem confining. Moreover, it is difficult for individual reporters to distinguish themselves in Washington because the competition is stiff. Many papers that have no have correspondents abroad have reporters in the capital, and veterans of the Washington beat have well-placed sources whom they have cultivated for years.

Another difficulty is that on any given day, a reporter in this job may be required to write about an entirely different issue or country from the subject of the previous day or the next. Sometimes the subject involves complicated matters of international finance in which only a relative handful of readers would be interested.

There was a stark example of this in Bigart's story of September 14, 1949. It was the lead article on page 1, the news item the editors considered the most important of the day, under this headline: "Accord Reached at Dollar Talks to End Ebb of British Reserves, / 4 Stopgap Measures Approved: Britain Gets Freer Use of E.R.P. Funds / U.S. to Cut Protection of Synthetic Rubber, Eases Customs Barriers."

This was indeed a major development. The United States had successfully brokered a resolution to a fiscal crisis in Britain, and Bigart had been following the talks for almost two weeks. But who was going to read that story? It was full of sentences such as "The United States agreed to waive temporarily Article 9 of the 1946 Anglo-American loan agreement, thus permitting Britain to discriminate in specific instances against American goods in its import program." He was a long way from Anzio and Okinawa.

During Bigart's time in Washington, he faced a neuralgic issue unique to that period—the "Red Scare," the domestic political fallout from the Cold War, which was beginning to grip the country. Fear of communists, suspicion of people who might harbor left-wing sympathies, and fear of being labeled "pro-communist," even if one was not, affected decisions all across politics and journalism.

As James Aronson wrote in *The Press and the Cold War*, "The atmosphere in the early 1950s was one of loyalty oaths and tapped telephones, suspicion and timidity engendered by inquisitors, and images of Bolshevik hordes fanning out from Europe to Asia."[1] The most fearsome of those "inquisitors" was Sen. Joseph R. McCarthy of Wisconsin, whose reckless accusations about communists here, there, and everywhere, and the fear he instilled among his targets, became part of the language: "McCarthyism" became permanent shorthand for investigations and purges based on flimsy evidence and guilt by association.

McCarthy, however, was a symptom, not a cause. He was a vulgar opportunist who took advantage of the country's legitimate fear of the spread of communism. It was a fact that a nuclear-armed Soviet Union had imposed communism on half of Europe and was working to spread Marxist ideology around the world. Mao Zedong's communists took over China in 1949, prompting a "Who lost China?" outcry in the United States and a purge at the State Department. The French were facing a communist-led rebellion across Indochina. Within the American population were pockets of people, especially in the intellectual classes, who were sympathetic to the ideal of socialism and who convinced themselves that Stalinist brutality was an aberration. The United States had a legal, organized Communist Party; its president, Gus Hall, ran for president four times. And some Americans actually spied for the Soviets, as the country learned through the trials of Julius Rosenberg, Ethel Rosenberg, and her brother, David Greenglass, who were convicted of espionage that aided the Soviet Union's acquisition of nuclear weapons. Plenty of people who wanted nothing to do with McCarthy were fearful of communism's gains.

Reporters for the *Herald Tribune* were in a doubly delicate position because the Reids, who owned the paper, wanted the contents edited to insulate them from any possible leftist taint. Westbrook Pegler and George Sokolsky, prominent opinion columnists in the Hearst newspapers, had branded the *Trib* as "the Uptown Daily Worker." That was ridiculous because the *Herald Tribune* was a pillar of country-club Republican respectability, but the Reids were hypersensitive on this subject. The young Ogden R. "Brownie" Reid was making militant, almost paranoid anti-communism the centerpiece of his campaign to become publisher.[2] Material in articles submitted by reporters that might be considered sympathetic to or even understanding of the Soviet Union or communism was excised.

Every newspaper that sought to be dispassionate and neutral confronted a conundrum: McCarthy was a US senator and the chairman of a subcommittee. What he said was news, and the papers were obliged to report it. If his accusations were unfounded or unsubstantiated by evidence, was it the responsibility of the papers to say so? If they did, would that not constitute "editorializing" and make them potential targets of the McCarthy blowtorch? Expressions that became familiar to newspaper readers during the presidency of Donald Trump—"said without evidence" or "said falsely"—rarely appeared in accounts of McCarthy's campaign.

Bigart got an early taste of the atmosphere in Washington in the spring of 1949. Secretary of State Dean Acheson wrote to the Senate Foreign Relations Committee to oppose a bill that would provide $1.5 billion in aid to the Nationalist government in China, which was losing its war against Mao Zedong's communists. The letter was leaked to the press.

Noting that Acheson had used blunt language that he would surely have toned down if he had known the letter would become public, Bigart reported "the gist" of it: The United States had already provided billions in assistance to Chiang Kai-Shek's Nationalists since 1945, and what had been the result? "There had only been a series of crushing defeats for the Nationalist armies, accompanied by a shocking decline of army and civilian morale and the capture or surrender of perhaps 80 percent of American-provided military supplies to the Red armies." Thus, there was no point in sending yet more money.[3]

Acheson's assessment was accurate, and the Nationalists would soon be ousted by Mao Zedong's communist forces, but Sen. Pat McCarran of Nevada, who had introduced the aid bill, was furious. He accused the State Department's Division of Far Eastern Affairs of "softness" on communism. Two other senators, Styles Bridges of New Hampshire and William F. Knowland of California, demanded "a full-dress investigation" of the State Department's policy in the Far East "while there is still time."

"The outcry against the State Department will be intensified in coming weeks as the China situation rapidly deteriorates," Bigart wrote.[4]

This "Who lost China?" furor escalated for months as Mao's communists completed their takeover. McCarthy's demands for scapegoats and a national obsession with ideological purity obliged Truman to create a "Loyalty Review Board" to scrutinize government employees.

One of the most prominent victims of the witch hunt was a distinguished Foreign Service officer named John Stewart Service. Raised in China by missionaries, he had the misfortune of being a China specialist and therefore one of the culprits who supposedly "lost" China. When he died in 1999, his obituary in the *Washington Post* said,

> Mr. Service was among the most celebrated Foreign Service officers whose careers were destroyed, interrupted or curtailed in the late 1940s and early 1950s in the wake of charges by Sen. Joseph R. McCarthy (R-Wis.) that the government, and especially the State Department, had been infiltrated by communist sympathizers. Few such accusations were ever proven, but scores of Foreign Service officers and other civil servants were forced into early retirements, resigned under pressure or saw their prospects for career advancement evaporate when their loyalty to the U.S. Government was questioned. Several, like Mr. Service, were fired; many were later exonerated.[5]

By January 1950, with Mao running China, the policy issue facing the Truman administration was no longer how to save China but what to do about Formosa, or Taiwan, the island to which Chiang and his Nationalist government had migrated. Some conservative politicians and commentators were clamoring for the United States to provide military assistance to Chiang so he could wage a campaign to regain control of the mainland.

The Truman administration was not going to do that, but Bigart found that the president and Secretary Acheson were hampered by an obsessive commitment to secrecy that undercut their ability to win public support for their policy.

Now a veteran of seven months in Washington, Bigart was able to describe the atmosphere with some confidence. "The State Department's inability to give a clear picture of even the broad outlines of a plan for preventing Soviet domination of Asia is a major cause for the present confusion in Congress," he told readers. "It has inspired the cry that the Department has no policy at all or a negative one at best."

Reporters assigned to write about this matter, he said, had never received "a comprehensive briefing on Far Eastern policy." Those who went daily to the State Department in search of information found it fruitless because they were always told that "the matter is under study" or that "it is not desirable to say anything at the moment." Bigart was learning why the State Department was commonly referred to as the "fudge factory." Perhaps, he mused, Acheson would clarify and explain in a speech he was scheduled to give two days later.[6]

Acheson did precisely that in a major policy address at the National Press Club. He declared that the United States was committed to protecting Japan and the Philippines but was not responsible for events elsewhere in South or Southeast Asia and could not prevent undesirable outcomes there. That policy seemed to satisfy no one but remained in place until Dwight D. Eisenhower succeeded Truman as president in early 1953.[7]

Creating NATO

Other than China, the biggest story before Bigart in those months in Washington was the creation of the North Atlantic Treaty Organization. Truman signed a proclamation putting the mutual defense alliance into effect on August 24, 1949. It was, Bigart noted, 12:42 p.m.

"At that historic moment," his story said, "the United States scrapped its traditional policy of non-participation in foreign alliances. From that moment on, this nation was morally committed to go to war should Soviet Russia attack any of the pact partners: Norway, Denmark, the Netherlands, Belgium, Luxemburg, France, Great Britain, Italy, Portugal, Iceland or Canada."[8]

Young reporters are taught that their articles should include a "so what?" paragraph to help readers understand why a development is news. Bigart was a master of it. In his classic account of the Japanese surrender ceremony, it had been the very first paragraph: "Japan, paying for her desperate throw of the dice at Pearl Harbor, passed from the ranks of the major power at 9:05 a.m. today." In the NATO story, it was the second paragraph, which made clear the significance of Truman's action: the United States was no longer a free agent in international affairs.

Through the late winter and early spring of 1950, much of Bigart's work concerned the hardening of Cold War divisions in Europe as the Soviets tightened their control and the implementation of the NATO agreement. Questions arose, such as whether Franco's Spain should be invited to join the alliance or who would command troops deployed by multiple nations.

Much of that reporting work was uncontroversial, but Bigart inadvertently set off a storm when he asked a simple question at one of Secretary Acheson's news conferences.

On January 22, 1950, Alger Hiss, a prominent State Department diplomat, was convicted of perjury in a case that is still controversial all these decades later. He had been accused of spying for the Soviets. By the time he was prosecuted, the statute of limitations had run out on the spying charge, but he was tried for perjury because of his denials of communist affiliation. His first trial ended in a hung jury, but he was convicted at a second trial. He served almost four years in federal prison, never admitting guilt.

A few days after Hiss was convicted, Acheson held a previously scheduled news conference. He had worked with Hiss at State, and Hiss's brother, Donald, had been his law partner. Because guilt by association was rampant in Washington, Acheson told his daughter that he feared he would be judged by his response to "some fool's question" about the Hiss case. That "fool" turned out to be Homer Bigart.

"Mr. Secretary," he asked, "do you have any comment on the Alger Hiss case?"

It was an obvious, neutral question that someone—if not Bigart then some other reporter—was sure to ask. Acheson knew it was coming, and he had had several days to prepare some anodyne response. Instead, he walked into a trap of his own making. The conviction was likely to be appealed, he said. Whatever the outcome, "I do not intend to turn my back on Alger Hiss." He went on about how thinking people had to judge for themselves and said he had been guided by the Sermon on the Mount, but nobody heard anything except his statement about not turning his back.

Within forty-eight hours, Republican senators who controlled the State Department's budget were demanding that Acheson appear before them as part of a full-fledged investigation of him and his department. Senator Knowland threatened to withhold the funding until the State Department "disgorged its traitors." Sen. Richard Nixon called Acheson's comment "disgusting."[9]

Acheson survived the episode because Truman backed him, and he remained secretary of state through the end of Truman's term. The atmosphere in Washington, however, did not calm down. McCarthy was just getting started.

Bigart was liberated temporarily from that foul environment by his assignment to Korea. For most of the next three years after that, he resumed his nomadic life as a roving correspondent overseas, including tours in Europe, North Africa, and East Asia. He was nominally based in Paris and had an apartment there, but he was seldom in it. In the summer and fall of 1952, he was back in Washington for a few months, writing mostly about the effect McCarthy was having on the presidential election campaign; then he returned to the road.

One of the articles he wrote during that 1952 Washington interlude demonstrated the pernicious effect of the *Herald Tribune*'s policy of not printing anything that might be construed as favorable to or tolerant of communists or communism. A Senate committee published the testimony of a witness who said communists were organizing students in public high schools in Brooklyn. Bigart's story about it listed by name and address the supposed student ringleaders in thirteen schools. Nowhere in the article is there any response or comment from any of them, a lapse that violated the basic rules of fairness that every young reporter is taught from the first day.[10] The thirteen students should have had the opportunity to deny the accusation or justify what they were doing, but if the *Trib* published such statements, it might have been perceived as protecting communists.

On his world travels before and after that summer, in Asia Bigart wrote a three-part series on Britain's war against a rebel insurgency in Malaya, reporting that would later shape his thinking about Vietnam. In Morocco he reported on a rebellion against French colonial rule and the parallel buildup of US military forces there. He went back to Korea, where he and Marguerite Higgins reported—separately—on the status of the stalemated war. And he stopped in Taiwan long enough to administer a reality check to those in Washington who were still promoting the notion that Chiang Kai-shek's Nationalists could retake mainland China if only the United States would support them.

"Attempting a reconquest of China from Formosa is a project as impertinent as trying to overrun the whole United States from Staten Island," he wrote. The Nationalists had convinced themselves that US aid for this impossible venture would soon come and had refused to send any troops to join the UN forces still fighting in Korea unless they were assured such aid would happen. But their army was tiny and poorly equipped compared to Mao's forces, and the Nationalists' navy "is in an even sorrier state," making an amphibious assault impossible, Bigart found.[11]

Crisis in Iran

One of the biggest stories Bigart covered during this period as a roving foreign correspondent was the crisis over the nationalization of the oil industry in Iran, beginning in the spring of 1951.

There, the head of state was the young, untested Shah Mohammed Reza Pahlavi, but the man running the government was Prime Minister Mohammed Mossadegh, a quirky populist whose French was better than his Farsi and who sometimes received visitors in his pajamas.

In that era, throughout the oil states of the Middle East it was common for the fields, wells, and export terminals to be controlled by the American or European corporations that had developed them. In Iran that foreign enterprise was the Anglo-Iranian Oil Company, a British venture. In March 1951, at the behest of Prime Minister Mossadegh, the Iranian majlis, or parliament, passed a law nationalizing the entire operation.

The British, naturally, resisted. The United States was in a difficult position. On the one hand, it was an ally of Britain's and feared that nationalization in Iran would set an unfortunate precedent for the vital American oil operation just across the Persian Gulf in Saudi Arabia. Moreover, Iranian oil was vital to the United States and its allies in Korea, where the war continued unabated, and no one knew what might happen to that flow if Mossadegh succeeded. On the other hand, President Eisenhower's overall policy was to support developing countries as they sought to take control of their own destinies in a postcolonial era.

As this drama unfolded, the *Herald Tribune* decided it required the attention of Homer Bigart. The paper informed its readers in an advertisement in the edition of May 24, "It's news when two-time Pulitzer-winner Homer Bigart arrives on any scene. As this is written, he has just arrived in Iran, to cover the world's newest balance-of-power crisis. Roving correspondent Bigart's first dispatch is expected presently. Herald Tribune readers can be sure of one thing: Bigart will report the facts fearlessly."

That same day, Bigart filed his first story from Tehran. It ran on the *Trib*'s front page on May 25, preceded by an extraordinary Editor's Note in italics: *"Homer Bigart, co-winner of the 1951 Pulitzer Prize for his dispatches from Korea, has arrived in Tehran to cover the crisis in the Middle East."* Bigart was a star reporter, but this notice, coupled with the advertisement that announced that he was going to Iran, amounted to a cult of personality in the newspaper business, especially because it was not the first time. The paper had run a similar promotion for Bigart's 1949 articles about the Franco government in Spain, and it sometimes ran his photograph with his articles.[12] It is hard to know what Bigart thought of these notices because he probably never saw them. He had no access to the paper while on the road, and in any case, he made a point of not reading his articles in print, knowing it would make him angry to see how his copy had been edited.

Bigart's reports from Iran that summer were marked by clarity, perception, and a full grasp of the issues. He understood almost immediately what the British could not or would not: the Iranians wanted them gone and would negotiate only the terms of their swift departure. His first article said that the Mossadegh government had given the British an ultimatum: send representatives to Iran within a week to negotiate terms of the takeover or the Iranians would act unilaterally. The British waited two weeks before sending that team, and then its mission was not to negotiate but to dictate. The message the British team delivered was that the Iranians were not competent to run their oil industry by themselves. But Mossadegh and his allies could not be bullied. The day before the British team's scheduled arrival, Bigart reported that the Iranians were preparing to reject its message and begin taking over the oil installations immediately.

That "may conceivably be a bluff," his report said, but it did not bode well for any coming negotiations. Some officials and diplomats believed Mossadegh "would be perfectly willing to see the flow of oil cut to a dribble if only he could force the British to surrender control."[13] That turned out to be a prescient assessment.

By the third week of June, Bigart had concluded that British stubbornness and arrogance were counterproductive because they only bolstered Mossadegh's popularity. The premier, often emotional to the point of weeping, was blaming the "wicked" Anglo-Iranian Oil Company for the poverty of the Iranian people, and it was working.

"With this theme as his sole political belief," Bigart wrote, "Mr. Mossadegh has risen as a triumphant popular figure. And while Western observers may be tempted to scoff at his melodramatic weeping and fainting in parliament and laugh at his long self-imposed confinement in the Majlis building when he feared assassination, the Premier is by no means an absurd figure. He is brave, sincere, and incorruptible."[14]

Bigart Takes a Bride

Bigart stayed in Iran for three months, reporting on the oil takeover and its aftermath, but it was an especially difficult time. He was now a married man, and his wife fell ill after she accompanied him to Tehran.

On March 15, 1951, Bigart married Alice Kirkwood Veit, a young woman from Queens, who was an assistant in the *Herald Tribune*'s editorial department. He was forty-three years old; she was thirty-two. It was the first marriage for both.

She was a graduate of the Katharine Gibbs School, a private, for-profit institution in midtown Manhattan. The school said its mission was "to provide its students with the foundation for lifelong learning. Whether they choose to continue their education or enter the workforce, Gibbs graduates are trained to succeed."[15] But it was generally known as a "finishing school," a place where proper young ladies learned what proper young ladies needed to know.

Alice moved with her new husband to a modest apartment in Auteuil, a quiet neighborhood in Paris's Sixteenth Arrondissement. On May 14, she wrote to his sister, Gladys, about her new life. Apologizing for not having written sooner, she said, "There has been so much to do—moving and getting settled—and so many parties!"

She included a sketch of the apartment's layout. It had a fireplace, a piano, and windows overlooking a small garden. Her sketch showed a kitchen with a stove and a sink but no refrigerator or icebox. There was a "W.C." but no bath or shower; as in many Parisian apartments of that day, those were down the hall, used by multiple tenants. The place was "very dirty" when they moved in, she said, but after a week of scrubbing and polishing, it was shaping up. The *Herald Tribune*'s Paris office was twenty minutes away by Metro.

As a first-time homemaker and a first-time visitor to Paris, she was flummoxed by grocery shopping. "You would laugh to see me buying groceries in the surrounding shops," she told Gladys. Her French was limited and so was her knowledge of cooking, other than breakfast, "but I am anxious to do more as soon as we have some kind of icebox." The French, also lacking iceboxes, "shop for one meal at a time, [and] seem never to store any food." She found that the shops all closed from noon to 2 p.m., just when she always needed something, and none of them carried the Wheaties or cornflakes her husband liked for breakfast.

She did not have to concern herself with such mundane domestic details for long because she was soon in Iran with her husband. In that long, hot summer in

Tehran, Bigart's reporting may have gone well, but their young marriage did not because she got very sick. She could not tolerate the intense heat. In late July she returned to Paris.

"Alice has been back in Paris two weeks now and I feel very lonely without her," Bigart wrote to Gladys on August 11. "Called her on the phone today. She is feeling better but was sick again last week. I'm afraid her heart is not too strong and may have been affected by so many weeks in this high altitude."

The heat was so intense that he wrote about it that same day for the *Herald Tribune*: "Furnace heat combined with the nearly mile-high altitude of Tehran plays like a dentist's drill on the nervous system. Anyone unlucky enough to endure week after wretched week of hellish heat, dust, glare and ennui may be excused if occasionally murderous thoughts invade his mind. Briefly, people go nuts here."[16]

As a roving correspondent not resident in Tehran, Bigart prepared to move on after five months. In a valedictory analysis published on August 26, he noted, "Political intelligence would have saved Anglo-Iranian. But its directors were too afflicted with the Sahib complex to pay much attention to the emotional and social forces at work in Iran. . . . In particular, the British paid too little attention to an old and obscure [parliament] deputy named Mohammed Mossadegh, an eccentric but courageous patriot who was rising to power on the single theme that all Iran's ills could be removed by kicking the British out of Abadan," the city at the center of the oil region. Bigart was contemptuous of Sir William Fraser, the chairman of Anglo-Iranian, whose high-handed inflexibility infuriated the Iranians. At a critical moment, "fed up with Oriental higgling and haggling, Sir William packed his bags and went grouse shooting." As a result of the company's obtuseness, Bigart said, "today with the Iranian press almost solidly anti-British, opinion is so hardened that the Mossadegh government would not dare reach an agreement with Britain."

The result was that the Iranians did nationalize their oil industry and booted out the British. In the short run, it was a Pyrrhic victory because, as Bigart had foreseen, major oil refiners all over the world responded by boycotting Iranian crude, cutting off the country's main source of income.

In mid-September, still struggling to recover, Alice went to Santa Margherita, an Italian resort town near Genoa, for about two weeks. Bigart joined her briefly. They strolled together in the rain and enjoyed the food, but after two days he was off again. This time he went to cover NATO maneuvers in Germany. Alice "looks much better and goes swimming every day," he wrote to Gladys.[17]

But the following week he told his sister,

Alice has gone home [to New York] for a few months for a complete rest and good medical treatment. Her heart was weakened by the Tehran ordeal and her recovery at Santa Margherita was, unfortunately, only superficial. Luckily her cousin, Col.

Perkins, was in town and is taking her home via Ireland. . . . It would have been dangerous for her to travel alone, for she had fainted on the trip up from Italy. I called her on the phone in London two days ago and got a letter from her today. Both of us are confident of her complete recovery but meanwhile she must have a long rest. Paris is too much of a strain, and I would have been away most of the time.[18]

The archive of Bigart's letters at the Wisconsin State Historical Society contains no record of what Alice thought when her husband of six months chose to stay apart from her and keep working in Europe during her recuperation.

Bigart fell ill himself that summer. He contracted malaria, the mosquito-borne disease that was then ubiquitous in hot climates. He lost weight, and his skin took on a yellowish tinge, but he assured his parents that medication had helped him recover quickly. He did not leave Iran for medical treatment.[19]

Before going to Santa Margherita, Bigart had lunch in Paris with Gardner Cowles Jr. A newspaper baron from Minneapolis, Cowles raised the possibility of a job at *LOOK* magazine, which was part of the Cowles media empire.

"He's been thinking of hiring me full time, but I haven't yet made up my mind whether to leave the paper. If I stay with the Trib I'll never make much more money than I'm getting now," he told Gladys, "and although 'Look' is a trashy magazine the Cowles are rolling in money. He's been sounding out Mrs. Reid on [the] possibility of buying the Tribune, but the paper will never be sold while Mrs. Reid is alive." He said he could not leave the *Herald Tribune* for less than $15,000 a year. "Having seen the Riviera," he wrote, "my one ambition was to have enough money to live there the year 'round."[20]

In another letter ten days later, he told Gladys that he was contemplating "the problem of what job I am going to do." *LOOK*, a popular magazine that competed with *LIFE*, had accepted an article of his about Iran and had paid him $1,500 for it, "which is darn good money," he said. "'Look' magazine wants me to work for them at a good deal more than I am making now on the Tribune. But I hate leaving the paper, so at the moment I can't make up my mind."

That was the first indication in the archives that he was contemplating a move to another news organization. It took him four years to make up his mind.

After the NATO war games in Germany, his itinerary confirmed what he had told Gladys after his wife went home—that is, having Alice with him in Paris was not workable because "I would have been away most of the time." Germany was just the first stop on a post-Iran reporting odyssey that lasted more than two years. He was overseas that whole time except for the fall of 1952, when he returned to the United States to cover Dwight Eisenhower's campaign for the presidency. By the time he resumed his full-time work in Washington in 1953, his marriage was all but over; he and Alice divorced not long afterward. They had no children.

From Mossadegh to McCarthy

While Bigart was away from Washington, the Red Scare did not subside. It intensified. The Republican Party's platform in the 1952 presidential election called for ridding the federal government of "subversives" who had supposedly infiltrated it. Eisenhower campaigned in Wisconsin with Senator McCarthy at his side. In the most absurd manifestation of the uproar, Major League Baseball's Cincinnati Reds changed their nickname to "Redlegs" so as not to be associated with communism. On a higher level, in the spring of 1954 the Atomic Energy Commission revoked the security clearance of J. Robert Oppenheimer, one of the country's most prominent nuclear scientists, because of suspected pro-communist sympathies.

In that atmosphere, Bigart took on an assignment that was a potential minefield—the political spectacle known as the Army-McCarthy hearings. The Reids had been purging *Trib* staff members who were known or suspected to be communists or communist sympathizers, going so far as to search desks in the newsroom for evidence of disloyalty.[21] Bigart's challenge was to convey the reality of McCarthy without crossing the publisher and his influential wife.

Throughout 1953, McCarthy, as the chairman of the Permanent Subcommittee on Investigations of the US Senate's Committee on Government Operations, had conducted vitriolic hearings in which he flogged the press, the State Department, the US Army, and even the Government Printing Office for alleged communist influence. One target was the army's Signal Corps Center at Fort Monmouth, New Jersey, where the security clearances of thirty-three civilian scientists and engineers were suspended after McCarthy accused them of espionage. Another was a respected, decorated army brigadier general, Ralph W. Zwicker. McCarthy said Zwicker was "unfit to wear the uniform" after the promotion of a dentist in his unit, Irving Peress, who had invoked his Fifth Amendment rights in declining to say whether he had been a communist.[22]

In April and May 1954, McCarthy presided over thirty-six days of subcommittee hearings into his charges against the army and the army's countercharges against him. Televised nationally in all their drama and melodrama, they became the first major political event about which Americans' primary source of information was television rather than newspapers. The coronation of Queen Elizabeth II of Britain in 1953 had shown Americans the power of television to convey a spectacle. Nearly a year later, the Army-McCarthy hearings conveyed human emotions and reactions as no printed words could.

The hearings made household names of previously obscure figures: Roy Cohn, McCarthy's counsel; G. David Schine, an army private for whom the army accused McCarthy and Cohn of demanding special privileges; and Joseph N. Welch, the army's chief lawyer.

The *Herald Tribune* asked Bigart to write what is known in newsrooms as a curtain-raiser, a thorough advance article about the issues and the stakes in an upcoming event. Bigart did so, but it never appeared in the paper. In a letter to Richard Kluger, Bigart said it was "almost too fair to McCarthy" and "very straightforward," but it also pointed out that nothing McCarthy had done or said had led to the actual trial and conviction of any suspected communists.[23] That was true, but saying so in the paper would have angered the Reids.

Bigart was well positioned to cover the hearings because he had been reporting about McCarthy for months. He was present in Wisconsin, for example, when the senator accused the Democratic Party and its unsuccessful 1952 presidential candidate, Adlai E. Stevenson, of "criminal stupidity or, at worst, treason." In a speech McCarthy gave in Milwaukee on March 19, 1954, one of his accusations in a twenty-count "indictment" was that Stevenson had been part of a plot to bring the Italian Communist Party leader Palmiro Togliatti into that country's postwar government. Another was that a leftist State Department had "hamstrung" General MacArthur in Korea. And another was that Dean Acheson, as a lawyer, had represented communists. A separate "count" of this "indictment" accused Democrats of issuing "a secret Army directive which authorized the granting of commissions in the United States Army to members of the Communist conspiracy."

With the flair of a gifted demagogue, McCarthy asked after each count, "How do you plead, Adlai, guilty or not guilty?" The audience got into the spirit and yelled "guilty" each time.[24]

When the Army-McCarthy hearings began on April 22, 1954, the hearing room was jammed with print and television reporters, camera crews, and spectators who had been waiting in line for hours. CBS ran an hour-long special about the hearings each evening; notably, the broadcasts were produced by Alice Weel, one of the first women to gain a major position in broadcast news.

When McCarthy entered the room, Bigart's report said, "he walked with a proprietary air, for this was the room in which he had built his reputation as the nation's most publicized investigator into communism. He strode confidently to the big casket-shaped table where members of the Senate Investigations subcommittee were already seated to hear the case of Army versus McCarthy."[25]

The three words "Army versus McCarthy" helped readers to understand the agenda of the hearings. McCarthy may have been the center of attention, but he was not the prosecutor or inquisitor; he was the defendant, accused of abusing his power to bully the army, malign innocent individuals, and extort favors. There was inherent drama in the proceedings, but much of the testimony was tediously detailed: who said what to whom and in what context? Could some comment reasonably be interpreted as a threat? Did Private Schine get far more weekend passes from Fort Dix, New Jersey, than other draftees? If so, why? Was it at the behest of Roy Cohn?

Still, there were moments of high tension and emotion, which Bigart conveyed in vivid but studiously neutral language.

On April 26, for example, "an Army charge that an enlarged photograph, introduced as evidence to show Army Secretary Robert T. Stevens standing alone with Pvt. G. David Schine, was 'shamefully altered,' threw the public hearings on the McCarthy-Army case into an uproar of angry shouting and desk-pounding today." The army produced what it said was the original photo, showing that Stevens and Schine were with two other people. The issue was whether Stevens had cultivated Schine to curry favor with McCarthy and Cohn, for whom the young soldier had worked before he was drafted.

When army counsel Welch described the first photo as "doctored," McCarthy demanded that he be put under oath.

At one point in the ensuing shouting match between McCarthy and committee chairman Karl Mundt, Sen. Stuart Symington objected that McCarthy was "out of order." McCarthy snapped, "Oh, be quiet."

"'I haven't the slightest intention of being quiet,' Sen. Symington replied, just as angrily. 'Counsel is running this committee and you are not running it.'"[26]

As that account showed, the hearings tended to generate more heat than light.

Two days later, Schine was called to testify about why he, a mere private, had met the secretary of the army and whether they were alone.

"The sudden appearance of the most highly publicized private in the history of the United States threw the place into bedlam," Bigart reported. "Photographers tore across the room, vaulting chairs and leaping tables. The predominantly female audience craned and tittered."[27]

After nine sessions in which, as Bigart noted, "little progress was evident," Republicans on the committee tried to terminate the hearings quickly by holding night and weekend sessions and by hearing from only one more sworn witness after Secretary Stevens had finished testifying—Senator McCarthy himself.

"The Republican maneuver," Bigart wrote, "was inspired by a growing anxiety among top [Eisenhower] administration officials, including Vice-President Richard M. Nixon, over the prospect of an interminable televised spectacle of an all-Republican squabble."[28] The Democrats naturally objected, and the ploy failed. The hearings went on for six more weeks.

Near their end, Bigart captured the angry outburst that is still remembered as the moment that marked the beginning of the end for McCarthy. Much of the day's testimony concerned Roy Cohn's relationship with Private Schine, including the question of whether the two had been seen drinking together at New York's Stork Club while Schine was supposedly on duty at Fort Dix.

Then McCarthy himself took the stand. He promptly went after Joseph Welch, the mild-mannered Boston lawyer whom the army had brought in as special counsel. The senator said Frederick Fisher, a lawyer in Welch's firm, was a member of the National Lawyers Guild, which had been declared subversive by the House Committee on Un-American Activities. McCarthy said Welch had brought Fisher to Washington to assist him with the hearings and accused Welch of trying to "foist on the committee" a man with a former communist affiliation.

That was too much for Welch. He denounced McCarthy as a "cruelly reckless character assassin" and demanded, "Have you no sense of decency, sir, at long last? Have you no sense of decency?"

Bigart used those rhetorical questions from Welch as the entire fourth paragraph of his article.[29] In the *Times*, the veteran reporter W. H. Lawrence used only part: "He asked Senator McCarthy if any 'sense of decency' remained in him." The impact was not the same.

The hearings concluded on June 17 after thirty-six days of acrimonious testimony and argument that left many issues unresolved. The special committee took no action, but the matter did not rest there.

According to a US Senate history, McCarthy "had appeared invincible when investigated by a Senate subcommittee in 1952, but by 1954 he had finally gone too far, convincing his Senate colleagues that his power must be curtailed." On July 30, 1954, Sen. Ralph Flanders, a Vermont Republican, introduced a resolution of censure.[30]

The issue was not whether McCarthy's accusations had been valid or whether there actually were communists in the government. It was whether McCarthy's behavior and tactics in pressing his charges were "contrary to senatorial traditions." The dignity and reputation of the Senate were at stake.

On August 2, the Senate appointed a bipartisan special committee to consider the matter and to issue a report before the end of the congressional session at the end of the year. On December 2, the Senate voted 67–22 to censure McCarthy and stripped him of his subcommittee chairmanship. His day of power was over.

Bigart said he had found time to write "a multi-part series on McCarthy" to run after the hearings, but it met the same fate as his curtain-raiser. "I don't know whether it was good or not," he told Richard Kluger, "but I never asked what happened and nobody told me." Why not ask? "I always hated confrontations with editors and never won any."[31]

As for Roy Cohn, the evil genius behind McCarthy's tactics, his career took off as he represented one high-profile client after another and hobnobbed with celebrities—until his own downfall. In 1964 federal prosecutors charged him with fraud and bribery in a case unrelated to his work for McCarthy. Bigart covered his trial, which ended in a mistrial after a juror's father died. Cohn was acquitted in two subsequent trials and never convicted of any crime, but he was later disbarred in New York when a court upheld an investigatory panel's findings of "dishonesty, fraud, deceit and misrepresentation."[32]

No Rest for the Weary

Bigart was not in Washington when the Senate voted to censure McCarthy. Within a day or two after the public hearings ended, he was on the road again. He went to Honduras to write about yet another war, or soon-to-be war, next door in Guatemala. He was not happy about it.

"I was really dead beat when they told me to come down here," he wrote to his father on the letterhead stationery of the Hotel Prado in Tegucigalpa. He said that after the McCarthy hearings concluded, he expected to have a long, restful weekend at a friend's cabin outside Luray in central Virginia. His hosts gave him a late supper, and they settled in for drinks around the fireplace.

The nearest telephone was at a crossroads general store six miles away, he told his father, but the *Trib* called the local sheriff, who sent the grocer to the cabin with a message: call New York right away. "So we went down to the store, called New York, and it was [senior editor] Everett Walker asking me if I wanted to go to Honduras. I didn't much want to go, but I had to say yes." His letter does not mention Alice.

He took a late-night bus back to Washington and a 2 a.m. flight to New Orleans, where he caught a connection to Tegucigalpa, the Honduran capital.[33]

In Guatemala, which borders Honduras, the United States was supporting a rebel named Carlos Castillo Armas in his effort to oust the leftist government of Jacobo Árbenz Guzmán. But at this point, there were not many reportable events. The rebel headquarters was an inaccessible encampment deep in the Guatemalan jungle. The Honduras-Guatemala border was reachable from Tegucigalpa only in a chartered small plane, and in the town nearest the rebels' camp there was no sign of them and no fighting. As a result, Bigart wrote, reporters trying to write about the rebellion worked mostly from the bar in his hotel.

"Normally," Bigart wrote in a *Scoop*-like account, "the gringo newspaper men would tear themselves away from the creature comforts of the Hotel Prado and attach themselves to the rebel leader. There are, however, good reasons why they prefer to sit tight and raise a glass to the revolution."

Finding the rebels was expensive, he said. It cost $200 an hour to charter a DC-3 to "the frontier town of Nueva Octopeque, already known here as New Octopus. There is no news at New Octopus," nor was there much in the interior of Guatemala. Even those who arrived at the border found that reaching the rebel headquarters in the interior was an arduous adventure, and Castillo didn't welcome them there, because he wanted his movement to appear entirely indigenous. "So you return to Tegucigalpa and find that a larger amount of blood has been spilled in a student riot not far from the Prado bar."[34]

Being Homer Bigart, he did manage to gather some news in New Octopus. He reported that the rebels captured their first airstrip inside Guatemala and flew planes from there to bomb a government garrison town and drop leaflets urging government troops to join the revolt. He noted that he obtained his information from rebel leaders who were still in Honduras and from radio broadcasts. "None of the American correspondents from the Honduran side have yet heard a shot fired in the elusive uprising," he acknowledged.[35]

When the rebels triumphed and took over Guatemala City two weeks later, Bigart and other "melancholy" reporters finally went there, only to find that all the fighting had ended and that Árbenz had fled several days before. The headline on that report said, "Dull Ending to Dull War for Press in Guatemala."[36]

EIGHT

LEAVING THE SINKING SHIP

After Bigart's work in Korea and his second Pulitzer Prize, he was in high favor with the *Herald Tribune* management and especially with the editor, Whitelaw Reid, who had joined the staff of his family's paper in 1938.

"Whitie" Reid came from a privileged background. He was a graduate of Yale, a pilot, a star athlete, and an adventurer. His grandfather, the first Whitelaw Reid, had succeeded Horace Greeley as the editor and publisher of the *New-York Tribune* in the 1870s, and the paper remained in the family after its merger with the *Herald*.

"All here deeply grateful for superb work since beginning of Korean war," Reid said in a telegram to Bigart on September 28, 1950. "Prestige of paper has been helped no end [by] you being credited with doing best news job on this grueling assignment." That message, sent in the euphoric moment after UN forces had taken Pyongyang and before the Chinese turned the war around, urged Bigart, "In present mopping up phase please don't take unnecessary chances." He said Bigart could pick his next assignment. By the following April, Bigart was based in Paris.

There, on May 17, 1951, he received another laudatory message from Reid: "Received Overseas Press Club Award for you last night. You can be sure all of paper is cheering your Pulitzer and Overseas honors. Never were they better deserved. Congratulations and very best wishes for your work ahead in Europe."[1]

In those early years of the 1950s, the *Herald Tribune* was to the *New York Times* as the Brooklyn Dodgers were to the New York Yankees: an excellent team, loaded with Hall of Famers and all-stars, but not the best in the city. The Dodgers gave up after the 1957 season and moved to Los Angeles. The *Trib* lasted a decade longer. With its roster of talented writers, it was still a serious competitor to the *Times*, so much so that when I first worked at the *Times* in 1959 as a copy boy on the night shift, one of us was dispatched to the *Trib*'s building two blocks away each night when its presses rolled to grab a copy of the first edition and see what

125

it had that we didn't. But the *Trib*'s struggles had been apparent for some years, even while Bigart was still in Korea.

After the *New York Sun* died in January 1950, its meager assets merged into the *World-Telegram*, and the city had seven daily newspapers. The *Herald Tribune*'s circulation, at 323,000 subscribers, was the smallest.[2] With the growth of television news, the *Times* and the *Wall Street Journal* were still prospering, but there was less demand for a third newspaper trying to deliver the same sort of sober, high-level coverage.

The *Times* was stuffy and beset by internal power struggles. Nevertheless, it "was unquestionably the best newspaper in sight," as Gay Talese wrote, "even though the *Tribune* in those days was a serious and interesting newspaper and was no doubt a more congenial place for reporters wanting literary freedom. For straight reporting, however, and for depth of coverage, the *Times* was incomparable."[3]

Talese and two other *Times* veterans who wrote books about the paper, David Halberstam and Turner Catledge, attributed the *Times*'s decisive advantage to decisions its publisher made during World War II. As wartime restrictions limited the availability of newsprint and ink, the *Times* and the *Herald Tribune* printed fewer pages. The publishers had to decide: print all the news that needed to be published at the cost of reduced advertising or print advertisements as usual at the expense of news coverage. Honoring his paper's front-page slogan, "All the News That's Fit to Print," *Times* publisher Arthur Hays Sulzberger chose to print as much news as possible while persuading advertisers to buy quarter- or half-page ads instead of full pages. The *Trib* made the opposite choice, with the result that its advertising lineage and revenue soared while its news coverage was limited. Readers noticed.

"Sulzberger's decision put the *Times* in a profit squeeze during the war years," Catledge wrote, "but its wisdom was seen after the war. We had won new readers with our war coverage and both our advertising and circulation far outstripped those of the *Herald Tribune*." Halberstam observed that the *Trib*'s wartime revenue surge was "a victory of the most Pyrrhic sort."[4]

To cover increasing costs, the *Trib* raised its newsstand price from three cents to a nickel. When the *Times* held on for three years without doing the same, it attracted still more readers away from its rival. *Trib* executives thrashed about in search of a formula for survival. Their ill-considered decision to create an "early bird" edition, which would reach newsstands by 8 p.m. to attract late commuters and compete with the *Daily News* and *Daily Mirror*, ran aground on the expanding evening news programs on television and precipitated organizational chaos in the newsroom. The rise of respectable suburban dailies such as *Newsday* also undercut the *Trib*'s circulation and advertising reach in the suburbs.

The *Trib* resorted to games and gimmicks. Its sports section was printed on green paper. Readers were invited to play "Tangle Towns," winning prizes for unscrambling the jumbled names of towns in New York. (As the game went on, the names got harder; Troy and Albany were easy, but Skaneateles was not.) More crime and divorce stories appeared in the paper, as did gossip columns and photos of "starlets." A. M. Rosenthal, who later became the executive editor of the *Times*, said uncharitably that "what they wound up with was a newspaper that was all dessert and no main course."[5]

On January 5, 1954, the *Herald Tribune* published an upbeat full-page "Report to Our Readers" celebrating its accomplishments of the year before, beginning with a reduction of an eighth of an inch in the width of each column. That decreased the width of each page by an inch. It saved money on newsprint, but the progress report put it as a matter of editorial improvement: it necessitated "tighter editing—and in turn resulted in greater ease of reading—on subways, trains or breakfast table." The report said the paper had added fourteen newspapers around the country as subscribers to its syndication service, bringing the total to forty-two. Despite two strikes that closed the paper briefly, the report said, "it should be noted that in 1953 the Herald Tribune received the largest advertising revenue in its 113-year history—and this for the second successive year."

The report listed other positive developments. Art Buchwald began his thrice-weekly humor column from Paris, where the *Trib*'s international edition was thriving. (Jean Seberg hawked that paper on the streets of Paris in the movie *Breathless*.) The Sunday magazine published works by John Gunther, Quentin Reynolds, and John Dos Passos. Several reporters and columnists, including Bigart and Marguerite Higgins, won prizes and awards for their work. The paper was the first to print a reproduction of Leonardo's *The Last Supper* in color. There was more in this optimistic vein.

It was all true, and to ordinary readers such as myself, perusing the *Trib* on the subway each day as I went to high school, it was difficult to discern that anything was wrong. The reality was that the *Times* kept gaining in readership and advertising, while the *Trib* was being undercut by the pressures of television and good suburban papers. Its Sunday magazine—which survives today in the form of *New York*—was excellent and highly popular but symptomatic of a larger problem. As Halberstam noted, the Sunday edition of the *Times*, laden with lucrative department store advertising, "made the entire paper richer and stronger; the *Trib* on Sunday drained the resources of the paper for the other six days."[6]

Despite its strong lineup of first-rate reporters and writers, the *Trib* was on an accelerating downward slide, and the staff could sense it. Peter Kihss, one of its star reporters, left for the *Times* in 1952. Bigart, working mostly overseas and in Washington and somewhat insulated from the environment in the New York newsroom, stuck it out until September 1955, when he called Turner Catledge, by then the managing editor of the *Times*.

Catledge had met Bigart during the Italian campaign in World War II. In his memoir, he described an encounter in which German artillery was firing on advancing American tanks: "All of us then scattered, the tanks included, except one correspondent with a passion for accuracy and the affliction of stammering who wouldn't leave until he'd gotten the correct spelling of the name of the Minneapolis lawyer who was commanding the tanks. His stammer grew worse as the shelling increased."[7]

David Halberstam, recounting the decline of the *Trib*, wrote that "in 1955, in what was to be a symbolic move, Homer Bigart, the greatest of the *Trib*'s reporters, Pulitzer Prize winner in World War II, Pulitzer Prize winner in Korea, the archetypal *Trib* man, fearless, tough-minded and irreverent, had become disgusted with the frustrations of his shop and walked across the street to ask for a job at the *Times*. When he called Turner Catledge, the *Times*'s managing editor, the response was, 'Homer, what took you so long?'"[8]

"If I was ever going to make a move, that was the time," Bigart said. "And I was not someone who could swing over easily to radio or TV," where his stutter would have been an impossible hurdle.[9]

Bigart later told an interviewer, "It was the easiest telephone call I ever had." Catledge had responded, "Come on over."[10]

On September 15, 1955, Bigart announced his departure from the *Trib* in a letter to Managing Editor George Cornish, whom he addressed as "Dear Mr. Cornish" although they had known each other for years.

"As I explained to you," the letter said, "I urgently need at least six months in New York to attend to personal affairs. Since my reputation at the Tribune has been built up largely as a foreign correspondent, I think the adjustment to another newspaper would be less difficult than adjusting to the city room here. I don't have to tell you how painful it is to leave the paper after twenty-seven happy years."[11]

He did not say what the urgent personal matters were, but it is fair to assume that they had to do with Alice and his marriage, which had broken up. She herself had moved from the *Herald Tribune* to the *Times*, and he admitted later that one of his motivations for doing the same was the possibility of winning her back.

"There were two reasons" for moving to the *Times*, he said. One was that he knew the *Trib* was going downhill financially and could no longer be what it had been. The other was that he "sheepishly" followed his former wife. "Don't ask me which one was the most important, which reason," he said.[12]

It is not clear how much interaction Bigart had with Alice at the *Times*, where she worked on a different floor of the building, but they never got back together. Bigart moved on, personally and professionally.

"I hated to leave the Tribune, in many ways," he said.[13] While the *Times* was the most prestigious newspaper in the country and one of the most prominent in the world, working at the *Trib* had been fun, and working at the *Times* was not, at least for Bigart. For one thing, he said, the *Tribune* had been "a hell of a lot more liberal" with expense account money than the *Times* was. "I traveled first class on the Herald Tribune. When I went over to the Times, it was steerage."[14]

"When Mr. Bigart left the Trib for the Times, there was no particular joy in it for him," his 1991 obituary in the *Times* said. "The Trib was a decade away from its demise, and its economic problems were not lost on Mr. Bigart. But it was a paper with a proud tradition of giving writers their head."

The obit quoted former *Times* managing editor Clifton Daniel: "It seemed to me that he always looked down on the Times, even when he worked there. Its main fault, in his eyes, was that it wasn't the Trib. It was too proud and stiff-necked for his taste. But he knew that if he couldn't work for the Trib, the next best thing was the Times. He was not disloyal to it; he just didn't love it."[15]

What Daniel may not have known was that Bigart came to detest him and other senior editors at the *Times* and to resent their attitude of superiority. He was particularly scornful of Daniel, whom he christened "the white rat" and described as "stuffy" and "the ultimate shit." When they were competitors in the Middle East, Bigart said, "I didn't like him. I beat his ass off. . . . I don't brag, usually, even in the cups, but I think I made his life fairly unpleasant there, and he made mine unpleasant, simply by existing."

Reminded that Daniel had married President Truman's daughter, Margaret, Bigart sneered, "Oh, I can't blame her for that."[16]

Daniel was not the only target of his scorn. Foreign Editor Emanuel Freedman was "that awful churl." Abe Rosenthal "was scary in the sense that you never knew when, if you said something light-veined to him, he would laugh at it, or sort of shrivel, and lash out at you later." Arthur Gelb, whom Rosenthal installed as city editor, "was a special plant that could only have survived, I think, in the Times newsroom, under Rosenthal."[17]

Bigart was annoyed by the *Times*'s self-important attitude and the rigid protocols of its vast, block-long newsroom—all of which were striking contrasts to the ramshackle environment at the *Herald Tribune*. "Accuracy, to the point of tedium! That's what the Times wanted and that's what the Times built its reputation on," he said.[18] Catledge and other *Times* editors were aware of the paper's reputation for heavy-handed editing that restricted lively writing; it proved another contrast to the *Trib*, where lively writing was the hallmark. Asked once by an editor how the *Times* could become more like the *Trib*, Bigart responded brusquely, "You could take out the air conditioning."[19]

Bigart had been happier in the *Trib*'s congenial newsroom, but several months after his move to the *Times*, already overseas, he told Gladys in a letter from Jerusalem that he had done the right thing.

> Joe Alsop is here. He gave me all the gossip about what's happening to the Washington Bureau of the Tribune. I think I told you that Walter Kerr [a reporter, not the celebrated drama critic] quit as bureau chief. He quit because Maggie Higgins was taking over. It seems that when she heard I was leaving the Tribune she went to Brownie [Reid] and demanded a fat contract, saying that Hearst had offered her a lot of money. Under the contract, she can take any assignment she likes, including the White House. When he heard of this, Walter said he could not run the bureau under these conditions, and quit. I guess I'm lucky to have quit when I did.[20]

"Pallid Clerks"

One reason Bigart was sometimes uncomfortable at the *Times* was that its editors, whom he described as "pallid clerks who are in charge of my destiny," were much more rigorous and demanding than *Trib* editors had been and gave him less room to express his own views.[21] Every article went through multiple editors, each of whom felt obliged to tinker with it. That proliferation of editors was symptomatic of another issue at the *Times*: it was absurdly overstaffed. Russell Baker, who was hired by the *Times* a year before Bigart, recalled that in his previous job at the *Baltimore Sun*, "I had written two thousand words a night without feeling overworked. At the Times, writing a six-hundred-word story seemed to be considered a whole week's work. Some reporters never seemed to write anything." Baker wrote that once when Peter Lisagor of the *Chicago Daily News* visited the *Times*, he "was talking to two Times reporters when he realized they didn't know each other and introduced them. There were editors who didn't know the names of reporters they passed in the corridors."[22]

Baker had been a Washington correspondent for the *Sun*, but in the vast *Times* newsroom, he was a nobody, receiving what he considered trivial assignments—an obituary here, a fire there. Bigart, who had earned multiple awards and widespread fame before he joined the *Times*, was not in the same category. The editors wanted to put him to work, but what was he going to do? The paper was so overstaffed, he said, that there were not enough good assignments to go around. He never asked to be assigned to any story, he said, waiting instead for an editor to take the initiative.

"What if you didn't get an assignment one day, what would you do?" he was asked.

"I'd sulk," he answered. He hid in the *Times*'s library, which was on a different floor from the newsroom, out of sight of the editors.[23]

He had been hired on to the city reporting staff, which was responsible for coverage of the city and its suburbs, but he had an understanding with Catledge: although he would be based in New York, he would also roam the world to report on major developments as they arose. Such an arrangement was difficult to reconcile with the bureaucratic realities at the *Times*, where each staff—city, national, foreign, business—had an assigned budget, a fixed number of positions, a separate payroll account, and a turf-conscious editor.

Bigart may have been a brand-name big shot by whom *Times* editors were "a little intimidated," as Betsy Wade put it,[24] but it would have been hard to tell from his first assignments. In his first bylined article, he recounted a speech by the police commissioner announcing the creation of a new "task force" assigned to cut the city's "horrifying" toll of traffic deaths. It was an important news story that appeared on page 1, but it was also a routine, static event that any rookie could have covered. He followed up with three stories recounting the distress in the city's neighborhoods caused by the transfer of foot-patrol officers to the new traffic unit.

That winter, he wrote about a new state test designed to determine if it was safe for epileptics to drive, about the will and estate of millionaire horse breeder William Woodward Jr., about the New York convention of the National Association of Manufacturers, about a labor dispute at Kings County Hospital in Brooklyn, and about a conference at Yale University on the future of labor in the "brave new world" of computers.

Throughout his years at the *Times*, he was unique on the staff as he rotated constantly between domestic and foreign coverage, just as Catledge had promised he could. When he was in the United States, editors used him as the principal reporter on natural disasters, strikes, plane crashes, and major crimes, such as the 1963 murders of "career girls" Janice Wylie and Emily Hoffert, a case that riveted New York for weeks. He covered one major high-profile trial after another: Albert DeSalvo, the "Boston strangler"; soybean oil swindler Billie Sol Estes; anti-war activists such as Philip Berrigan, a Catholic priest, and Benjamin Spock, the renowned pediatrician; Arthur Bremer, who shot George Wallace during the 1972 presidential election campaign; Roy Cohn; civil rights agitator H. Rap Brown; and other well-known defendants. He also conducted extensive examinations of student dissent and faculty politics at Cornell and Columbia Universities.

In his letter of resignation to Cornish, Bigart had said he needed at least six months in New York to deal with personal matters. The *Times* gave him less than four. Then he was sent overseas. In early February 1956, he began a six-month tour in the eastern Mediterranean. He started with a week in Cyprus, reporting on unrest over British rule, and then went on to Israel, where a decade earlier he had recounted the Zionist campaign to defy the British and establish an independent Jewish state. From then through July, he shuttled between Israel and Cyprus. That first full year at the *Times* set a pattern for his life for the next decade: constantly moving from one hot spot to another with intervals in New York, chronicling events cataclysmic and mundane and describing the people involved.

In one of his early articles from Israel, about an uproar at a meeting of the World Zionist Congress, he referred to the Israeli politician Menachem Begin as "a former terrorist." It was true—Begin had organized the infamous bombing of the King David Hotel during the Jewish rebellion against British rule in Palestine[25]—but by 1956 he had turned to more conventional politics and two decades later would become prime minister. Bigart's description prompted a furious retort from Yaakov Lieberman, Israel's representative in New York, saying Begin was held in high esteem in Israel, where he was "one of the legendary figures" of the young country. Bigart had joked when he accepted this assignment that while at the *Herald Tribune* he had been criticized as pro-Zionist, now it was the opposite.[26]

Rebellion in Cyprus

His reporting on the Greek Cypriots' rebellion against British rule was especially insightful. When the British exiled their nationalist hero, Archbishop Makarios III, violent protests erupted, which the British tried to suppress by sheer force. That policy "could not possibly work," Bigart concluded, "because the British cannot for long periods be sufficiently coldblooded and ruthless." The British had armored vehicles and barbed wire everywhere and were baffled when the local people greeted them politely.

"The contrast between appearance and actuality never ceases to surprise the British," Bigart reported. "Because people smile and don't hate with their eyes and are polite, the British cherish the delusion that most of the 400,000 Greek Cypriotes—four-fifths of the population—reject E.O.K.A. [the rebel organization Ethniki Organosis Kyprion Agoniston, or "National Organization of Cypriot Fighters"] and would readily collaborate with the British once the threat of terrorism were removed." But the British efforts to combat terrorism—a strict curfew, closure of schools, collective fines—were only stoking anger and provoking restless young people into anti-British action, he found.[27]

He was in Jerusalem in mid-May when he received a letter from Foreign Editor Freedman about who would succeed him there after he completed his six-month tour to which he had agreed.

"Your performance in your first foreign assignment for the New York Times has been just what we expected it to be—excellent," Freedman said. "I will be frank and say that we would like to keep you in the field, and I hope we can tempt you with a new assignment." He raised the possibility of North Africa, where "the Algerian situation is a very interesting, complex and active one, and we would like to have a really first-rate and experienced man covering it." He assured Bigart that "this is not an attempt to hornswoggle you. If you feel strongly that you want to return to the United States, our commitment to bring you back will be honored."[28]

Three days later, Bigart responded that he did indeed want to go back to New York.

There are, I'm afraid, pressing personal reasons for my wanting to return to New York at the end of July or by mid-August at the latest. But of course I do want more foreign assignments in the future. What I would like is the arrangement suggested by Mr. Catledge when I came to the Times last October. He suggested that I base in New York and be available for short-term assignments anywhere. That arrangement would be most appealing. I have always thought that the ideal job would be one that allowed me to spend roughly half the year in the United States on the city or national staffs. The rest of the time I'd be happy to go anywhere you wanted to send me, no matter how tough the assignment.[29]

In that, Bigart may have been unique among foreign correspondents. Most want a tour of at least three years based in some foreign capital, similar to what Keyes Beech had in Tokyo, for three reasons: They like the life, traveling to exotic places on an expense account and dining with diplomats and cabinet officers; they prefer a fixed residence so their families can be with them; and they know it usually takes several months at least to understand the intricacies of whatever place or region they are assigned to.

Not Bigart. He was always restless. He never sought the three- or four-year assignment as a resident correspondent in a foreign capital that was, for colleagues such as Beech, the admission ticket to some higher status.

"I never wanted to be stuck in one foreign capital," he said, "I could never learn another language in my life and I didn't feel qualified." The overseas stories he covered with such distinction were "mainly troubles and war stories, things like that," and "those stories don't last too long. Then, when they end, you're back on covering routine State Department stuff, that sort of thing, which can be pretty boring."[30]

Whether this was false modesty or a sincere self-appraisal, it was hardly an accurate assessment of his ability. In Europe, the Middle East, and Asia, he demonstrated time and again his ability to write deftly and warmly about people and about matters of politics, culture, religion, food, and economics, as any good foreign correspondent does when there is no shooting.

It did not take him long to realize that even in the tightly edited *Times*, he could find room to express his own views in the Sunday paper's News of the Week in Review section, which was created and controlled by Lester Markel, an editor who was largely independent from the editors in the main newsroom and often at odds with them. The Review section did not have its own reporting staff, so Markel had to ask for contributions from reporters who worked for other editors. He was difficult to get along with—Arthur Gelb described him as "jealous of his superiors and contemptuous of his subordinates"[31]—but Bigart often found the Review a useful channel for expressing views and analyses that had no place in the weekday edition. Throughout his years at the *Times*, Bigart would find room to roam in writing for Markel, but he also had angry spats with him when he thought Markel's requests were interfering with his coverage of breaking developments for the daily paper.

The Sunday Review of February 5, 1956, published a long assessment by Bigart about the mood in Cyprus, saying that the British tactics such as house-to-house searches were only alienating the populace even more. Resentment of the British was driving young men who could have been placated to join the rebel underground. He was right, but the British could not see it. He found the British as obtuse in Cyprus as they had been in Iran.

From the last week of January 1956 through the end of July, Bigart shuttled between Jerusalem and Nicosia. At the end of July, he returned to New York and to the Metropolitan News staff, where he reported on the first transatlantic telephone call by cable, a fire on a bridge over the Harlem River that halted subway traffic, and the appointment of President Eisenhower's brother Milton as the president of Johns Hopkins University—a story for which he traveled not to some remote foreign capital but to Baltimore. Then an anti-Soviet uprising broke out in Hungary, and by late October, Bigart was on his way back to Europe. From a base in Vienna, he patrolled the Hungarian border, struggling to recount events in a country that Western reporters were not permitted to enter.

On the one occasion when "friendly Hungarian border guards" did allow reporters to cross the border, he saw "the mass funeral of eighty-five students and workers" who had been gunned down by the pro-Soviet government's secret police in Magyaróvár, a town of sixteen thousand people. Bigart found it was "completely in the hands of the 'liberation forces.' Everyone wore a small ribbon of the national colors—red, white and green—or carried a flag from which the red star had been removed. Not a single red star or hammer and sickle device was seen anywhere. The hated symbols had been wrenched from the Communist headquarters, police station and City Hall and torn to bits."[32]

The rebellion was inspiring but doomed. Soviet troops soon put an end to it, but by then Bigart was gone from the scene. The story from Magyaróvár was his last about Hungary because Israeli troops invaded Egypt, and Bigart was on his way back to the Middle East.

The Suez War

The story of the Suez war of 1956 has filled many books, but the conflict is easily summarized.

In July Egypt's charismatic leader Gamal Abdel Nasser, the embodiment of Arab aspirations, nationalized the Suez Canal, which British and French interests had built and British troops still controlled even after Nasser's revolution of 1952. Nasser, determined to get rid of the last vestiges of colonial rule, proclaimed Egyptian sovereignty over the vital waterway, ordered the British out, and closed the canal and the Gulf of Aqaba to Israeli shipping.

In late October, senior officials of Britain, France, and Israel met secretly in France to plan military action to retake the canal. Israeli forces would invade Egypt's Sinai Peninsula on October 29 and aim to reach the canal within twenty-four hours. Britain and France would then call on Israel to withdraw, on the understanding that it was a sham gesture, and the Israelis, by prearrangement, would not do so. Britain and France would then have a concocted threat to justify their own military intervention. They also issued an ultimatum to Egypt to open the canal to all international shipping, including Israel's. If Nasser refused to comply, as they knew he would, British and French forces would enter the conflict on the side of Israel.

As planned, the Israelis attacked and rejected the sham British-French demand that they withdraw. British and French paratroopers landed in Egypt two days later.[33]

The Suez adventure, known to the Arabs as the "Tripartite Aggression," developed into a humiliating debacle for the invaders when the United States condemned it and the Soviet Union threatened to send its own troops into the conflict on the side of Nasser, whom it was assiduously courting in its quest for new alliances in the Middle East. But when the Israelis first attacked, nobody could foretell the outcome, and an international crisis erupted. The *Times* of course had resident correspondents in Jerusalem and Cairo, but they were fully occupied with diplomatic and political issues. The editors thought the paper needed close-up coverage of military developments; hence they deployed a veteran war correspondent. By November 1, three days after his visit to Magyaróvár in Hungary,

Bigart was filing front-page war reports from the Israeli Defense Ministry in Tel Aviv. (The ministry was and is in Tel Aviv even though the rest of the government operates out of Jerusalem.)

On the battlefield, Egypt was no match for the combined forces of Israel, France, and Britain, and its troops were quickly overwhelmed. On November 3, after less than a week of action, Bigart described the rout: "Israel's lightning conquest of Egypt's Sinai Peninsula and the Gaza Strip is complete except for mopping-up operations. The ancient Philistine capital of Gaza was the last town to fall. In its drive, Maj. Gen. Moshe Dayan's tough Army had killed, captured or put to flight 30,000 Egyptian troops east of the Suez Canal."[34]

On November 13, as Bigart was reporting on the arrival of a UN truce coordinator and on Israel's assertion of sovereignty over Gaza, Foreign Editor Freedman wrote him a cautionary letter. "Many people have remarked on the speed with which you got from Vienna to Tel Aviv when the war blew up out there. It was an impressive performance and we were very glad to have you on the scene in Israel," the letter said. "Your reporting has been excellent, and greatly appreciated."

Then came the "but": "Please be careful about commenting on the news in a way that might be interpreted as editorial." Freedman cited the last sentence of a story Bigart had filed the previous day, as international outrage mounted, saying that Israel "had put herself 'up the creek.'" Bigart had written—in cable-speak— about the Israelis that the "whole plaint is that big powers have 'sold Israel down river.' No one asks why Israel put itself so far up creek." The editors deleted that comment. It was a small episode but symptomatic of what would become a long-running argument between Bigart, who had learned in Poland and Spain the necessity of incorporating his own observations into his copy to convey the full picture, and *Times* editors—other than Markel—who wanted opinions limited to the opinion pages.[35]

In the same letter, Freedman asked Bigart to remain in the region for a while because the situation was still unsettled and the ultimate outcome still unclear. Bigart stayed until that fall, reporting mostly on international efforts to stabilize Egypt and reopen the Suez Canal.

On November 16, Bigart flew home because his father had died, but his time in the United States was brief. By January 1957 he was back in the Middle East, exploring the Kingdom of Yemen.

Yemen the Unknown

Except for the British protectorate of Aden along the southern coast, Yemen was terra incognita even for the Middle East specialists of the State Department. Few

Americans had ever been to its remote mountain cities. The ruling regime there had been in place for a millennium, but the United States had no official relations of any kind with it until President Truman sent a special envoy in 1946.

Then in January 1957, the aging sultan, or imam, invited Western reporters, including Bigart, to visit and tour his realm. Bigart was one of twelve who took him up on it. Their Jeeps took eight hours to cover the 125 miles from Aden to the mountain city of Taiz. The reason for this extraordinary overture, Bigart reported, was that the sultan was seeking support for a growing border conflict with the British in Aden.

Much of what Bigart wrote on that trip was basically travelogue about what he called "a pastoral kingdom just emerging from the twelfth century." He described the mountainous terrain, the people's clothing, the bad roads, the absence of electricity, and the national addiction to qat, or khat, a mild narcotic leaf that is ubiquitous in Yemen. But he also reported that the imam was an absolute ruler who, "like the Queen of Hearts in 'Alice in Wonderland,' may order anyone who offends him beheaded." Yemen's stability, Bigart concluded, "rests solely on terror inspired by the Imam."

Bigart investigated reports that the imam still held slaves. His conclusion was that there still were a small number of slaves, but their status was preferable to that of Yemeni peasant farmers because they paid no taxes.[36]

After Yemen, Bigart crossed the Red Sea to Ethiopia. He spent just a few days there, listening to Emperor Haile Selassie's complaints about British meddling. Then Bigart went on to Sudan and back to Egypt.

Brief as his stay in Ethiopia was, it led to an angry dressing down from Foreign Editor Freedman. The Foreign Desk was planning a package of articles about countries in the Red Sea region and had asked Bigart to do the piece on Ethiopia because he had just been there.

As the planned publication date for the articles approached, Bigart had not filed his, so Freedman asked him about it. Bigart, who was covering Egypt full time while the resident correspondent was on leave, was already unhappy because Freedman had been asking for more than he was able to do. Now he blew up.

He cabled on March 20: "EYVE HAD NO TIME FOR BLOCKBUSTER STOP ALL MY TIME REQUIRED IN PROVIDING DAILY COVERAGE IN COMPETITIVE SITUATION STOP IF THIS INSUFFICIENT EYE SHALL BE GLAD RESIGN WHEN CARRUTHERS RETURNS." (Osgood Carruthers was the resident correspondent in Cairo.)

Freedman responded in kind: "FLABBERGASTED BY YOU WAITING UNTIL MARCH 20 DEADLINE TO TELL US YOU NOT DOING SURVEY ASSIGNMENT [WHICH] YOU ACKNOWLEDGED FEB 26 STOP APPRECIATE FINE DAILY JOB YOU BEEN DOING BUT DO YOU AGREE WE WERE ENTITLED TO KNOW SO WE COULD MAKE OTHER ARRANGEMENTS STOP."

Freedman's irritation was justified, and a chastened Bigart agreed to submit the Ethiopia article within three days.[37]

He stayed in the region, reluctantly. But three weeks later, on April 18, denied entry to Lebanon and Jordan, and told by the Egyptians that he had to go, he cabled Freedman, saying he was "FED UP WITH THE MIDDLE EAST" and wanted to return to New York.

Freedman replied.

NOT YET. NEEDLESS TO SAY, WE CAN WELL UNDERSTAND YOUR UNHAPPINESS, AND YOU HAVE OUR SYMPATHY. WE SHALL DO OUR BEST TO RELIEVE YOU AS SOON AS IT IS POSSIBLE. UNFORTUNATELY, IT IS NOT POSSIBLE RIGHT NOW, AS I AM SURE YOU WILL AGREE. PLEASE TRY TO BE OF GOOD CHEER. YOU CAN HAVE THE SATISFACTION OF KNOWING THAT YOU ARE MAKING US AND COUNTLESS READERS OF THE NEW YORK TIMES HAPPY, EVEN IF THE SITUATION IS UNCOMFORTABLE FROM YOUR POINT OF VIEW.

He raised the possibility of Bigart's spending a month or so in North Africa when Bigart was finally on his way back to the United States.[38]

In Istanbul, Bigart was able to renew his Egyptian visa, so he stayed on. In June he returned briefly to Tehran. Then, as Freedman had suggested, he went to Algeria, where rebels demanding independence were waging a guerrilla war against the French.

There, for some reason, he apparently made no effort to use any of the French he had studied at NYU; he told a colleague he was "hopelessly handicapped" by his inability to speak the language. Still, he managed to write some illuminating articles about the conflict, most notably a report that the *Times* published on the front page on June 17, 1957. The dateline was Tébessa, Algeria.

"Algerian prisoners were exhibited to silent Moslem crowds in this ancient walled city near the Tunisian frontier today as French troops celebrated yesterday's victory over rebel forces. Six ragged young rebels, one wearing a dirty, bloodstained bandage on his left arm were put in an open truck and driven through the city. They were preceded by a loudspeaker truck that broadcast tape-recorded statements that the prisoners had made a few hours earlier."

In those tapes, the prisoners said they had been forced by the rebels under pain of death to join the insurrection. Attracted by the broadcast, "Moslems emerged from stalls and mud huts in the Casbah section and lined the narrow streets as the strange procession went by. The prisoners were made to stand in the truck back-to-back, three facing each side of the street. Squatting in the rear of the truck were French paratroopers armed with submachine guns."

The faces of the prisoners and of those in the crowds in the street were "equally expressionless."

Bigart stayed in Algiers until late July and then left for a holiday in Mallorca. On September 1, he transferred back to city reporting staff while resuming the nomadic career that took him from Arkansas to Cuba to the Bronx and points west. He covered many stories that may have been worthy of space in the *Times* but did not make full use of his talent and experience: an investigation of waste in New York's public schools; a bicentennial celebration in Pittsburgh; an inquiry into New York's market for "black market babies," featuring testimony by Pearl Buck; an effort by judges to crack down on ambulance-chasing lawyers. Anyone in that newsroom could have taken those stories. Then came the trial of Adolf Eichmann.

The Eichmann Trial

On July 6, 2000, Hawley, Pennsylvania, celebrated the 175th anniversary of its founding. Among the ceremonies was a tribute to one of the town's favorite sons, Homer Bigart. At that event, a local resident named Art Glantz read a letter he had received from Dieter Wechtenbruch, a German lawyer who had been part of the legal defense team at the trial of Adolf Eichmann.

Eichmann was perhaps history's most infamous war criminal because of his central role in Nazi Germany's effort to eradicate Europe's Jews. He sought refuge in Argentina after Germany's surrender in 1945, but Israeli agents tracked him down there and transported him to Jerusalem, where he was put on trial in 1961. The *New York Times* assigned Bigart to cover the trial.

As it proceeded, he interviewed Eichmann's chief defense counsel, Robert Servatius. In his letter to Glantz, Wechtenbruch said, "Instead of asking Dr. Servatius why he was defending a mass murderer, as most journalists did," Bigart wanted to know the details of the defense team's legal strategy. "It was easy to compare Mr. Bigart with other journalists, which may explain my great admiration and esteem for a man who was true and just, severe without being offensive, and friendly without being condescending. It is true that young men sometimes in their lives meet older men who show them the right way. Homer Bigart was one of the few I met."[39]

Perhaps Bigart would not have welcomed a tribute from a person who had helped to defend Eichmann, but what Wechtenbruch said was an accurate reflection of Bigart's coverage of the trial. He conveyed vividly, but not judgmentally, the details of the atrocities, the suffering of survivors who testified, and the implacable ordinariness of the defendant, the man who personified, in Hannah Arendt's famous phrase, "the banality of evil." Bigart treated the defense lawyers not as amoral monsters but as professionals doing a necessary job.

In fact, one of his articles, six weeks into the trial, reported that Servatius "has won the grudging respect and admiration of the Israelis for the way he has conducted an apparently hopeless case." Servatius was on his feet for hours on end, doggedly cross-examining prosecution witnesses and "taking abuse from Eichmann, who has accused him of skipping some documents that the former Nazi regards as significant." As the trial plodded on, Bigart wrote in the *Times* edition of July 3, "Dr. Servatius, who is in his mid-sixties, has been averaging about five hours of sleep since April 11. There are bags of fatigue under his watery blue eyes. His jowls have lost their pinkness. But he stands solid as an ox behind the defense table, tenaciously analyzing every document submitted by the prosecution that suggests Eichmann had any power of decision affecting the Nazi annihilation of European Jews."

Alert readers of the *Times* could see that the editors had already rendered judgment on Eichmann: the articles about the trial referred to him only as "Eichmann," not "Mr. Eichmann." The *Times* ordinarily used the title with every man it wrote about other than convicted felons or the athletes in the Sports section. And in truth the outcome was never in doubt; it was, as Bigart said, "a foregone conclusion."[40] The trial's drama lay in the horrifying stories told by prosecution witnesses.

In one session, Bigart reported, "the sinister world of Auschwitz, greatest of the Nazi death camps, was revived today in all its insane terror at the trial of Adolf Eichmann. The testimony was surpassingly dreadful" as the prosecution presented grim details about the Nazis' extermination campaign.

The first witness, an author named Yehiel De-Nur, "gave a choked cry shortly after he began to testify and fell headlong from the witness stand. He was carried off on a stretcher. Hardier witnesses . . . told how human ashes from the Auschwitz crematories were scattered on icy roads from a cart pulled by twenty children." Other witnesses described being sterilized in the Nazi doctor Josef Mengele's medical experiments. Mengele, they said, "rode around the vast camp on a bicycle whistling tunes by Mozart." He indicated "with a motion of his finger who should be gassed and who should live a little longer," not just among the Jews but also among the "Gypsies," whom the Nazis had rounded up as well.

"Most of the testimony was of filthy quarters, hunger, and the stench of burning bodies," Bigart's account said. "Eichmann was hardly mentioned at all," except when "a bearded, black-garbed Jew shouted hysterically at the prisoner's cage. 'Murderer!' he screamed. 'Your wife and children should burn in fire!'"[41]

On most days, however, "this lengthy proceeding lacks drama mainly because the chief character is as drab as a ribbon clerk," Bigart observed. Spectators came to the courtroom expecting "someone resembling Erich von Stroheim, the monocled Prussian villain of the silent films," but saw instead "a shriveled, ashen-faced individual whose only special feature is a tight mouth. It is hard to feel any stirring reaction about this completely colorless person."[42]

The trial lasted until mid-August. Bigart returned to Jerusalem in December for the verdict—guilty—and again, months later, for the sentencing.

Bigart never expressed his feeling about the trial while it was in progress. But two years later, reviewing a book about the Eichmann case in the *Times*, he reflected on the experience: "Few who sat in the Jerusalem courtroom during the long trial of Adolf Eichmann in the spring and summer of 1961 can bring themselves to read about it even now. At times a demented nightmare, at times just a punishing bore, the trial failed to produce any new, significant truths about the most ghastly phenomenon of our times: the attempt to murder all the Jews of Europe. Also, the accused seemed an exceedingly dull specimen of the Nazi bureaucracy."

Before the trial, he observed, writers who had never laid eyes on Eichmann portrayed him as a fanatical Nazi with blood on his hands. "But the facile image of a sadistic jack-booted monster did not survive long once the accused was on display on the bullet-proof glass dock of the Jerusalem court. Whatever Eichmann had been in the days of Nazi grandeur, at the time of the trial he had the look of a pallid bureaucrat, the ordinary, unimaginative, clerkish individual one can meet every day in government, business, and the tamer branches of the armed forces."[43] The most interesting part of the book he was reviewing, Bigart wrote, was not about the trial but about the "cloak-and-dagger operation" that brought about his capture.[44]

After the trial, two journalism teachers at a high school in New Jersey wrote to the *Times* that their students had been upset by some of the language Bigart had used to describe Eichmann, such as "pallid figure" and "suddenly bolted to his feet." They said such words were a better fit for the tabloids.

Clifton Daniel wrote a response. Bigart, he said,

is a man in his fifties who has devoted more than 30 years to the profession of journalism. He has won two Pulitzer Prizes for his reporting. He has been through two major wars and a number of minor ones. He has worked all over the world. In brief, he is a man of experience and knowledge and he writes from that background.

He is able to bring to his reporting of the news a certain extra dimension and depth that is perhaps not available to the ordinary reporter. He feels a confidence in his powers of analysis and description that would perhaps not be justifiable in a younger, less knowledgeable man.

The trial, Daniel said, was a historic drama in which the defendant "stood before the court in Jerusalem as the symbol of a vast upheaval in human experience. It was an event that called for the maximum descriptive powers of a great reporter."[45]

Searching for Michael Rockefeller

The cavernous *Times* newsroom was mostly quiet on the late afternoon of November 19, 1961. It was Sunday, and while the Sports department was busy with football and hockey, there was not much local news. The few reporters on duty had little to do. I was there because I worked every Sunday; my days off were Tuesday and Wednesday.

Bigart was in the newsroom at that weekend hour because he was still working on a final version of a long story, which would run on the next morning's front page, about horrifying conditions on the Bowery, Manhattan's skid row. He and Betsy Wade, who was editing his article, were arguing with senior editors over his use of the word "bums" to describe denizens of the street.

"Why do I always have to write derelict?" Bigart demanded. "Why can't the *Times* just use the word 'bum'?"[46]

Then a telephone rang, and there was a sudden stir. Shortly afterward, Bigart was on his feet, putting on his jacket and heading for the exit. Michael Rockefeller, the twenty-three-year-old son of New York governor Nelson A. Rockefeller, had been reported missing on an extended expedition to a remote jungle in New Guinea, where he was looking for primitive art. The governor was going to New Guinea to join the search, and Bigart was going with him.

As Wade recalled the moment, "The entire machinery of the paper suddenly focused on getting Homer on the plane with the Governor—suitcase, visas, shirts, tickets, money—not easy to do on a Sunday."[47]

We, the young people of the support staff—copyboys, clerks, and news assistants aspiring to become reporters—were awestruck. We would have been thrilled to be sent on assignment to the Bronx. New Guinea? Who even knew where that was? Bigart knew, of course, having been there on a reporting trip earlier that year.

For me it was an important moment. I had aspired since high school to become a newspaper reporter. I knew I would never want a job in which I went to the same place and performed the same tasks every day. This episode cemented my career decision. What could be more exhilarating than what had just happened to Homer Bigart?

The New Guinea mission was emblematic of the *Times* at its wealthy best. If anyone questioned how much it would cost to send a reporter halfway around the world for however long the governor would be away, we never heard about it. The story demanded coverage, and no one doubted that Bigart would handle it adroitly.

Bigart left in such a hurry that he did not have time to write the immediate story for that Monday's paper about Michael's disappearance. That was handled by Peter Kihss, another refugee from the *Herald Tribune*, the fastest typist in the newsroom, a veteran reporter known for his skill at tackling any subject and turning it into coherent copy on deadline. Colleagues did not hear from Bigart until Tuesday, when he reported from Honolulu that the governor, "gray with fatigue," had somehow arranged during a refueling stop to charter a larger, faster plane for the rest of the transpacific flight. Rockefeller also received a sympathetic telegram from President John F. Kennedy offering whatever assistance the government could provide.

Bigart's November 21 article said that the governor "clung to the hope" that his son, last seen trying to swim ashore from an overturned boat, had reached the shore safely. His son, Rockefeller said, was a resourceful young man and a powerful swimmer.

Bigart was one of the few American reporters who knew anything about what was then Dutch New Guinea; he had met several senior officials there earlier that year after a long swing through Australia and New Zealand. He knew how forbidding the terrain was, how desolate the coast, but neither his knowledge nor Governor Rockefeller's money, nor the president's offer to help, produced any results.

In a dramatic account Bigart filed on Thursday, datelined Merauke, Netherlands New Guinea, a Dutch scientist who had been with Michael when their motorized catamaran was swamped in a storm reported that the governor's son was last seen trying to swim to shore, against the current, supported only by two gasoline cans tied together. The scientist, René S. Wassing, said he had tried to persuade young Rockefeller to stay with the boat because there was a "50-50 chance" of being rescued, but Michael "took off his pants and jumped into the sea."[48]

Hearing nothing encouraging from Dutch officials for a week, the governor was prepared to accept reality and fly home when a Dutch naval vessel found one of the gasoline cans many miles away. Rockefeller delayed his departure briefly, but no further clues turned up.

Wassing had been rescued when a plane spotted him clinging to wreckage and dropped a life raft. Michael Rockefeller was never found. In January 1963, the Rockefeller family petitioned a court in White Plains, New York, to declare Michael legally dead.

Research conducted decades after his disappearance indicated that he had been killed and dismembered by indigenous people, the people whose lives he was there to study and whose art he was collecting. The artifacts he had shipped home before his disappearance are in the Michael C. Rockefeller Wing of New York's Metropolitan Museum of Art.

Bigart did not fly back to New York with the governor. He went to Port Moresby, the capital of the Australian sector of New Guinea, to write a brief but sour piece about how art collectors and missionaries were exploiting the indigenous people. He then went on to Jerusalem for the sentencing of Adolf Eichmann. To no one's surprise, the sentence was death by hanging.

The Bowery article that Bigart and Wade had been finalizing ran on the front page of the November 20 edition of the *Times*. With unpalatable details, it described the street on the Lower East Side as "the last refuge of the defeated, the embittered, the alcoholic," living in cruel squalor. It did indeed use the word "bums." Only many weeks later did Bigart return to the newsroom to discover that he and Wade had won the argument about the use of the word. He had apparently forgotten about it. "Bum?" he responded. "It's unsuitable for the Times to use the word bum."[49]

The Bowery article was honored with one of the "Merit Awards" bestowed periodically by the publisher. It was $100.[50]

Bigart received accolades from the publisher again in August 1966, when his editors assigned him to write about a murder in Harlem. That was the height of the civil rights era, but it was still highly unusual for any of the mainstream New York papers, let alone the *Times*, to show interest in crime in African American neighborhoods such as Harlem. To send a reporter of Bigart's stature was almost unheard of. But this murder was different: the victim was White.

Bigart wrote a straightforward story about the death of Helen Berman, who operated a "hole-in-the-wall haberdashery" on West 125th Street. He found that the "tiny shopmistress" usually kept the door locked, admitting only potential customers who did not look threatening, but she had apparently guessed wrong this time and paid with her life.[51]

In the scope of Bigart's career, this story was negligible, but it brought tributes from the paper's leadership. Publisher Arthur O. Sulzberger said it was "really first rate" and sent his congratulations. Catledge sent a note saying, "You have gone and done it again" with the story and repeating Sulzberger's congratulations. No such messages would have been sent if the shopkeeper had been Black because no reporter would have written about it.

NINE

CUBA, CONGO, AND CANNIBALS

In the two decades after World War II, the noncommunist world experienced one upheaval after another as colonies threw off their masters and nationalist firebrands rose to power. Bigart had seen this wave up close as he reported on Mossadegh's Iran, Nasser's Egypt, and Makarios's Cyprus. It was logical for the *Times*'s editors to dispatch him to new uprisings.

By the winter of 1958, news editors at the *Times* were not comfortable with the paper's coverage of the dramatic events unfolding in Cuba, where a rebel army led by the charismatic young Fidel Castro was threatening the right-wing regime of President Fulgencio Batista. The *Times* had published the biggest scoop about that conflict the year before in an interview that proved Castro was still alive, despite government claims to the contrary, but the paper was not getting the definitive coverage it wanted. Other papers, including the *Chicago Tribune*, were publishing dramatic accounts that underscored the importance of the story, but the *Times* had not found a reliable correspondent to provide the authoritative, balanced reporting on which the *Times* prided itself.

Its resident correspondent in Havana, Ruby Hart Phillips, had received that assignment by accident, literally: her husband, James D. Phillips, held the post from 1931 to 1937, when he died in an automobile accident. She spoke Spanish and knew the country, so the *Times* gave her the job, despite her scant experience in journalism. Using the byline R. Hart Phillips to disguise the fact that she was a woman, she wrote about Cuba competently and sometimes perceptively for the next twenty years. But she had little experience in war reporting, and she had become so close to the Batista regime that it was difficult for her to write impartially about Castro's rebellion. "Such was her influence in Havana in the 1950's that whenever Mrs. Phillips heard from sources that dissidents had been picked up by Fulgencio Batista's secret police, a call from her with a promise to write an article could usually set the prisoners free," according to her obituary in the *Times*.[1] That access was useful when she was writing about the Cuban government and politics, but it undermined her credibility when writing about the rebels.

When the Batista government put out the story in December 1956 that government troops had killed Castro, the rebel leader understood that it would cripple his movement if people believed its leader was dead. He sent word to a trusted agent in Havana that he wanted a foreign correspondent to come see him—an invitation to a sure-fire scoop. The go-between chose a representative of the *Times*, but it was not Ruby Phillips. The writer who would risk the treacherous trip into the mountains of Oriente Province to meet Castro was Herbert L. Matthews.

Matthews was everything Phillips was not as a foreign correspondent—a well-traveled veteran of international reporting in dangerous environments, perhaps best known for his coverage of the Spanish Civil War—but in early 1958, he was no longer a member of the *Times*'s international news reporting staff. He was an editorial writer, paid to offer his opinion rather than to report the news objectively. At the time, it was not unusual for members of the editorial staff to write for the news pages, and the prospect of an interview with Castro was a prize the paper could not turn down. Matthews, who happened to be in Cuba anyway to make his own assessment of the state of play, put his reporting hat back on and ventured into rebel territory.

The result—after a clandestine journey that resembled Bigart's hard trip to find Markos Vafiadis a decade earlier—was a dramatic three-part series that Matthews waited to write until he was safely out of Cuba. The *Times* printed the first article at the top of the front page under the headline "Cuban Rebel Is Visited in Hideout / Castro Is Still Alive and Still Fighting in the Mountains." The article was accompanied by a photograph of Castro that the rebel leader had signed and dated to verify its authenticity.

Matthews used more of the article than was necessary to blow his own horn. "This is the first sure news that Fidel Castro is still alive and still in Cuba," it said. "No one connected with the outside world, let alone with the press, has seen Señor Castro except this writer. No one in Havana, not even at the United States Embassy . . . will know until this report is published that Fidel Castro is really in the Sierra Maestra. This account, among other things, will break the tightest censorship in the history of the Cuban Republic."

Matthews left no doubt that he was captivated by Castro and his movement. "The personality of the man is overpowering," he wrote. "It was easy to see that his men adored him and also easy to see why he has caught the imagination of the youth of Cuba all over the island. Here was an educated, dedicated fanatic, a man of ideals, of courage, and of remarkable qualities of leadership."

Was Castro a communist, as some in the US government suspected? He could not be, Matthews wrote, because his economic and social program, while vague, "amounts to a new deal for Cuba, radical, democratic, and therefore anti-communist."[2]

There was more in that vein in those articles and in another series Matthews wrote after returning to Cuba in June. "From poor farmers and workers to the highest levels of conservative, religious elements of society, business and the professions, Señor Castro has become the leader and symbol of the struggle against the dictatorship of General Batista," he reported. "No figure has attained this stature in Cuba since the struggle for independence from Spain."[3]

A biographical sketch with Matthews's papers at Columbia University says that the interview helped to "undermine the Batista regime and revive the struggle of Castro, making him appear as the best hope for democracy and social justice in Cuba."

This adulatory coverage drew strong criticism from writers and analysts who thought Castro was a menace, not a hero—especially after Castro gained power and revealed his true colors. In one notable example, William F. Buckley Jr. lampooned the *Times* and pilloried Matthews in an article cleverly titled "I Got My Job through the New York Times," a sendup of a *Times* advertising slogan. Matthews, Buckley wrote, "became the Number One unbearded enthusiast for Fidel Castro. Castro, he told the world in a series of articles that made journalistic and international history, is a big, brave, strong, relentless, dedicated, tough idealist."[4]

Inside the Eisenhower administration, opinion about Castro's movement was divided. Some officials believed, as the historian Hugh Thomas wrote, that "Castro always had been a communist and should therefore be destroyed as soon as possible." Another faction, led by Roy Rubottom Jr., the assistant secretary of state for Western Hemisphere affairs, "had high hopes for Castro," believing that he might turn out to be a political and economic liberal. Rubottom used Matthews's articles to persuade the administration to impose an arms embargo on the Batista government.[5]

As 1958 began, Catledge and other editors in the newsroom decided they could not continue with the pro-government coverage they were getting from Phillips or the paeans to Castro they were getting from Matthews. It was time to send a correspondent they trusted. Homer Bigart was soon on his way.

His assignment, Foreign Editor Emanuel Freedman told him, was to "take a look at the situation." He was not to concern himself with daily events but to review larger issues such as the status of individual liberties under Batista's rule, the importance—if any—of Castro's rebellion, and the attitude of the business community. He should "not be influenced by our previous coverage," Freedman's memo said.[6] He did not specifically tell Bigart to try to interview Castro, but that was what Bigart wanted to do.

Bigart often complained, when assigned to French-speaking countries, that his inability to speak French was a handicap, although he must have known at least the basics. He had made no such complaint about his lack of Spanish when reporting from Honduras, nor did he in Cuba. "I made contact with some Castro people, then flew to Santiago to a safe house and waited there," Bigart recalled. "Remember, in those days Castro had wide support among the intellectuals, among the middle class, and it was an engineer who took me from Santiago down to the base of the mountains, and then up to see Castro." He said editors at the *Times* knew what he was up to, but he did not tell Phillips, to whom he referred as "some awful woman there who was the correspondent in Havana."[7]

In that pre-cellphone era, Bigart was "outtapocket"; that is, his editors could not reach him nor he them. Alarmed as days went by with no word from him, the editors asked Matthews to make inquiries.

"Herbert Matthews has been in touch with one of Fidel Castro's prominent adherents who has just arrived in New York from Santiago, Cuba"—the capital of Oriente Province—Foreign Editor Freedman informed Catledge and other senior newsroom executives. "He reports that Homer Bigart had to wait in Santiago four or five days before he was able to take off to Fidel's headquarters—which means that he has been up there about ten days. This informant feels that this is not excessive and that we should be hearing from Homer within a few days." The informant called his mother, who lived in Santiago, and learned that "for the past five days nobody had been able to go into Fidel Castro's area or come out because of fighting and military patrol activity." Ruby Phillips had no information, this same memo said, but she hoped to hear some news from the US consul in Santiago.[8]

In fact, Bigart was in no danger, at least not from the rebels. Government security forces were another matter. Bigart complained that Freedman "stupidly sent a cable to the American embassy, or to this woman, who practically worked for the American embassy, saying, 'Look out for Bigart, he's disappeared!' Well, if there's one thing that could sign a death warrant for you, it's to alert Batista's people that I am at large."[9]

Despite the need to maneuver and avoid detection by government forces, Bigart told an official of the US Embassy afterward that he "was impressed with the ease and comparative freedom of travel into and within the Sierra Maestra. His group had no trouble in evading the few army patrols in the area." He found Castro and his men living in a "semi-permanent" camp where "living conditions were primitive." Hygiene was poor, the food was "plentiful but monotonous," and many of the men had intestinal parasites, but medical care was available from "an excellent surgeon and physician."[10]

More than two weeks passed before Bigart emerged to file his article about his interview with Castro and the strength of his movement. It was published on the paper's front page on February 26, 1958.

It said that Castro had sent Batista a proposal to end the war based on specific conditions: government military forces would withdraw from Oriente, after which Castro would agree to participate in nationwide elections, provided that they were supervised by the Organization of American States. Castro wanted Batista's troops out of Oriente, he said, because he believed that with polls there under his control and with supporters liberally scattered all across the country, "his 26th of July movement would sweep the elections."

Bigart made clear that Castro was not making this offer from a position of strength. He might control the mountains of Oriente, Bigart wrote, but "in fifteen days in the sierra this observer saw no evidence of rebel strength sufficient to win a decisive action on the plains." Castro understood that, but he believed that Batista's political support was eroding and that he could be toppled by a campaign of sabotage capped by a general strike.

Bigart reported what little Castro said about his economic and social program, but he was considerably less enthusiastic than Matthews had been. He said Castro "showed some uneasiness when questioned" about this for an "obvious" reason: he did not want to alienate his many wealthy and middle-class supporters, who saw him as "a symbol of a middle-class reform movement rather than of economic and social revolution." But he also needed the support of the laboring classes and their trade unions, to whom "he may have to promise reforms that could frighten other groups" of his backers. Castro said no public utilities or other industries would be nationalized under his government if they were "operating efficiently" and that "no expropriation of privately owned lands would be necessary."

The neutral tone of Bigart's article did not indicate whether he believed what Castro told him about nationalization of industry and land. The word "communist" did not appear in the published text.

In a separate article assessing Castro's military strength, Bigart said that even if Castro could deploy as many fighters and weapons as he claimed, there was no way those forces could defeat a government army equipped with tanks and artillery. The maximum number of fighters Castro could commit to any one engagement was four hundred. Success would depend on widespread defections by Batista's officers, but "his program offers no attractions for power-hungry officers."

"To see our victory," Castro told him, "it is necessary to have faith."

When Bigart arrived at his camp, Castro said he and his men were resting after what he described as their biggest battle of the war—an attempt to overrun a government outpost at Piña del Agua. He positioned three columns of about a hundred fighters each, one commanded by himself, one by his brother Raúl, and one by "a young Argentine physician, Ernesto Guevara," later famous as Che Guevara. The plan was to make a surprise dawn attack on a government outpost and then ambush the reinforcements that were expected to rush to the scene of the fighting.

One government patrol of sixteen soldiers was wiped out, but most of the outpost's defenders fled into the woods. No column of reinforcements arrived. "Clearly this phase of the rebel plan failed to come off well," Bigart wrote. This engagement, he observed dryly, "will never make an addition to Sir Edward Creasy's 'Fifteen Decisive Battles of the World.'"[11]

That comment drew criticism from Matthews's biographer, Anthony DePalma, a former *Times* reporter himself. "Bigart failed to understand the dynamics of guerrilla war, which was not surprising, given his experience with conventional war. Castro did not need to win one of the world's fifteen decisive battles," DePalma wrote. "Though he had been sent to Cuba to correct what the editors believed was Matthews' biased reporting, Bigart also apparently took sides, downplaying Castro's chances of winning the war."[12]

It is true that in 1958 Bigart had little experience in reporting on unconventional or guerrilla warfare. He had written a series about the rebellion against British rule in Malaya, and he had been to French-ruled Vietnam, but those articles were based mostly on reporting in the capital cities. In Greece's civil war, most of the military action he had seen was from the government's side. But it is also true that his military assessment in Cuba was undoubtedly correct: Castro prevailed because the Batista regime was corrupt, unpopular, and incompetent, not because of his rebels' military strength. The aim of guerrilla warfare is to foment dissent and disrupt economic activity, not to win set-piece battles, as Bigart himself would see in Vietnam. DePalma was writing decades later, when unconventional warfare had become widely understood.

Three days after Bigart's account of the Piña del Agua attack appeared, the *Times* published a brief report about a statement from the Batista government that said the story was completely erroneous. "Such insidious and lying propaganda to confuse the Cuban people must stop. Combats are won on the field of action, not by printed words," the statement said.[13]

Despite his instructions from Freedman to explore larger issues in depth, Bigart then left Cuba. He filed one more report, from Miami, on tactical differences among Castro's allies about his planned general strike; then Bigart flew to New York. His respite did not last long.

Within a few weeks, Catledge decided that reporting events in Cuba again required reinforcements. In a terse memo to the publisher, he said, "On account of the stirrings in Cuba, we think we had better get another man down there. We have had Homer Bigart poised for several days and feel that now is the time for him to be on his way."[14] Bigart returned to Havana on April 1.

He promptly went back to Santiago, where several American reporters, defying a declaration of martial law, were trying to report on the increasing military pressure from Castro's rebel troops. On April 7 and 8, the Cuban military arrested seven of the correspondents, including Bigart. Three were held overnight; Bigart and the others were kept in custody for several hours. When they appeared at the US consulate in Santiago after their release, the consul, Park F. Wollam, told them he could offer little help because under martial law "the security forces could do anything they pleased." He pleaded with them to return to Havana.[15]

A week later, Castro played what he thought was his trump card: he called the general strike that he believed would bring down the government. It was a total failure. In the first sentence of his account, Bigart made clear why: "Unrealistic planning, poor coordination, and shockingly inadequate communications were mainly responsible for the collapse of the Cuban revolutionary strike."[16] Bigart did not linger in Cuba for long after that debacle. By the last week of April, he was back in New York, and by July he was again in the Middle East.

When Castro rode into Havana in triumph after Batista fled the country the following January, Ruby Phillips wrote the *Times*'s story. Castro became supreme commander of Cuba's armed forces and officially took power as prime minister on February 16, 1959.

In April, Castro visited Washington for the first time. It was an unusual arrangement because he was invited not by the State Department or the White House but by the American Society of Newspaper Editors, whose members wanted to know more about him.

In a ceremony at the Cuban Embassy, Castro awarded eighteen-karat gold medals, his signature engraved on each, to thirteen American journalists who had interviewed him while he was leading his rebels in the war. Nine of them, including Herbert L. Matthews, were present to accept their medals in person. Four were not: Wendell Hoffman of CBS, Charles Shaw of WCAU radio in Philadelphia, Karl Meyer of the *Washington Post*, and Homer Bigart.[17]

"Bigart's absence from the gold medal ceremony was understandable," Leonard Ray Teel wrote in his book about the press coverage of Castro and not just because he was thousands of miles away. "Assigned to Cuba by news desk editors as a high-caliber substitute for Herbert Matthews, Bigart had none of Matthews's enthusiasm for the revolution."[18]

After Castro took power and showed his true colors, Catledge wrote in his memoir, the criticism of the *Times* "troubled" him and Sulzberger. The source of the "trouble" was not the criticism itself but "a belief that the critics were in part correct, that Matthews had used poor judgment and lost his cool in his coverage of Castro, and that his articles had to some degree misled our readers." When Matthews went back to Cuba in 1961, after the Bay of Pigs fiasco, and again in 1963, Catledge refused to print anything he wrote in the news section.[19]

"The Dark Continent"

Bigart was less successful in his next extended foray into the developing world. He spent seven grueling months in late 1959 and the first half of 1960 roaming Africa from Mauritania to South Africa as colonial rule by France, Britain, and Belgium neared its end. If there was a chapter in Bigart's illustrious career that inspires cringes and criticism as much as admiration, it was his coverage of what was known as "the dark continent" on the eve of independence.

The *Times* had resident correspondents in Nairobi and Johannesburg, but so much was happening across Africa that the paper sent Bigart to supplement them. Belgian Congo by itself presented a daunting challenge for a reporter. It was a vast land of jungle and savannah with few roads and occupied by multiple tribes with their own languages, largely cut off from the modern world, and often hostile to each other.

Throughout his time in Africa, Bigart struggled to find the right balance between forthright accounts of the difficulties facing the emerging countries after the abuses of colonialism and his editors' desire for travelogue-style depictions of strange African customs and cruel rituals. Having covered many civil rights conflicts at home, Bigart was quite familiar with the phenomenon of Black people having been abused and oppressed by Whites, but the Blacks of the southern United States were Americans, wearing the same clothes and speaking the same language as White people. Those of Africa were apparently a different order of being.

Much of his reporting was perceptive and even prescient. He was among the first, for example, to spot Patrice Lumumba as a rising force in Congolese affairs and to explore the evils of apartheid in South Africa. But he spent entirely too much energy and time writing about "cannibals," "pygmies," "sorcerers," and the supposed inability of many Africans to comprehend the concepts of independence or poly-tribal nationhood. In the aggregate, his dispatches from Africa reflect a deep sense that Africans were violence-prone primitives and that White settlers represented a veneer of civilization on a continent that had none of its own.

After all, he wrote in one early file from Leopoldville, the Belgians had brought running water, electricity, and paved streets. Congo's capital, known since independence as Kinshasa, "has skyscrapers, tree-lined boulevards and landscaped lawns, luxury shops and supermarkets. Elevators run. Plumbing works. Tap water is potable. Efficiency prevails. Even the African districts are not bad."[20] What more could the Congolese want?

Six months later, near the end of his Africa assignment, he found Leopoldville considerably less attractive: "spotless, up to date, but intolerably stolid," characterized by "heavy architecture, dull food, a steamy climate, humorless Belgians [and] scowling natives."[21]

He noted in early dispatches that the Belgian settlers felt bewildered and besieged after widespread riots the previous January and apprehensive about their future. They had expected to stay. He wrote, "Having provided the Congolese with the best schools, best housing, best medical services and highest standard of living for any Africans south of the Sahara, the Belgians found it impossible to believe that any serious discontent would arise."[22] That article said nothing about the previous century, when the Belgians had exploited Congo's resources and ruled its people with unparalleled brutality.

I happened to be living in Brussels that summer of Congolese independence and encountered many of the displaced and uprooted settlers whose bewilderment Bigart had described. It was natural to feel sympathetic. But Bigart was not in Europe; he was in Africa, surrounded by people whom these settlers had abused. Yet he seemed more interested in the Africans' exotic beliefs and habits than in their opinions about the departing Whites.

In these attitudes he was encouraged by his editors in New York, who were amused by his descriptions of what he viewed as primitive savagery and quaint folk beliefs. Just a few weeks into his tour, he received a letter from Turner Catledge praising his coverage. "It's a real pleasure to watch an old pro work," wrote Catledge, who was raised in segregated Mississippi. "It has been particularly worthwhile when you have gone into the back country and told us what these Africans who are aspiring to independence are really like and what vestiges of pagan and primitive culture still exist among them. It all makes mighty good reading and is very educational in the bargain."[23]

Bigart had not been enthusiastic about the Africa assignment. "On Dec. 3, I set out from New York for West Africa, a region I had always viewed with deepest apathy," he wrote in *Times Talk*, the paper's house organ.[24] Once he arrived and began to travel extensively, he was exasperated by the inconvenient plane schedules and poor telecommunications that characterized networks that had been installed to link the colonies with their home countries rather than with their neighbors. The difficulties of travel were exacerbated by the need to obtain visas for countries he wanted to visit. In one episode, he was in Accra, Ghana, on March 30 when he received a message from the Foreign Desk asking him to go to South Africa "immediately." It would take a week to get there, he replied, because he would have to stop in Leopoldville to pick up a visa.

Any correspondent assigned to West Africa, he wrote on March 2 in a "Dear Frank" letter (presumably to City Editor Frank Adams), "should (1) be young and healthy and (2) have a fluent command of French. I'm too old. My lack of French is a terrible handicap in Belgian Congo, Cameroon and Guinea. . . . I think I'll survive, but the days do drag." He was looking forward to the end of his assignment, he wrote, but "meanwhile I get a perverse kick out of exposing myself to the most godawful hellholes in creation." Nor was he inspired by the prospect that millions of people would be liberated from White colonialism to take control of their own fate. "I'm afraid I can't work up any enthusiasm for the emerging republics," he said.[25]

He encountered several of the rising Africans who would become founding leaders of those "emerging republics" and, except for Lumumba, generally came away unimpressed. "The politicians are either crooks or mystics," he wrote to Frank. Ghana's Kwame Nkrumah, he wrote, "is a Henry Wallace in burnt cork. I vastly prefer the primitive bush people. After all, cannibalism may be the logical antidote to this population explosion everyone talks about."[26] (Henry A. Wallace was a populist politician who was vice president of the United States in Franklin Roosevelt's third term.)

These attitudes did not arise from malevolence or from hostility to non-White people in general, as his sympathetic coverage of the plight of American Blacks and Native Americans would later demonstrate. They were the product of Bigart's life and his time. He grew up and went to school in environments that were almost entirely White, as were almost all the troops he had written about in World War II and in Korea. Most of his readers were unaware that there were educated, sophisticated Africans. Most of the places in Africa he was describing did not even have educated diplomats at the United Nations who might impress New Yorkers because they were not yet independent countries and therefore were not represented at UN headquarters. The news staffs of the *Herald Tribune* and the *Times* were virtually all White, and their pages reflected it. Articles on any topic other than sports were almost entirely about White people. Any murder was news, unless it occurred in Harlem or some other mostly Black neighborhood, in which case the major papers ignored it. Schools in the South and many northern cities were mostly segregated in fact if no longer in law. Children still read *Little Black Sambo*.

In Bigart's seven months in Africa, he reported at least briefly from Nigeria, South Africa, Belgian Congo, Cameroon, Togo, Ivory Coast, Ghana, Liberia, Mauritania, Rhodesia (now Zimbabwe), and Ruanda-Urundi, which upon independence became the separate countries of Rwanda and Burundi. His first stop, Lagos, Nigeria, "smelled like Secaucus," he wrote in *Times Talk*, referring to the northern New Jersey town then notable for its pig farms. He also noted that his hotel "is run by Greeks who have mastered all too well the secrets of British colonial cooking. . . . There is not a good saloon or restaurant in town." He described other capitals such as Freetown, Sierra Leone, as even worse.

He wrote to a colleague:

I think I hit bottom in Freetown. You may remember Graham Greene's "The Heart of the Matter," a very depressing novel—but he caught the flavor of the place. I could not find a room in the Central Hotel, the dump Greene describes so vividly in the opening chapter, and I may have fared somewhat better at Lucy Bishop's Guest House, although one morning I did have to shake a couple of mice from my carpet bag. I think they were trying to smuggle themselves out of Sierra Leone.[27]

The press of events across a vast continent, the difficulties of travel, and the logistics of sending his output to New York often left him angry or depressed and in no mood to deal with requests from Sunday editor Lester Markel for additional material. On February 26, he cabled Markel: "AM SUFFERING DEPRESSIVE FATIGUE THAT MAKES EVEN DAILY STUFF DIFFICULT UNLESS EXPOSED TO REAL SHOCKER. HOPE MOOD IMPROVES BUT MEANWHILE CANNOT UNDERTAKE ADDED WORK."[28]

Throughout his tour, Bigart was less than laudatory about the hotels, food, and hygiene, except in a few French-speaking outposts. His favorite was Abidjan, the capital of Côte d'Ivoire, or Ivory Coast, where he found respite from the squalor he experienced elsewhere.

"Abidjan is the prettiest town I've seen all up and down the coast," he wrote to his sister Gladys on March 27, "and I appreciate it all the more after two weeks in Freetown and Monrovia. . . . The food is wonderful here, and I'm getting awfully fat. Except for the sticky heat, this could be Paris. The hotel has a sidewalk café and I sat there this morning and had coffee and croissants and watched the people strolling through the park across the street."

French Africa in general offered better "creature comforts" than British Africa, he wrote, except at the telegraph office where he tried to send articles by cable; it was "complete chaos," operated by Africans who seemed to enjoy making life difficult for White clients.

One of his early dispatches captured the tone of much of his reporting from Africa. It appeared in the *Times* on January 31, 1960, under the headline "Barbarian Cult Feared in Nigeria."

It described life among the much-abused Izi people of eastern Nigeria, where "a pocket of barbarism still exists . . . despite some success by the regional government in extending a crust of civilization over the tribe." There had been a "momentary lapse into cannibalism" the previous year, this article said, "but what bothers the police more than this is a constant threat of revival of a secret society called Ndozi Obudu," a murderous gang he likened to the Ku Klux Klan. The police thought they had crushed it eighteen months before, Bigart found, but it had reemerged as "a society for violence and extortion."

"Garroting was the society's favored method of execution," the article said. "None of the victims was eaten, at least not by society members. Less lurid but equally effective ways were found to dispose of them. According to the police, about twenty-six were weighted with stones and timber and thrown into flooded rivers. No trace has been found of these bodies. A few were buried in ant heaps. But most became human fertilizer for the yam crop."

All that might have been true, but the article described life among the Izi in condescending tones, reflecting the fact that Bigart did not interview any of them. He got all his information from the police and the colonial authorities, including a "native court judge" installed by the British.

"Here a man is deemed rich if he has three wives, ten rows of yams, and a cow or ten dogs," he reported. "Daughters at age 12 are sometimes sent to a 'fattening house,' where they are stuffed with yams and peanuts and allowed no exercise. Emerging three months later, fat and sullen as baby hippos, they are paraded on market day in hopes of marriage bids."

Peculiar as their customs may have been, Bigart found, the Izi "have a pathological hatred of thieves, particularly yam thieves." The police rarely went to the countryside because there were no roads, so the Izi organized "vigilante" groups to secure their crops against the Ndozi Obudu and to protect the farmers' wives from "enticement and adultery."

In the back country of Liberia, Bigart interviewed George Way Harley, an American missionary doctor who was going home after thirty-four years. The hardest part of the work, Harley said, was "the unending struggle against ignorance, sloth, avarice and superstition," as if those qualities were unique to Africans. "Only recently he had to face down the Society of Witch Smellers, which sent a delegation to the hospital demanding that he turn over a patient known to them as an evil witch." These witch smellers not only believed in witches but also thought they could identify them by their scent.[29]

The response from Foreign Editor Freedman to this sort of reporting was glowing. "This is just a note to say hello and to tell you how much pleasure your reporting from the badlands is continuing to give us and the public," he wrote to Bigart on March 3, 1960. "By now you must be American journalism's leading expert on the sorcery, witchcraft, cannibalism and all the other exotic phenomena indigenous to darkest Africa. All this and nationalism too! Where else but in the New York Times can you get all this for a nickel?"[30]

Bigart was happy to comply with the editors' requests for more. He even joked about it to colleagues. In his *Times Talk* piece, headlined "Cocoa and Cannibals," he said that while he had been unable to complete a thorough story about the cocoa crop, "I was able to obtain a story about cannibalism. Just a potboiler, of course."

In one letter to Freedman, as the Congolese were voting on independence, he wrote, "from Stanleyville last week I went to Usumbura, Bukavu and Albert National Park. I had hoped to find pygmies voting and interview them on the meaning of independence, but they were still in the bush. I did see several lions, however, and I sent a long mailer about the Watusi giants."[31] (A "mailer" was an article that was not time sensitive, so it was sent by mail instead of by cable to save money.)

Bigart wrote more along these lines, interspersed with thoughtful, realistic reports about the difficulties facing these emerging nations, whose colonial rulers were leaving them ill-prepared for the task of running modern countries on their own. In one analytical article for the Sunday paper, he noted that Belgian king Leopold II "had a simple and direct approach to Congo and the Congolese. They existed to be exploited. The treatment that accompanied this exploitation was something special. Leopold's agents cut off the hands or feet of Africans who failed to fulfill rubber or ivory quotas," and they proved their worth to Leopold's overseers by bringing in from the bush "baskets of hands, salted and smoked to preserve them in the dank climate."[32]

Otherwise, he did not seriously address until the end of his tour the question of why the Africans were so ill-prepared for independence. If the Izi and other tribes were still uneducated and living primitively in the bush, whose responsibility was that? Was it not because the colonists were busy enriching themselves at the expense of the local people? Leopoldville and Abidjan may have had electricity and hospitals and paved streets, but that was because the White settlers lived in those cities. Outside the capitals, conditions were considerably less benign.

Bigart was especially pessimistic about Cameroon. "Of all emerging African nations Cameroon, which achieved independence Jan. 1, seems least likely to succeed," he reported.[33]

Cameroon was beset by a separatist rebellion in the south, which Bigart said was probably inevitable because of the way the colonial powers had set up the country. Cameroon was split between Muslims and Christians and between French- and English-speaking regions. It also "makes little sense geographically, consisting of widely diverse northern and southern regions divided by a central plateau that effectively discourages communication." His gloomy assessment has been validated by Cameroon's unhappy record of division, corruption, and conflict.

Apartheid Comes to South Africa

At the end of March, the Foreign Desk asked Bigart to go to South Africa, where the new status that was unfolding was not independence for the indigenous Africans but apartheid—the imposition of strict racial separation on the multiracial population. The *Times* had a resident correspondent there, Leonard Ingalls, but Assistant Foreign Editor Nat Gerstenzang told him the editors wanted Bigart "available for coverage of trouble spots throughout country with you remaining Johannesburg to handle main story." Only a profitable newspaper with an encouraging publisher would have the luxury of double coverage.[34]

From Cape Town, Bigart sent vivid accounts of the fear and disruption among non-Whites as the ruling White Afrikaners sorted out residents by skin color and created reservations in the countryside for "Bantus," who, the Afrikaners explained, would feel safer and happier away from the tensions of the big city.

In reports from Durban, Bigart showed flashes of the sensitivity to racial injustice that he would display through the rest of the decade in the United States. His concern was not so much for the Black people confined by apartheid as for the Cape Coloreds, as people of mixed race were called. In one story from Durban, published on May 1, he wrote that "a ruthless drive to purge white neighborhoods of persons of mixed blood is under way here."

The Afrikaners, he found, had nurtured "acute sensitivity" about skin color ever since an early leader had "allowed one of his men to marry a Hottentot." Because of that episode, he said, most of the Afrikaners of 1960 did not welcome the rigorous scrutiny of their family trees to which the government-appointed zealots of the Group Areas Board were subjecting them. In the Durban area, about eighty thousand people deemed contaminated by Black or Indian blood were being forced to move. This campaign demonstrated what Bigart called "the inhumanity of apartheid."

In the middle-class neighborhood of Greenwood Park, he reported, "families of mixed racial origin have lived peaceably alongside whites for many years. Now Greenwood Park has been rezoned for Europeans. Only pure whites can live there." To enforce the rules, he wrote, "government agents have been working overtime, acting on tips [from] spiteful neighbors and interrogating Afrikaners whose ancestry seems indisputably white."

After Durban, Bigart returned to Belgian Congo, where independence would be proclaimed on June 30. He found the Congolese thrilled and fascinated by the imminence of independence, even if most of them did not understand what it meant. "Independence is an abstraction not easily grasped by the Congolese and they are seeking concrete interpretations. All seem to agree that it means an easier life," his article of June 5 said.

"To the forest pygmy, independence means a little more salt, a little more beer," this front-page article said. How did Bigart know that? For a foreign correspondent, generalizing from small samples is an occupational hazard—three days after arriving in Damascus for the first time, I wrote a paragraph that began, "Most Syrians believe . . ."—but in this case, what was the sample? Bigart had told Freedman earlier that he was unable to interview Pygmies about independence because they were "still in the bush."

He didn't stop there with the Pygmies and their beer. "To meat-starved tribes living near the national parks," his article reported, independence is the "freedom to invade the game preserves and slaughter the magnificent herds of antelope and buffalo, and the hippopotamus, elephant, warthog and lion."

"Among the proud Bakuba, the most artistic of all Congolese tribes, independence means a revival of illicit practices such as ordeal by poison, the traditional way to eliminate the witches and sorcerers that have proliferated among them under Belgian rule."

The implication of such assertions is that when White rule ended, the veneer of civilization and order that the Europeans had imposed would vanish along with it, freeing the Africans to revert to their natural state of barbarism and paganism. It is a safe bet that editors of the *New York Times* today would at least attach some qualifiers to those negative depictions rather than displaying them unquestioned on the front page.

On June 25, the *Times* ran an in-house advertisement promoting articles that would appear in the next day's *Sunday Magazine*. "'In-de-pen-DANCE comes to the Congo," the ad said, reflecting the French pronunciation of the word. "Will the Congolese use their new independent powers wisely? Times correspondent Homer Bigart reports on the excited state of the next African nation to become independent."

That article, described in a brief editor's introduction as "one reporter's impressions of the new nation," was the last major piece from Bigart's sojourn in Africa. It combined the best and worst features of his work of the previous seven months—shrewd observations and thoughtful analysis mixed with racial stereotypes and generalizations. Of the first eight paragraphs, four were about the Pygmies even though, as the article said, there were "fewer than 30,000 pure-blooded Pygmies left in the Congo" among a population of 13.6 million.

After the Pygmies came the description of "a native girl walking with languid grace across a field. She would put something to her lips and expel an airy, gossamer substance that floated away like soap bubbles. Then I saw what she was doing. She was eating a fistful of flying ants, one by one, and delicately rejecting the wings. The Congo is not for the squeamish." What would that "native girl" have thought about the ingredients in the scrapple widely consumed in Bigart's native Pennsylvania?

With these bits of local color, so to speak, out of the way, Bigart's article turned to more substantive assessments of the difficulties the Congolese would face in running their new country. Here, he finally addressed in detail the grim record of the Belgians.

In all those decades of Belgian rule, he reported, the colonizers made "no effort to train the Congolese for self-government. After eighty-four years of Belgian tutelage, barely half the Congolese can read and write. Only sixteen Congolese are university or college graduates. . . . The Congo has not even one Negro doctor or lawyer or engineer."

The British had done a far better job in training Ghanaians to administer that country at independence. The Belgians' mistake, Bigart found, was "believing they had another fifty years to rule Congo while the natives were hoisted slowly up the economic ladder," a necessary prelude, the Belgians said, to political progress. They were caught unprepared when France's Charles de Gaulle promised imminent independence to French Congo, a separate colony on the other side of the mighty Congo River. News of de Gaulle's promise almost immediately stirred demands for independence among the previously quiescent people on the Belgian side. The Belgian governor-general, Bigart reported, "saw quickly that Belgium could not maintain rigid colonialism on its side of the river while the French side went free."

Unfortunately for the Congolese, Bigart found, the approach of independence led many Belgian settlers to flee, taking their money back to the home country with them. This flight of capital took the equivalent of $182 million out of Congo in the first three months of 1960, dropping the reserves of the Central Bank to $50 million, "the legal minimum required to cover the currency."

Who among the Congolese would emerge to lead them in the challenge of running their country? The most likely candidate, Bigart said, was Lumumba, "who looks and talks like a provincial schoolmaster. He has been described in the world press as a demagogue, yet he never hollers or jumps about, and usually sounds no more inflammatory than a board chairman at the annual stockholders' luncheon. Nevertheless, the crowds hang on his every word."

Aside from Lumumba, Bigart said, only his rival, Joseph Kasavubu, was "interesting. He is intelligent, responsible, and honest, but terribly shy and suspicious, and he has little strength outside his tribal association."

Congo's "immediate outlook is poor," Bigart judged, but the country was rich in minerals and other resources and could succeed if well led. To this day, the wise, responsible, honest leadership the country required has never emerged.

Upon independence, Kasavubu became president and Lumumba prime minister, but Lumumba was assassinated the following January. Rival factions became proxies for the great powers in the first great battle of the African theater of the Cold War.[35]

That was Bigart's last report from Africa. He left a few days later, never to return. By July 12, he was back in New York.

TEN

REALITY CHECK IN VIETNAM

One morning in December 1961, a *TIME* magazine writer named Stanley Karnow was having coffee with a US Army officer at the Hotel Majestic in Saigon, South Vietnam. They were sitting on the terrace, which looks out over the Saigon River. Suddenly a US Navy aircraft carrier appeared around a bend. Strapped to its deck were forty-seven helicopters.

"Look at that carrier!" Karnow exclaimed.

The officer looked out at the imposing vessel and responded, "I don't see nothing."[1]

The reason he didn't "see nothing" was that officially there was nothing to see. Even as the administration of President John F. Kennedy was inexorably being sucked into South Vietnam's war against a communist-supported insurgency, the administration's position was that no such thing was happening. The official position was that a small number of US military advisers were in Saigon to help the government, but the United States was not participating and would not participate beyond that and would certainly not take part in any combat.

In Laos, next door to Vietnam, the United States was openly providing military backing to a royal government that was facing an uprising by Soviet-supported guerrillas. In Vietnam, however, the administration insisted that the US role was strictly limited.

By the time Karnow spotted those helicopters, as Kennedy was finishing his first year in the White House, it was becoming more and more difficult to sustain the official fiction. News reporters and independent observers in Saigon and Washington were becoming aware of an escalating US commitment to the government of President Ngo Dinh Diem and increasing US military involvement.

Karnow, who was based in Hong Kong, could see it as he traveled around the region. So could the *New York Times* correspondent in Hong Kong, Robert Trumbull, a longtime Asia hand. He sent a story from Saigon in March 1961 that said, "South Vietnam, regarded here as the key to Southeast Asian defense against Communist aggression, has become a testing ground for new United States Army guerrilla tactics designed for fighting in tropical jungles." A US Military Assistance Advisory Group (MAAG) in Saigon was commanded by a major general experienced in jungle warfare.[2]

That was only a preview. By the end of 1961, Trumbull reported from Saigon that "observers" were warning that "growing American participation in the anti-guerrilla campaign may draw massive intervention by Communist North Vietnam." He said the arrival of the troop-carrying helicopters Karnow had spotted was "only the beginning of direct American assistance for a tactical role." In addition to MAAG, "probably at least 1,500 more United States airmen and other military personnel are now participating more or less directly in the conflict."[3]

At the same time, it was becoming increasingly apparent that the Diem government was incompetent, corrupt, distant from the population, and thus ill-equipped to stave off an insurgency that wielded terror and propaganda with equal effectiveness. The United States backed him through Kennedy's first two years because at that time the administration could see no alternative. This was the tropical equivalent of Washington's predicament during the Greek Civil War.

Editors at the *Times* could see that the administration's official position on Vietnam could not be reconciled with what appeared to be happening on the ground. They wanted more coverage. The news services had reporters based in Saigon, but the *Times* as usual wanted its own person. Trumbull had his hands full with the Laos crisis and with trying to follow events in China. It was time to send a correspondent who would be based in Saigon, preferably one who knew something about the country and something about war. The obvious choice was Homer Bigart.

He agreed to go for six months, and by January 2, 1962, he was on his way. The assignment turned out to be the most unpleasant six months of his career, but he also produced some of his most important work. His reporting influenced virtually all the American correspondents who followed him over the next decade.

Sending Bigart to Vietnam was significant far beyond the *Times*'s newsroom. The *Times* was read each morning throughout official and political Washington. Reports in the *Times* carried extra weight because at the time no other major newspaper had a resident correspondent in Saigon. Television coverage was not yet a factor in the public's perception of the war because there was almost none at that early phase. No network had a correspondent or camera crew in Saigon, partly because there was no way to transmit any pictures; film had to be packed in cans and flown to Hong Kong to be sent back to the United States.

Malcolm Browne, whom the AP sent to Saigon while Bigart was there and became his friend, wrote,

In 1962 Homer was overweight, wore glasses, often dressed in business suits despite the heat, and stuttered more than usual when he was angry, which was most of the time. He had none of the egotistic flamboyance of some of the star correspondents of World War II and Korea, who sometimes succumbed to the temptation to see themselves as their own heroes. Throughout his career he avoided that snare; he never visited the Saigon tailor shops that outfitted American network correspondents with safari suits.

He hated Vietnam—the country as well as the war. What really galled him was that all the major participants in Vietnam, Americans as well as Vietnamese, were playing deceitful games that left no room for trust in anyone. . . . Toward the end of his tour he told me that he had come to think of the place as a snake pit, where nothing was as it seemed and no one told the truth.[4]

For the *Herald Tribune*, Bigart had reported from Vietnam in 1945 after the surrender of Japan, in 1950 after Korea, and in 1953, when he spent several weeks there looking at France's war against the indigenous pro-communist rebels seeking to throw off colonial rule.

That war was stalemated, his articles in 1953 reported; neither side was able to strike a knockout blow. (That was the year before the decisive French defeat at Dien Bien Phu.) People in the countryside lived in constant fear. The major cities appeared secure, but elsewhere even the main roads were closed at night as the rebels known as Viet Minh roamed freely. The rebels had been building political support for years, and their charismatic leader, Ho Chi Minh, "Uncle Ho," had become a folk hero.

As Bigart studied the conflict for those 1953 articles, he concluded that it had been a strategic mistake for the United States and Britain to help France restore its colonial rule over Indochina after the end of Japanese occupation. Ho had gone to Paris in 1946 to ask for a united Vietnam, independence within the French union, and creation of a national army. He would have welcomed American support but did not get it. When France rebuffed him, he took up arms.

Bigart recalled that he had met an American intelligence operative during his 1945 trip to Vietnam who was "utterly disgusted with the way we had given in to the British and the French on this and reinstated the French. Reinstated the French!" Bigart said he had hoped at the time that "some sort of deal could be made with Ho Chi Minh which might have avoided all the involvements, the terrible tragic involvement of the United States in Southeast Asia."[5]

Bigart was not an ideologue, anti-war activist, or "peacenik," as opponents of the war came to be called; he was still the correspondent who had referred to American troops in previous wars as "we." He was in Vietnam to report what was happening, for better or for worse, not to oppose the war as a matter of policy or principle. At the time, it never entered his mind that by 1969 US troop strength in Vietnam would be more than half a million or that more than fifty-eight thousand Americans would be killed in a decade of war. Committing ground troops was "incredibly stupid," he said later, but "after we started getting a lot of bodies in there, it was inevitable. It was inevitable that we would commit ground troops, but we never should have."

The main reason, he said, was that American troops and their equipment and training were incompatible with jungle warfare against elusive guerrillas who were familiar with the terrain and indistinguishable from civilians. "We have never been able to fight a guerrilla war. We can't do it, we're not trained to do it. We're too big and clumsy and awkward," he said. Even when the American troops knew where the Vietcong (VC) were, he said, "we would go into an area where they had been, slowly and with great din—clanking of tanks and all that sort of thing. Well, they could easily slip away."[6]

Bigart could justly claim to have been the first American correspondent to discern that the military track was the wrong track, especially when compounded by ineptitude and misguided policy on the civilian side of the campaign. All the upbeat statistics and "body counts" delivered by Robert S. McNamara, Kennedy's defense secretary, turned out to be as meaningless as Bigart had seen them to be.

Bigart's dismay at US military tactics, his skepticism about everything American officers and diplomats were saying about the conflict, and the contempt he quickly developed for the Saigon government had impact far beyond him and his six-month tour. The seeds of doubt he sowed among his young colleagues set a tone for press coverage throughout the war and stoked the anti-war sentiment at home that truncated the presidency of Lyndon B. Johnson.

By the time I arrived in Vietnam a decade after he was there, Bigart's fears had long since been realized. It was no longer a guerrilla war. Since the Tet Offensive in 1968, the Americans had mostly been fighting North Vietnamese regulars in set-piece battles. But victory, whatever that would have meant, was still not in sight. Not even the diplomats at the US Embassy or the officers at the US Military Assistance Command, Vietnam (MACV) talked of victory. Ho was dead, but his successors were undeterred, and no amount of bombing could persuade them to quit. President Richard Nixon had accepted reality and was rapidly dismantling the US military presence, the so-called Big Green Machine. None of my press corps colleagues and competitors referred to the American troops as "we."

As he began his six-month tour, Bigart quickly found himself in a situation that was bound to stir his outrage. Military strategy was just one item on his grievance list.

He was writing about a war with no beachheads, no front line, and no obvious territorial objectives; thus, there was no way other than the specious body counts to measure success or failure. Diplomats at the US Embassy and officers in the military units either lied to the press or really believed the fiction about limited involvement; either way, they did their best to prevent reporters from learning the truth. The South Vietnamese government was worse, corrupt as well as untruthful. It was nominally led by President Diem, a French-speaking mandarin who seemed to live in some parallel universe of unreality, but the real powers in the palace were Diem's arrogant brother, Ngo Dinh Nhu, and his wife, Tran Le Xuan, who was also known as Madame Nhu, the notorious "Dragon Lady." They took unfavorable press coverage as personal affronts, not as constructive criticism. And by Bigart's reckoning, his editors were part of the problem, overediting his copy, prohibiting use of the first person, and so committed to balanced coverage that they printed reports from Washington repeating the official line along with his articles revealing the truth, leaving readers to figure out for themselves what to believe.

"Homer had never played the role of cheerleader for the home team," Mal Browne wrote, "but however critical his reporting of such military blunders as the Anzio beachhead could be, there was never any doubt which side had his sympathies. In Vietnam, by contrast, Homer could never wholeheartedly identify himself with an American team that often looked arrogant and wrongheaded, and whose cause seemed questionable to him."[7]

"Confusion and Despair"

Bigart had been in Saigon only ten days when he said in a message to Foreign Editor Freedman, "I know you will understand if my copy sometimes reflects confusion and despair."[8]

The most immediate issue was the refusal of the Americans or the Vietnamese to let reporters ride with the troops on helicopters to combat areas. "I had not realized there was so much red tape and planning needed to leave Saigon," his note to Freedman said. Much of the Mekong Delta region was reachable by automobile and boat, but getting to the northern provinces or the Central Highlands without air transportation was very difficult.

He was especially annoyed when a photographer for *LIFE* got permission to travel on the helicopters "because of a direct order from [Secretary of State Dean] Rusk," while Bigart and other reporters were receiving "minimum cooperation" from US Embassy and military officials "who apparently feel gagged by state department directives." He asked that the *Times* join the Associated Press in an appeal to Washington.

The *Times* did so, through its Washington bureau, and appeared to get quick results. On February 2, Freedman messaged Bigart: "STATE DEPARTMENT HAS

CABLED EMBASSY URGING ALL FACILITIES FOR YOU STOP PLEASE ADVISE IF ANY FUR-
THER TROUBLE."[9]

But the issue remained unresolved. Bigart grew more and more furious as visiting opinion columnists and celebrity television correspondents got special treatment and preferred access. He finally exploded when Joe Alsop got this VIP welcome. Alsop was in favor with the embassy and MACV because after each visit
to the country, he reported that things were going swimmingly and that a handful
of reporters with leftist sympathies were giving a distorted picture.

On April 12, Bigart fired off an intemperate cable to Freedman: "ALSOP NYK
TRIBUNE GETS TO RIDE ON HELICOPTER MISSION AFTER TWO DAYS IN SAIGON SUPER-
CEDING [*sic*] CORRESPONDENTS WHO BEEN WAITING THEIR TURN FOR WEEKS STOP IF
NYKTIMES CANNOT SAFEGUARD ITS CORRESPONDENTS AGAINST THIS KIND OF FAVOR-
ITISM EYE WANT TO QUIT."[10]

He might have been even angrier if he had known that Freedman's February 2
message had been accurate, as far as it went: the State Department had indeed
instructed the US ambassador in Saigon, Frederick "Fritz" Nolting, to be more
helpful to American reporters and give them more access. But Nolting was in an
awkward position.

The ambassador had been distressed by some of what he read in Bigart's early
dispatches. Despite his difficulties in getting to combat zones, Bigart was moving
around where he could and within two weeks of his arrival was poking holes in
the official position. Evidently Bigart was not getting the message that this was
not America's war and that the South Vietnamese military was getting better.

On the fashionable Tu Do Street (the former Rue Catinat), once a favored
promenade of French officers and their Asian girlfriends, Bigart found that the
Americans had taken over, quite visibly. Rowdy bars were proliferating. Juke-
boxes were playing country music. Boys sold the *Times of Vietnam,* an English-
language newspaper that featured four pages of comic strips on Sunday. At the
same time, more Americans became targets of Vietcong attacks. A day before
Bigart wrote this article, a contractor at the airport had been killed in an ambush.[11]

Around the important city of My Tho, gateway to the Mekong Delta, Bigart
found that the guerrillas were gaining strength while the government's local chiefs
confined their troops to "static defense chores." Those tactics had "completely
frustrated American hopes for vigorous, aggressive action. So far, the politicians
have prevailed over the younger military leaders who would like to take the soldiers out of their useless, dangerously immobile mud forts and train them in aggressive patrolling by small units."[12] Static defensive positions left the guerrillas
free to roam the countryside, as had happened in Greece.

One of Bigart's articles bore the headline "Saigon Is Losing the Propaganda
War," despite the US aid program. He said American workers had told him, "Gov-

ernment representatives spend only a few hours in a village while clandestine Viet Cong agents live among the villagers and learn to exploit their local grievances. The Government representatives dress well and look well fed, whereas the Viet Cong agents go barefoot and dress like peasants," which many of them were.[13]

The next day, he reported that "United States planes have sprayed jungle growth along the Saigon-Saint Jacques road to remove foliage hiding Communist guerrillas." This was the first Americans at home had heard about the Agent Orange defoliation campaign.

Bigart managed to get to Quang Ngai Province, on South Vietnam's central coast, to see what happened when planes sprayed the insecticide DDT to kill mosquitoes that spread malaria. His dispatch began, "American DDT spray killed the cats that ate the rats that devoured the crops that were the main props against Communist agitation in the central lowlands. The result: the hungry, embittered rural population is tending to support the Communist insurgents." That was what the local people believed had happened to them, he reported, but the real reason for the proliferation of rats was not the death of all those cats but "the Government's failure to ensure adequate supplies of rat poison. Through some glaring lapse of judgment, pesticides were removed from the commodity import list in 1959. The price of rat poison doubled . . . rats two-thirds the size of cottontail rabbits and weighing up to four pounds began devouring rice, sugar cane, and vegetables in the coastal provinces."[14] That was hardly the upbeat message the US Embassy and MACV wanted to deliver.

In February, Bigart posted a long report for the Sunday paper. The first sentence said, "The United States is involved in a war in Vietnam." The article said that US warships were helping the "embryonic" South Vietnamese navy guard the long coastline, army helicopter crews had come under fire while ferrying Vietnamese troops and supplies to combat areas, and US Air Force pilots had flown with Vietnamese air crews on bombing runs. In short, Americans were doing everything in combat except pulling the trigger. About three thousand American troops and sailors were participating in these military actions, and two thousand more were in the country in support roles.[15]

In another article he wrote that the US military presence had reached the point where "billets are so scarce that the men sleep three in a room at the Hotel Majestic," but American officials would not acknowledge the presence of any number of troops that exceeded 685. That was the maximum military manpower strength permitted by the 1954 agreement at Geneva that ended the French war and divided the country into North and South Vietnam.[16]

A few weeks later, Bigart reported that Americans were advising, equipping, and going on patrols with an irregular army of twelve hundred men organized by a Catholic priest. "Legally, United States military aid cannot be given to an irregular force," his story said. "It would require an act of Congress," but the Americans were doing it anyway because the irregulars, known as Sea Swallows, were effective fighters.[17]

Nolting asked the State Department for guidance on dealing with the troublesome press corps—not just Bigart but also François Sully of *Newsweek* and the news agency reporters. "We are running into increasing difficulties here with US newsmen," he said. "They claim they are not being given sufficient opportunity to cover US participation in operations against VC, alleging embassy [is] responsible for 'blackout.'" In particular, the reporters were unhappy about being excluded from helicopter missions, he said, but that was not the embassy's doing. The order had come from US military headquarters for the Pacific, he said.

"I had thought we were making some progress with US correspondents here and am concerned at their present attitude." He asked for "Washington's urgent consideration and advice" about giving him the "authority to decide on local correspondents' requests to cover field operations in which US [is] participating."[18]

Secretary Rusk replied two weeks later. His long cable showed a remarkable misunderstanding of what reporters do and how they operate.

The State and Defense Departments and the US Information Agency had concluded, Rusk said, that "in absence of rigid censorship, US interests best be protected through policy of maximum feasible cooperation, guidance and appeal to good faith of correspondents. Recent press and magazine reports are convincing evidence that speculation stories by hostile reporters [are] often more damaging than facts they might report."

The issue was not the "good faith" of the correspondents, nor were those who reported bad news "hostile." The reporters' job was to find out as much as possible about what was happening in South Vietnam and why, not to support US policy or the war effort. If what they found indicated that US policy was effective and the conflict was going well, they would report that. If they found otherwise, they would report that too.

Rusk's cable revealed a peculiar understanding of "maximum feasible cooperation" with the press. It said Nolting and everyone who worked for him should adhere to certain "guidelines" to "avoid harmful press repercussions." These guidelines included the following:

> Reiterate "this is not a US war," and all military and civilian personnel should refrain from giving interviews suggesting otherwise. "Our participation is only in training, advisory and support phases."
> Keep in mind "it is not in our interest . . . to have stories indicating that Americans are leading and directing combat missions against the Viet Cong."

Emphasize to reporters that military operations make "every effort to avoid" harm to civilians. "Sensational press stories about children or civilians who become unfortunate victims of military operations are clearly inimical to national interest."

Discuss operations in "general terms," without specific numbers of troops or equipment.

Stress that success requires high-level cooperation between the American and South Vietnamese governments and that "frivolous, thoughtless criticism" of the Diem regime makes that cooperation difficult.

Do not take correspondents "on missions whose nature [is] such that undesirable dispatches would be highly probable."

In addition, Nolting and Gen. Paul Harkins, the US military commander, should talk to reporters frequently to seek "voluntary undertakings" that they would refrain from writing about "sensitive matters" and to "adopt self-policing machinery." They should explain that this would be a long war, and therefore reporters should not expect "decisive battles."[19]

Bigart and other reporters guffawed at those "guidelines," which were unrealistic and unenforceable, and prioritized image over fact, but the State Department had little choice because President Kennedy had dictated the message.

At a news conference on February 14, 1962, a reporter asked Kennedy if he and his administration had told the American people "as much as can be told" about the American role in Vietnam.

"We have increased our assistance to the government—its logistics," he replied. "We have not sent combat troops there, although the training missions that we have there have been instructed if they are fired upon to—they would, of course, fire back, to protect themselves. But we have not sent combat troops in the generally understood sense of the word." He said the purpose of everything the United States was doing was "to prevent a communist takeover of Vietnam," as had been its policy since 1954, "and we are attempting to make all the information available that we can consistent with our security needs in the area. So that I feel that we are being as frank as we can be."[20]

Nolting was the president's representative in Saigon. Rusk was Kennedy's chief foreign policy officer. They were not in a position to get out in front of the boss, no matter how unhappy the reporters were.

Besides, Nolting was hearing from people on his embassy staff who were sharply critical of Bigart and his press corps colleagues and who felt that negative press coverage was undermining their work.

A "Terrible, Terrible Press Corps"

One of them was James D. Rosenthal, a Vietnamese-speaking political officer, who deplored the "terrible, terrible press corps." The most important engagements of the war were not taking place in the Mekong Delta, he said, but "the correspondents would just get in their jeeps and go down there." One reason reporters spent so much time in the Delta, of course, was that they could indeed drive down there, while reporting from the Central Highlands or the coastal area north of Da Nang would have required the air transport that the Americans refused to provide.

Of Bigart in particular, Rosenthal said, "I didn't like him. I thought he was an opinionated, arrogant old cuss, who I'm sure had great credentials as a combat correspondent in Korea and World War II. But he was very perverse. Everything that was going badly he would report—it seemed to me anyway—and everything that was going well was just not reportable."[21]

Bigart was just as unhappy with Nolting and his team as they were with him. "This is a most frustrating place to work," he wrote to Betsy Wade on February 12. "The Americans and Vietnamese both seem to view reporters with deepest suspicion."

The previous day, he said, an American C-47 transport plane with eight crew members aboard had disappeared while dropping propaganda leaflets on Vietcong-controlled areas. "We don't know to this minute what happened to them. Apparently the plane had Vietnamese air force markings. Why then was it piloted by Americans? Apparently we are bashful about being involved in propaganda drops. I found out too that we are jamming Radio Hanoi. But this was kept secret because we always held jamming was immoral when the Russians did it. I'm afraid all this nonsense is too hypocritical for me."[22]

On two occasions when he did succeed in getting aboard a helicopter to accompany Americans on a mission, the results did not reflect the upbeat outlook the embassy and MACV were looking for.

In the first, he was aboard as US Army helicopters braved "Communist sniper fire" to deliver seven live pigs, several chickens, and other food to hungry Vietnamese troops at a besieged, remote outpost. But there was no point because the outpost, deep in a valley surrounded by high peaks, was to be abandoned soon anyway; it was too difficult to supply and probably indefensible.[23]

In the second, two days after his eruption about Alsop, he was on one of several American helicopters ferrying Vietnamese troops to a cluster of huts called Cai Ngai, deep in the Delta near the southern tip of the country. He watched as a Vietnamese battalion conducted "a successful raid" against the dug-in Vietcong. The VC were caught by surprise; nearly twenty were captured, and the rest fled.

"A communist armament factory, a food supply depot and a first aid station were captured and destroyed," Bigart wrote.

"But as usual the main enemy force got away" because "the government troops failed to exploit the Viet Cong state of shock. They bunched up and dawdled in drainage ditches and under the shade of coconut trees until an American adviser cried out in exasperation, 'Let's move this thing forward.'"[24]

By that time, Bigart had fallen into disfavor with Foreign Editor Freedman.

A rough patch in relations with New York began with the story he sent about Nolting's new press guidelines. It was a straightforward, factual account—except for the lede, in which he likened the new rules to the words of a popular song: "You've got to accentuate the positive, eliminate the negative."

Freedman "spiked" the story, literally impaling the paper on a copy spike after writing on it: "Unused. Treatment unsuitable." Then he told Bigart he had done so.[25]

Then on February 27 two planes of the South Vietnamese air force piloted by dissident officers dropped bombs on the presidential palace in an apparent attempt to kill Diem, and Bigart missed the story. The *Times* used an Associated Press dispatch because no file arrived from Bigart.

He later described this episode as "the most humiliating experience that ever happened to me." The bombs fell at about 7 a.m. Saigon time, he said, "and I slept through it." Once he woke up and caught on, because of the time difference, he still had time to get a story to New York for the next morning's paper. He ran to the palace and gathered what material he could, but by the time he had an article ready to send, the government had shut the central post office and the telegraph service. "All I could do was hand the copy to a hotel clerk and hope that he would get through." He did not, but the clerk did not tell Bigart, who received the next morning what he called "a nasty cable" from Freedman about his failure to file.

"Anyhow, I really felt awful," he said. "The worst occasion. The worst day of my career as a journalist."[26]

Then his follow-up story the next day began with the words "after yesterday's thrilling bombing of the Presidential Palace," according to Wade, who was a copy editor on the Foreign Desk.[27] That prompted a letter of reprimand from Freedman, the same editor who had chastised Bigart about a slant in his reporting on the Suez crisis six years earlier.

"I notice increasing signs of a polemical approach in your reporting," the foreign editor wrote. "Fun is fun, and objective reporting ought to be serious business. It ought to be unemotional. The reasons for this little sermon are specifically the story on lifting the ban on helicopter rides by correspondents (story spiked) and your Wednesday story on the palace attack (story being sterilized). I think you know us well enough to know that we do not want to limit correspondents in any way in legitimate reporting, no matter whom it helps or hurts. But there is a right way and a wrong way. Agreed?"[28]

Expelled

The Vietnamese government was even more unhappy with Bigart. On March 23, the Ministry of Interior ordered him out of the country.

By his account, he was summoned to the "Department of Information" and knew that such a summons always portended unpleasantness.

> Wondering where my copy had been found repellent, I stopped first at the shop of Dang Duc Khoi, who is a special press adviser to the Presidency. Khoi is a Buddhist, but he seems more attuned to reality than most Christians here. [Diem and the Nhus were Catholics.] Khoi assured me that my stories were jewels of objectivity. Suspecting perhaps that my intimations of deportation were based on wishful thinking, Khoi exhorted me to banish such thoughts. Besides, the director general would never dare to try to oust me. Here he was wrong.

This director general, who had "just returned from a symposium on the Free Press in India," told Bigart that the interior minister had signed an expulsion degree and he would have to leave the next day.[29] *Newsweek*'s Sully also was ordered to leave.

According to Wade, the article that precipitated Bigart's expulsion was a chatty, substance-free "Talk of Saigon" piece. It began with a brief account of "Laugh with the Girls," the first USO (United Service Organizations) show for the troops in Vietnam. The theaters downtown and at the airport were full, but his story noted that official attendance figures were not released so that "the International Control Commission, which is in charge of policing the [1954] cease-fire, cannot complain" that the number of troops exceeded the limit set at Geneva.

The last part of the article was about the activities of Madame Nhu, who was about to go abroad. Her schedule was not made public, but Bigart cited "some sources" who said she would return to fight for passage in the National Assembly of her "purification bill." That measure would outlaw "cockfights, fishfights (between Siamese fighting fish), prizefights, beauty contests and other 'vain' entertainment, including Western dances" such as the twist.

That article was never published, probably because it contained no urgent information and grew stale as it sat around for more than a week.[30] But the system by which reporters transmitted their articles enabled Vietnamese officials to read them as they were sent, so the government knew what it said.

As Bigart's reference in his conversation with Khoi to "wishful thinking" indicated, he would have been happy to comply with the expulsion order because he detested the place, but this was not about his personal feelings. The institutions of the free press and the *New York Times* were being challenged. He immediately notified the US Embassy and the editors in New York. Bigart told them the Vietnamese had accused him of "false and tendentious reporting."[31] He later told an interviewer that the Vietnamese never said specifically what upset them but ordered him out because "they didn't like my attitude."[32]

Freedman and Turner Catledge instructed the Washington bureau to take the matter up with the State Department and the Pentagon. The bureau's leaders doubted that they would receive a positive response, given the administration's antipathy to what Turner Catledge called "Mr. Bigart's aggressive reporting." Hearing promises that administration officials will assist "in any way possible," bureau chief James "Scotty" Reston scoffed, "Assist? At what? Packing his bags?" Nevertheless, the expulsion order was lifted two days later. The Vietnamese, Bigart reported to Freedman, "said 'twas all a mistake due to 'erroneous translation.'" Because of the translation error, the Vietnamese interpreted his article as suggesting some improper relationship between Madame Nhu and her brother-in-law, the president.[33]

The expulsion of Sully was also rescinded, although at the end of that year, he was ordered out again. (He returned later in the war and was killed in a helicopter crash near the Cambodian border in 1971.)

The move to expel the correspondents of two major American news organizations was newsworthy, but Bigart said he did not want to write about the episode because doing so would inflame the "irrational atmosphere" in Saigon. The expulsion orders, he said, were part of a "general campaign of press harassment" by Madame Nhu. He said the "irrational atmosphere" in Saigon "could only be worsened by any publication now of expulsion story while government groping for facesaving explanation."[34]

The State Department had intervened against Bigart's expulsion because there really was no alternative. It could not sit by while a government dependent on the United States for military and political support threw out correspondents such as Bigart and Sully. But the department was still unhappy with what he was writing and still failed to grasp the importance of substance over image.

On April 1, Lester Markel's Sunday Review section printed a long report by Bigart about the early stages of the Saigon government's "strategic hamlet" program. People who lived in remote areas where the Vietcong roamed at will were to be relocated into fortified communities that the government could protect. "The measure involves the resettlement—by force if necessary—of thousands of

Vietnamese rural families that live in areas susceptible to Communist domination," Bigart's report said.

The uprooted people were moved off their land into fortified communal villages. They would receive patches of land, a small amount of money, and government services that had not been available in their rural communities, which were burned down as they left. The Americans were providing the cash and assisting Vietnamese troops in the logistics of relocation, which was officially known as Operation Sunrise. They were assuming "moral responsibility," Bigart wrote, for "a drastic program that was certain to be bitterly resented by the peasantry, whose allegiance must be won."

This turned out to be, as Frances FitzGerald wrote in *Fire in the Lake*, her landmark book about the war, "by far the most ambitious of the Diemist land programs and by far the most destructive." The rural Vietnamese were spiritually bound to their land and to their ancestors buried there, and they had no reason to trust the government officials who were herding them away. Thus, the forced relocations alienated many of the people the government was trying to win over.[35]

Bigart's piece also noted that the Americans sometimes gave the impression that they were in charge as the moves were made and that Vietcong propaganda was already stirring up resentment about that, telling the peasants that "the Americans have simply replaced the French as rulers of Vietnam."

The article prompted Averell Harriman, then assistant secretary of state for Far Eastern affairs, to fire off a warning message to Ambassador Nolting. The State Department, he said, was "increasingly concerned over constant implications in [the] press generally of U.S. participation and direction" in the conflict rather than simply training and equipping the Vietnamese. "Part of this press picture is probably developed by observing support and advisory activities in which American presence is conspicuous."

Harriman cited the fifth paragraph of Bigart's Sunday article: "Last Wednesday, a large group of American colonels from the military advisory mission and civilian observers from the United States operations mission inspected the stockade where the first group of families uprooted by Operation Sunrise were sitting dejectedly under temporary shelters in a rubber plantation. Nobody looked happy."

"Why do large groups of Americans inspect anything?" Harriman asked Nolting. It was that sort of thing that led Bigart to report that Americans were taking on responsibility for an unpopular program that the Vietcong could exploit.

"It cannot be overstressed," Harriman said, "that the conduct and utterances public and private of all U.S. personnel must reflect the basic policy of this government." That is, Washington was in "full support" of Diem's war but "we do not assume responsibility" for it.[36]

To Harriman and other American officials, including McNamara, the problem was not that the policy was misguided and ineffective but that the public's perception was the United States was responsible for it. It was absurd: the people of rural Vietnam were not getting their information from the *New York Times*; they could see what was happening all around them. What bothered the Kennedy administration was that the people of the United States might discern the truth.

Barbecue Pits and Tennis Courts

It is not hard to imagine Harriman's reaction to a story Bigart wrote in June that began, "Americans are digging in for a long war in Vietnam." He based that conclusion not on any combat action but on what he could see all around Saigon, unconcealed: Americans were building a bowling alley, a swimming pool, a picnic park with barbecue pits, a high school, tennis courts, and a gymnasium with basketball, volleyball, and handball courts. They were even constructing a radio station to entertain the troops—the one later made famous in the Robin Williams movie *Good Morning, Vietnam.*

That contradiction between fact and official fiction plagued Bigart throughout his tour in Vietnam because American officials would not level with him; sometimes they embarrassed themselves as they tried to manage the information. In April, for example, Bigart discovered that the army had refused to award a Purple Heart medal to a soldier wounded by Vietcong fire during a helicopter raid because "Washington does not recognize this as a combat zone for Americans."[37] The day after his article appeared and military men and veterans' groups complained, President Kennedy—who had received that medal himself after he was wounded in the South Pacific during World War II—reversed the policy.

By that time, the embassy had hired a new public affairs officer, John Mecklin, who had reported from Indochina for *TIME* during the French period. He was unable to turn Bigart and the other reporters around, he acknowledged later, because the facts were not on the embassy's side, and the policy was flawed.

"The root of the problem was that much of what the newsmen took to be lies was exactly what the Mission genuinely believed, and was reporting to Washington," he found. "The government figures on Viet Cong casualties—which the Mission accepted—became a joke around Saigon."

The deeper problem, he found, "was the fact that the U.S. had bet all its chips on Diem. There was no alternate, fall-back policy if Diem failed us. . . . It had to work, like a Catholic marriage or a parachute." Therefore, the Diem government could not be perceived or depicted as failing.[38]

Bigart dubbed that policy "Sink or Swim with Ngo Dinh Diem."

A month after his original reprimand of Bigart, Freedman sent a note to Catledge, who was about to embark on a round-the-world tour of *Times* bureaus. He urged Catledge to give Bigart a medal because "his copy has been good as always, although we have had to slap him down once or twice on editorialization. It might be worthwhile to sermonize briefly on this point."[39]

Catledge did deliver a critical message but not from himself. "He confided that John D. Rockefeller 3d, who was through here a couple of months ago, had told him in New York I was too critical of the regime," Bigart wrote to his sister, "and that if only I would start writing nice things all the other correspondents would follow suit. He [Catledge] says he backed me, telling Rockefeller the paper had confidence in my judgment."[40] Catledge knew perfectly well that Bigart was not interested in persuading other reporters to write "nice things" about the Diem regime.

The next night Catledge organized a party for the foreign press corps in Saigon, but Bigart missed it because he was exhausted after a day of flirting with death in a battle in the Plain of Reeds. He was in a helicopter watching the action as American gunners opened fire on green-clad Vietcong whom they had caught out in the open, which they rarely were. "They were beautifully disciplined," he told Gladys. "They returned fire and we caught two .30 calibre bullets in the nose of the helicopter." One of those rounds hit the commander of the chopper in the arm, and two crew members were punctured by flying shards of glass and aluminum. "I could barely stay awake writing the story," he said.[41]

In an account of the expulsion order that he wrote for *Times Talk*, Bigart said that Saigon was "a nice place to spend a few days in," with air-conditioned hotels and good restaurants. "But to work here is particularly depressing" because when reporters deviated from the official line, the officials they needed to talk to shunned them. "I am sick of it," he wrote. "Each morning I take a pen and blot off another day on the calendar. At this writing I have 83 more days to go."[42]

Those eighty-three days were just as unpleasant as the time up to then. He was fifty-four years old, unmarried, and childless. In Saigon he had little social life. He was out of shape physically: he ate, drank, and smoked too much, and he never exercised. Then he got sick, afflicted by some stomach bug. He did not tell Freedman, who had to learn about it from Betsy Wade. She wrote a memo to Freedman reporting what Bigart had told her: he felt "quite ill" and "can hardly drag himself around."

Freedman dispatched Jacques Nevard, another correspondent in the region, to Saigon to cover for Bigart. Nevard found him "weak from two weeks of diarrhea." By the time he recovered, with the aid of paregoric supplied by Robert Shaplen of the *New Yorker*, it was well into April.[43]

No wonder he was out of sorts when the Foreign Desk told him in an urgent message, or "rocket," that one of his stories had been bumped to an inside page as a "shirttail," a follow-up to a front-page story by Neil Sheehan of United Press International (UPI).

Sheehan, who later gained fame as a reporter for the *Times* by obtaining the Pentagon Papers, was then a neophyte half Bigart's age. He had been in Vietnam only two weeks when he got a tip from a US Army major about a supposed big victory by the South Vietnamese army's Seventh Division. His source told him that three hundred Vietcong had been killed in a battle in the Delta and that the Saigon government troops had been transported in American helicopters. Sheehan filed an urgent dispatch to UPI and went to bed at 4 a.m.

What followed has been recounted many times by Bigart's friends and colleagues. This is Harrison Salisbury's version.

Four hours after Sheehan went to sleep, Bigart telephoned him. It was 8 a.m. in Saigon and 8 p.m. the previous night in New York, where the *Times*'s editors were making the final decisions about displaying the articles for the next day's paper and had informed Bigart about their plan to use Sheehan's story on the front page.

"Bigart's stutter always became worse when he was angry," Salisbury recalled. "This is Bigart. Sh-hee-han, y-you wiped me off the f-f-front page. Y-y-you shirt-tailed me, you s-s-son of a bitch. I-I-I h-h-have this rocket from New York. It says U-P-I has 200 Vietcong killed in the D-D-Delta by waves of attacking Vietnamese troops. Sheehan, there better be two hundred bodies there because you and I are going down to have a look. I have a car and I'll pick you up in five minutes."

There had indeed been a substantial battle, they found, but the number of VC killed was twelve, not three hundred, the number Sheehan had actually reported. Sheehan, the most junior correspondent in Saigon, knew he would have to file a new story with the revised account and feared he would be fired.

"D-d-don't worry about it, kid," Bigart told him on the road back to Saigon. "They're not going to fire you. I've done it many times myself. But—just don't do it again."

Bigart's article the next day about the operation noted, "The first reports of 300 guerrillas, or Vietcong, dead were drastically reduced this morning." One government soldier was killed in an attack by "a water buffalo apparently crazed by the whirring of the helicopters."[44]

This, Salisbury observed, was "Sheehan's first lesson in the Bigart school of journalism." He got another when he and Bigart went to the field four days in a row without finding any action.

"Every time," Salisbury wrote, "Bigart extensively questioned officers and enlisted men, endless detailed questions. After the fourth of these expeditions, Sheehan groused, 'Jesus—all that time and there's no story.'

"'Really?' Bigart replied. 'There's no story?'

"'Well, what story is there?' Sheehan wanted to know.

"'It doesn't work, kid. It doesn't work anymore.'"[45]

Sheehan understood. US-guided operations against the Vietcong were not useful in suppressing the insurgency.

Right to the end of his six-month tour, Bigart kept writing about the growing, and increasingly visible, US involvement in the escalating conflict.

Just before he left, he wrote about an incident in which the wives of Nolting, Harkins, and three other senior officials of the US mission had a close call while riding in a helicopter convoy toward Bien Hoa, about twenty miles northeast of Saigon. They planned to inspect housing and schools built for Vietnamese soldiers, but low-lying clouds prevented them from landing. Alert to the sound of the rotors, guerrillas in the forest opened fire, missing the wives but hitting a seven-year-old boy in another chopper. That night two of the wives took flowers to the boy in a hospital, only to find that he had died. That incident was not exactly the low profile for the US team that the State Department had ordered.

Bigart had no desire to extend his tour and left Vietnam as scheduled at the end of June 1962. As he was leaving, his press corps colleagues bade him farewell with seven verses of doggerel, including this:

> Helpful Homer, says Fritz Nolting,
> Life will not now be the same.
> Everything has been revolting
> Since the day that Homer came.[46]

If Nolting and the other Americans thought Bigart's departure would make their lives easier, they were wrong. For one thing, Sheehan had absorbed his lessons well, and by that time he was writing dispatches for UPI and its subscribers worldwide about the sputtering campaign against the Vietcong and about US policy mistakes. "Despite a massive dose of further military aid and an influx of some six thousand American military advisers since December of 1961," he wrote in May 1962, "the situation has still not improved and may even have deteriorated in certain aspects."[47]

Then the *Times*'s editors selected David Halberstam to succeed Bigart as the paper's correspondent in Saigon. He arrived in time to attend the farewell party for *Newsweek*'s Sully, who had been ordered out for the second time. Halberstam's first sentence in his book about the experience says, "I arrived in Saigon at a time of singularly bad feeling toward foreign correspondents."[48]

Halberstam turned out to be even more enraged at the US mission's policies and strategy than Bigart had been, and more confrontational. In January 1963, he, Sheehan, and Mal Browne of the AP reported that a major battle in the Delta village of Ap Bac had resulted in a resounding victory for the outnumbered Vietcong, with heavy losses of aircraft and vehicles on the government side, partly because the South Vietnamese commander refused to do what the Americans told him to do. Three Americans and a hundred South Vietnamese soldiers died, and five American helicopters were shot down. After Ap Bac, there was no more room for happy talk by Americans about how well the South Vietnamese military was performing.

Before long, other prominent newspapers began to send resident correspondents to Saigon, including the *Los Angeles Times*, the *Baltimore Sun*, the *Washington Post*, and the *Christian Science Monitor*. None of those organizations was interested in reporting only what the embassy and MACV wanted reported. *TIME* magazine, however, hewed to the official line. Its Saigon correspondent, Charles Mohr, who had been reporting the truth only to be overruled in New York, quit in frustration and joined the *Times*, where he became one of the most aggressive and respected correspondents in Vietnam.

Freedman had asked Bigart before he left Vietnam to write a comprehensive assessment of the military, political, and diplomatic situation there. Bigart said he would do so after he returned to New York and took a little time off. On July 25, he unloaded, under a two-column headline on the front page: "Vietnam Victory Remote / Despite U.S. Aid to Diem."

The military campaign was making some progress, he reported, as the South Vietnamese forces grew and learned. "There would seem to be valid reason for optimism" unless the rebels received substantial aid from outside, as the North Koreans had from China. Nevertheless, he wrote, "the issue remains in doubt because the Vietnamese President seems incapable of winning the loyalty of his people."

The South Vietnamese military had overwhelming advantages in manpower, weaponry, and mobility. "Yet visions of ultimate victory are obscured by a secretive, suspicious, dictatorial regime. American officers are frustrated and irritated by the constant, whimsical meddling of the president and his brother, Ngo Dinh Nhu, in the military chain of command."

Two American officers had been killed when the Vietcong wiped out a convoy on the heavily traveled road to the garrison town of Ben Tre, his report said. "This incident was a bitter revelation" for the Americans because the VC had set up the ambush in broad daylight in full view of peasants in nearby fields. "Yet no one informed the garrison at Bentre. Could this have happened if peasants felt any real identification with the regime?"

The Story That Would Not End

After his 1962 reporting tour in Vietnam, Bigart returned there only once, briefly. In 1968 he traveled with retired US Air Force general Curtis LeMay, then running for vice president of the United States on the third-party ticket of George C. Wallace.

LeMay was a colorful character, to put it mildly. He was notoriously hawkish on the Vietnam War and war in general. Bigart had known him in London during World War II, so it was reasonable for the *Times*'s editors to assume that his campaign whistle-stop in Saigon would produce interesting stories. It did not. LeMay kept a low profile during his time in Saigon and said little to his traveling press contingent. But the trip was illustrative of a fact of journalistic life in the United States in the 1960s and the first half of the 1970s: the Vietnam issue was everywhere—in politics, in academia, within the armed forces, on the streets. Bigart, with his experience, wrote about many of these developments.

His assignments often were single-day events, such as anti-war demonstrations, which any competent reporter could have handled. Others, such as allegations of war crimes by American troops, relied more on his expertise. In 1970, for example, he went to Fort Bragg, North Carolina, to write about the first officers graduating from a new training program designed to give them some knowledge of Vietnamese life and culture before they went there. "Like the fictional Ugly American in the 1958 best-seller," his story said, "the men will be sent to Southeast Asia to do good works: advising the Vietnamese on health and sanitary facilities and improving such ventures as rice production, currency control, psychological operations and medical aid." Unlike many civilian aid workers, he noted, military personnel had received little training in such matters; they were trained to fight, not to assist. These new military advisers would receive at least rudimentary instruction about "the demography, geography, history, culture, religions and philosophies of the Vietnamese."[49] The obvious implication was that such training should have commenced several years earlier.

Then in late 1971 he went to Fort Benning, Georgia, to chronicle the sensational court-martial of 1st Lt. William L. Calley Jr. The diminutive officer was accused of premeditated murder in the deaths of 102 Vietnamese civilians in what was known as the My Lai Massacre of 1968, but in a larger sense the US Army itself was on trial, as it well knew. The My Lai scandal was a major impetus for creating the training program Bigart had observed at Fort Bragg. Bigart, by then a veteran of covering major trials and deeply experienced in war, was a logical choice for the Calley assignment.

As one historical narrative put it,

> The My Lai massacre was one of the most horrific incidents of violence committed against unarmed civilians during the Vietnam War. A company of American soldiers brutally killed most of the people—women, children and old men—in the village of My Lai on March 16, 1968. More than 500 people were slaughtered in the My Lai massacre, including young girls and women who were raped and mutilated before being killed. U.S. Army officers covered up the carnage for a year before it was reported

in the American press, sparking a firestorm of international outrage. The brutality of the My Lai killings and the official cover-up fueled anti-war sentiment and further divided the United States over the Vietnam War.[50]

The court-martial raised disturbing questions in Congress, in the press, and in the army itself. Calley was a low-ranking officer. If he was guilty, what about the officers above him in the chain of command? What were the troops being taught before they were sent through the jungles and rice paddies to fight in villages where civilians were often indistinguishable from Vietcong cadres? What was justice in such a case?

"This boy is a product of the system," his lawyer said. "He was taken out of his own home, given automatic weapons, taught to kill. They ordered him to kill. And then the same Government tries him for killing, and selects the judge, the court and the prosecutor."[51]

The trial lasted more than four months, during which the *Times* gave front-page play to many of Bigart's reports. In one of the most dramatic, Calley's lawyers tried to shift the blame to his immediate superior, Capt. Ernest Medina. A former squad leader among Calley's troops, Charles A. West—whom Bigart described as "a tall, lanky black from Chicago"—testified that Medina exhorted the men to "leave nothing, walking, crawling, or growing" in the village. Another witness, Michael A. Bernhardt, told the court that Medina "warned him not to disclose to his Congressman or anyone else the facts of the Mylai incident."[52]

The court heard ghastly testimony from soldiers whom Calley had commanded at My Lai. One witness told the court that Calley ordered him and another soldier to gun down more than thirty unarmed people who had been rounded up and were squatting in a rice paddy, unresisting. "They were pretty well messed up," the witness said. "Lots of heads were shot off and pieces of heads. Pieces of flesh flew off the sides and arms. They was all messed up." When only a few children were still alive, and the soldiers pleaded that they could not shoot any more defenseless people, Calley shot the rest himself, the witness said.[53]

On March 29, 1971, the court-martial convicted Calley of premeditated murder in the deaths of twenty-two civilians. At the age of twenty-seven, he faced a possible death sentence; if the court spared his life, the mandatory alternative was life in prison. The following day the court gave Calley and his lawyer the opportunity to state the case for sparing his life.

Bigart's account of that session was a textbook example of detailed, dispassionate, insightful reporting. It began,

Gasping for breath, First Lieut. William L. Calley Jr. made a final plea for understanding today as he faced the military jury that convicted him yesterday of the premeditated murder of at least 22 South Vietnamese civilians at Mylai. The 5-foot 3-inch platoon leader, who has described himself in an interview as "just a finger, a fragment, of a Frankenstein monster," said he never "wantonly" killed anyone. Shaken with sobs, he said the Army never told him that his enemies were human.

The army never described the Vietnamese as anything but communists, Calley said. They had no race, sex, or age. As a result of this dehumanization of people, he said, he did what he thought he had to do: "Apparently I valued my troops' lives more than that of the enemy."

Noting that Calley was "too short to use the lectern," Bigart wrote that he stood erect during his plea, which lasted two minutes and twelve seconds. "He wheezed noisily through the microphone and had to pause a number of times."

At the end, Bigart reported, "in a choked voice, he made his last statement: 'Yesterday you stripped me of all my honor. Please, by your actions that you take here today, don't strip future soldiers of their honor, I beg of you.'"

To which the prosecutor, Capt. Aubrey M. Daniel III, said to the members of the court, "You did not strip him of his honor. What he did stripped him of his honor. It is not an honor—it has never been an honor—to kill unarmed men, women and children."[54]

The court sentenced Calley to life in prison, and he was locked up in the stockade while he appealed the conviction. Ultimately his appeals prevailed when federal courts ruled that his conviction was tainted by unfavorable publicity, and he became a free man in September 1974. He married and became manager of a jewelry store in Georgia.[55]

A few months after the Calley trial, Bigart was back in Georgia, at Fort McPherson, for the court-martial of Captain Medina, the only other officer prosecuted in the My Lai case. He was acquitted on all counts.

ELEVEN

THE GREAT STRIKE AND A NEW ALICE

L abor unrest was a fact of life in the New York newspaper business. Each of the general circulation daily papers, including the *Times* and the *Herald Tribune*, was fully unionized, and the collective strength of those unions was bolstered by the way the papers were printed and delivered. It was a complicated industrial operation.

Editors sent articles deemed ready for publication to the composing room, a large, noisy chamber on a different floor of the building, where the text was converted into lines of cast lead on giant machines called Linotypes. Then the lines of lead were assembled into page-size frames along with photos engraved on metal; the frames were then pressed onto mats that would form impressions on plates to be mounted on the printing presses. (Newsroom editors making a final check of the frames before they were pressed were prohibited by union rules from touching them or going around to the printers' side of the metal tables on which they were assembled; the editors had to learn to read the lead type upside down.) Once printed and assembled, the papers were loaded onto delivery trucks for distribution around the metropolitan area.

Each of the ten trades and crafts involved in that process had its own union. Reporters, photographers, copyboys, and some editors were represented by the Newspaper Guild of New York. The Linotype operators and composing room printers were members of New York Local Six of the International Typographical Union, known as "Big Six." Other unions represented the press operators, the photoengravers, the mailroom operators who assembled the papers, and the deliverers—17,761 workers at nine papers.[1] The unions sometimes cooperated in the mutual interest of their members, but they were also rivals, often led by ambitious men with strong personalities. At the top of that roster was Bertram A. Powers, the president of Big Six. He was an ambitious, handsome man who walked with a pronounced limp because of multiple fractures he had suffered in a fall off a truck.

Among members of the blue-collar unions, as Gay Talese wrote in his book about the *Times*, "their loyalty was not to their newspaper but to their union." Their jobs were the same no matter what the content or which newspaper they worked for. A Linotype machine worked the same way at the tabloid *Mirror* as it did at the *Times*. There was also an element of class warfare as the unions confronted management. The publishers and senior executives were rich people who attended tony schools and had second homes on Martha's Vineyard or in the Hamptons; the printers and their craft union colleagues were blue-collar guys who lived in working-class neighborhoods of Queens or the Bronx. They cared more about the price of groceries and the quality of the local public school than they did about the European Common Market or any threat from communist China.[2]

Each of the unions went out on strike from time to time. The walkouts were usually brief, ending after the union had made its point. The photoengravers walked out for eleven days in 1953, the delivery drivers for seventeen days in 1958.[3] In October 1962, the Newspaper Guild struck the *Daily News* over administrative issues such as the union's request for a union dues deduction from paychecks and management's efforts to exempt four hundred jobs from union jurisdiction. The strike ended after a week, when Labor Secretary Willard Wirtz intervened, on orders from President Kennedy.[4] That outcome did not resolve any of the major issues facing all the papers and unions, issues that surfaced simultaneously in the fall of 1962.

The workers wanted more money and shorter hours, of course, but they also wanted job security. Newspapers were beginning to automate the production process—the nonunion *Los Angeles Times* was almost entirely automated—and the craft union workers knew their jobs were in peril. The publishers naturally wanted to pay as little as possible, but they also wanted the right to streamline production through automation. Their first goal was to eliminate "bogus type," the rule by which even material from outside sources that came in ready for printing, such as advertisements or the stock market tables, had to be reset into type by the printers anyway. The printers wanted to maintain the bogus type system and fend off an innovation known as teletypesetting, in which low-wage, nonunion typists converted typed articles into perforated tape that was then fed into the Linotype machines, eliminating the need for a human Linotype operator.[5] The International Typographical Union knew automation was inevitable—it had already established a training center in Colorado where its members could learn to use whatever new equipment was introduced—but it wanted a share of the cost savings the publishers would reap from increased productivity.[6]

The unions themselves were divided over another issue—the date on which their contracts would expire. The Guild's contract traditionally expired on October 31, while the others expired on December 7. That gave the Guild the lead in labor negotiations as its settlement became the basis on which the publishers negotiated with the other unions. The contract the Guild accepted then became a template for the others. But the Guild had less leverage than the craft unions because newspaper management could produce papers without the Guild, using copy generated by news syndicates and wire services, but could not produce papers without the printers or press operators. Bert Powers did not want the printers' leverage diluted by the Guild; instead, he wanted all the unions' contracts to expire on the same October 31 date because November 1 marked the beginning of the Christmas advertising season. Powers understood that Christmas advertising was crucial to the newspapers' bottom lines and that publishers might be more forthcoming on October 31, when Christmas season ads were just coming in, than on December 7, when most of that advertising had been booked and a strike would be less painful.

In October 1962, the Guild, after its strike at the *News*, had accepted a new contract increasing pay by eight dollars per week, but Powers was unwilling to settle for that. He wanted a package of pay and benefits worth thirty-eight dollars, which was beyond the limits for most of the publishers because, other than the *Times* and the *News*, their papers were already unprofitable. They were subsidized by the chains that owned them, such as Hearst, or by the personal wealth of their publishers.[7]

The unions formed a solidarity pact: if one struck, the others would all honor the picket line. The publishers did the same, agreeing that if one paper were shut down by a strike, the others would cease publishing in solidarity. The irresistible force was about to hit the immovable object.

Bert Powers of Big Six was a high school dropout. The chief labor negotiator for the publishers was Amory Bradford, a patrician graduate of Yale and Yale Law School, who failed to hide his disdain for people who rode the subway to work.

Powers and Bradford had worked opposite each other previously and gotten along as best they could, but this time, according to Powers, Bradford "seemed outraged that we'd actually close down the New York Times." In the negotiations, Powers said, Bradford "began to lose his temper and I'd help him do it. I was definitely baiting him."[8]

Instead of accepting what he regarded as the meager package negotiated by the Guild in its strike at the *News*, Powers asked the members of Big Six to authorize their own strike when their contract expired in December. They did so by a vote of 2,003 to 47.[9]

The publishers waited until the evening of December 7, a few hours before the printers' contract would expire, to make a counteroffer to Powers's demand for a thirty-eight-dollar-per-week package. They offered $9.20 a week in wages and benefits. Powers, who believed that an extended strike was necessary and was in no mood to yield, still insisted on thirty-eight dollars. The gap was too wide to be bridged by incremental last-minute tweaks.

Shortly after midnight on December 8, 1963, the printers at the *Times* turned off their Linotype machines and walked out. The great strike that began at that moment shut down New York's newspapers for 114 days. Officially, Bix Six called the strike only at the *Times*, the *Daily News*, the *Journal-American*, and the *World-Telegram and Sun*. Powers did not call out his members at the other papers because they were financially weaker; he did not want them to die and take their jobs down with them. Because of the publishers' solidarity agreement, however, the *Post*, *Daily Mirror*, and *Herald Tribune* shut down anyway. The *Long Island Press* and the *Long Island Star Journal*, which did not distribute their papers in any borough other than Queens, continued to publish, but the *Press* stopped distributing inside the city limits. The *Wall Street Journal* and specialty papers such as *Women's Wear Daily* continued to publish, but they could not fill the void for most readers.

Life in New York was transformed overnight. The strike eliminated 5.7 million papers that would have appeared each weekday and 7.2 million on Sunday.[10] Subway commuters had nothing to read. Major advertisers such as department stores and automobile dealers had nowhere to advertise. Sports events came and went without news coverage. Broadway shows opened without reviews. Civil rights demonstrations fizzled because potential participants did not know about them. City officials held back important announcements and decisions on public policy because they had no effective way to make residents aware of them. By one account, "three hundred and fifty blind, crippled and elderly newsdealers were forced out of business; 5,000 hotel and restaurant workers were discharged; welfare agencies reported that, without the ads they placed in newspapers, offers to take in orphaned and needy children dropped from roughly 100 per month to zero; charity balls were canceled. Without printed obituaries, attendance at wakes and funerals declined, and flower shops suffered."[11]

News, like nature, abhors a vacuum, so in that pre-internet era, news producers and consumers scrambled to improvise. Enterprising news dealers began trucking papers into Manhattan from the New Jersey suburbs and even Philadelphia. People with friends in California got them to mail copies of the *Times*'s West Coast edition, which was not shut down. Circulation of the *Brooklyn Eagle* sextupled. Television and radio stations, including the *Times*-owned WQXR, increased their news coverage, hiring some of the striking newspaper reporters and editors to provide the content. (On WCBS television, the celebrated newscaster Harry Reasoner read the comics for children.) A group of literary editors created the *New York Review of Books* with the support of major book publishers who normally counted on the *Times* and *Herald Tribune* for reviews. Among the writers in its first issue were Norman Mailer, Gore Vidal, Mary McCarthy, William Styron, and Robert Penn Warren. Two credit card entrepreneurs raised enough money to create a whole new paper, the *New York Standard*, which at the peak of its brief life reached a circulation of 400,000. It was printed at the *Elizabeth (NJ) Daily Journal*. Ethnic papers such as the *Jewish Daily Forward* also continued to appear. Their readership was obviously limited by their foreign languages, but the Italian-language *Il Progresso* put out a daily sixteen-page English version, the *New York Daily Report*. Even the Harvard *Crimson* published a special New York edition.

Some community weeklies around the city switched to daily publication. Charles G. Hagedorn, the publisher of *Town & Village*—a community paper serving Manhattan's Stuyvesant Town and the Lower East Side—converted to a six-day-a-week schedule, using nonunion print shops. To fill its pages, he hired seven displaced reporters and some newsroom support staffers from the *Times*, including me.

In any crisis, people do what they have to do, but Hagedorn's was the definition of a fly-by-night operation. As a little paper with large ambition, it had access through its expanded staff to plenty of news about the city, but where was it going to get news from Washington and overseas? No problem. Twice a day, I, or some-one else of my lowly rank, was dispatched to the office of the *Jewish Daily For-ward* to collect the carbon copies of articles that paper had received from United Press International, the worldwide news agency. We never asked if Hagedorn was paying the *Forward* for this material or if either paper was paying UPI.

My last assignment at the end of each day was to get off the subway on my way home and go to the newsroom of the *Daily Racing Form*, the bible of the horse-racing business. I was to find out that day's "handle," or total amount bet, at a particular track and phone it in. It was essential to print that figure because it was the basis for payoffs in New York's thriving, if illegal, numbers racket.

Many of the workers who had been out on the streets survived the first two months of the shutdown with support from their unions' strike funds. After six weeks, the printers' fund was running low on money because of a simultaneous strike in Cleveland, but on February 6, International Typographical Union members nationwide voted to allow the union to deduct 3 percent from their wages at every paper to support their striking comrades. At about the same time, the state of New York began paying unemployment benefits to the strikers—not just to the printers but to all who were not getting paid. In effect, the state subsidized the strike. Between their union benefits and their unemployment checks, the printers were taking home almost as much money as when they were working. At the *Times*, news staff members who continued to work—in the Washington and over-seas bureaus and at the West Coast edition—were less fortunate. In early January, the *Times*'s publisher, Orvil Dryfoos, issued what he called "the most difficult memo to the staff that I have ever had to write": those still working would have their salaries reduced by 20 to 50 percent.[12]

Meanwhile, a strike by longshoremen paralyzed the Port of New York. The papers could not have obtained enough shipments of newsprint to resume full publication anyway, so the stalemate continued through the winter.

The *New York Post* Breaks Away

The first break came at the end of February, when Dorothy Schiff, the colorful, liberal publisher of the *Post*, resigned from the Publishers Association and called her workers back. Her paper resumed publication on March 4. A few days later Mayor Robert F. Wagner Jr.'s intermediary, the celebrated labor lawyer Theodore W. Kheel, finally cajoled and bullied the two sides into sullen agreement. Powers, who had infuriated the publishers with what they regarded as his ego trip, got much of what he wanted: a uniform contract expiration date, a thirty-five-hour work week, and a pay raise of $12.63 a week, with more for the night shift. The publishers, however, won a major breakthrough—the right to use automated type to print the stock tables. The door to automation swung open. The agreement said that workers would share in the savings, but the amount of that benefit was not specified.

It took three more weeks for other unions to set aside their own squabbles and agree to the deal. The papers were back on the streets on April 1, 1963.[13]

When the strike began, Homer Bigart was about to travel to Pennsylvania to write about a coal mine disaster. That assignment was scrubbed by the shutdown. Through Alice Weel, whom he knew from the Army-McCarthy hearings, he worked for a time writing news for CBS and its local affiliate, although, oddly, a news release from the network proudly listing well-known newspaper people who had signed on for the duration did not mention him.[14] Then he spent a good part of the 114 days in Nashville, writing an article for the *Saturday Evening Post* about another trial of Jimmy Hoffa, the notoriously corrupt and thuggish boss of the International Brotherhood of Teamsters. Bigart's article, titled "Will the Law Ever Get Hoffa?," appeared in the magazine's edition of March 30, 1963.

Hoffa had beaten several criminal cases filed against him by the US Justice Department, which was run by one enemy he could not bully into submission, Attorney General Robert F. Kennedy. This time Hoffa was accused of sharing a million-dollar payoff from a trucking company, the price of labor peace.

During the trial, Bigart noted, Hoffa maintained his practice of rigorous exercise, including a four-to-six-mile hike through Nashville before court each morning. Never one to watch from the sidelines or the rear command post, Bigart accompanied him on some of those walks. One morning, Hoffa stopped to watch and listen as the driver of a big rig shifted gears on an upslope. "Just like music," Hoffa said.

"Standing there bareheaded on that Nashville corner grinning with boyish delight at the sound of a diesel being goosed, Hoffa seemed not to have the least qualm about the treachery to his own union members which Kennedy regarded as clearly evident," Bigart wrote.

Bigart was not charmed. Noting the vast economic power Hoffa exerted through teamster control of trucking nationwide—even the drivers of hearses at many funeral homes were teamsters—Bigart observed, "The thought that any one man . . . should wield such unprecedented power has alarmed thoughtful Americans in and out of government. And that the man should be Jimmy Hoffa, notoriously arrogant and greedy for power, often accused of misuse of funds, and infamous for his toleration of hoodlum associates, makes the prospect still more perilous for the country."

That trial ended in a hung jury after weeks of boring testimony in which, Bigart reported, each day's proceedings "inevitably seemed more tedious than before." When the judge declared a mistrial, "Hoffa, cocky and exuberant, strutted out of the courtroom, leaving the Government lawyers crushed and despondent. It was unlikely, everyone knew, that the case would be brought to trial again." Hoffa still faced prosecution in federal cases in Orlando and Chicago, but Bigart concluded that the government's lawyers would need to do better, presenting "solid," comprehensible evidence, or he could beat those raps as he had all previous ones.

During the strike, talented reporters such as Tom Wolfe and Gay Talese had found new careers in what came to be known as "the new journalism." Liberated from the constraints of time and space at the daily newspaper, they found artistic life in books and in magazines such as *Esquire* and never went back. Bigart had no desire to make that break. Other than a dozen or so book reviews, he wrote for magazines only sparingly, usually because he needed the money. The Hoffa assignment would bring a payday and give him something to do that he thought was worth doing.

The article demonstrated that he was quite capable of long-form, opinionated writing, and he could have made a second career of doing that. Editors at *Collier's*, *LOOK*, and other magazines, as well as the *Saturday Evening Post*, had made clear that they would welcome contributions from him. He never made the transition, partly because he was emotionally attached to the newspaper business and partly because the *Times*, evolving with the trend, increasingly assigned him to write magazine-style series and major articles known as "takeouts" that gave him some stylistic running room.

The Pope Comes to Town

It was fortunate for the *Times* that Bigart stayed, because the paper needed him when another strike, this time by the Guild, shut down the paper again in the fall of 1965. In solidarity with the Guild, the craft unions walked out at all the other papers except the *Post*.

Arthur Gelb, the city editor at the *Times*, was one of several newsroom editors who qualified as management and were therefore exempt from Guild jurisdiction. He went to work each day in the vast, empty newsroom along with his boss, Abe Rosenthal.

Gelb wrote in his memoir,

> Day after day, Abe and I sat staring out at a sea of empty desks. Even Homer Bigart's glares would have been welcome. We felt miserable and frustrated missing story after story in the mayoral [election] campaign," which was then in full swing.
>
> Causing us even greater concern was the imminent approach of an unprecedented local event, so far-reaching that we figured the story would require the services of most of our staff. Set for October 4, the event was Pope Paul VI's arrival in New York to address the United Nations, the first time a pontiff would be setting foot in the New World.

Hoping that the strike would soon end, Rosenthal and Gelb planned the paper's coverage of the historic visit. They set up a roster of reporters, showing who would cover which aspect of the story. John Cogley, the religion reporter, was dispatched to Rome, where he would join the pope aboard his plane.

But the strike did not end. As the days went by, the editors fell into despair. Then, as Gelb wrote, "Abe received a phone call that turned out to be a miracle of sorts."

Bantam Books proposed that the *Times* call back to work the reporters and photographers who would have covered the story and assemble them in a make-shift newsroom at the book publisher's office, where they would produce an "instant book" about the event. The Guild assented because the fifty-one staff members would technically not be reporting for the *Times* but writing under contract for Bantam. They would not be crossing picket lines. All who were asked to work "eagerly agreed, Homer Bigart the most enthusiastic among them," Gelb recalled.[15]

On October 4, the day of the pope's arrival, the *Times* had reporters all along the twenty-four-mile route from the airport to St. Patrick's Cathedral, at the United Nations, and at Yankee Stadium, where the pope celebrated Mass. More reporters worked the phones to the police and other news sources. It was a long day's work:

the pope was in New York for fourteen hours, and Bantam had set a deadline of 5 a.m. the next day for the entire report to be written, edited, and submitted to its production department.

Bigart, assigned to write the lead chapter, handed in his typescript at 4:15 a.m. It was a straightforward narrative summarizing the day's events, filling seven printed pages in the instant book, mostly written as he would have written it for the newspaper. "Pope Paul VI journeyed to the United Nations on October 4, 1965, to appeal to the leaders of the world for peace," it began. "It was a historic mission that transfixed a great city, seized the attention of millions of Americans throughout the country, of people around the globe." The pope saw the best of fashionable New York as his motorcade passed through the Upper East Side, but he also saw "the endless dreary blocks of rotting tenements" in Harlem.[16]

After reading Bigart's typed article and passing it to the copy editors, Gelb wrote, "Abe poured Bigart and me the last of the whiskey that had helped sustain the staff through the night, and clicked his own paper cup against ours." None of the three had actually laid eyes on the pontiff.

Bantam's 160-page book, *The Pope's Journey to the United States*, came off the presses two days later, and half a million copies went out to bookstores in a feat listed for several years in the *Guinness Book of Records* under "fastest publishing." Four days after that, the strike ended.

Once again the other papers, except the *Post*, had closed in solidarity with the *Times*, but after ten days, the *Herald Tribune* broke ranks. John Hay "Jock" Whitney, the polo-playing, art-collecting aristocrat who had become the publisher in 1961, and Walter Thayer, the president of the company, "decided they had had enough—that it was the *Times*'s own ineptness and stubbornness that had caused the Guild walkout and it was suicidal for the *Tribune* to stay down to honor a principle that the *Times* had not absolutely pledged to support," Richard Kluger wrote.[17]

With the pope's visit and an intense, hard-fought campaign for mayor unfolding, the public was clamoring for news, and the *Trib* was briefly the city's only morning newspaper. Circulation tripled from its prestrike level to more than 900,000 per day. *Herald Tribune* executives were ecstatic, hoping that the paper's lively writing and creative features would retain some former *Times* and *Daily News* readers after the strike, but the moment did not last. Within a month, daily sales were back down to 305,000.

The writing was on the wall. The wounds inflicted on papers by the great strike of 1962–63 turned out to be fatal to four of them, including the *Trib*, as readers moved on to other sources of information, advertising declined, and costs of production went up. The papers raised the per-copy price to cover the additional labor costs, driving away some readers. Even the august, profitable *Times* was staggered. Three months after publication resumed, *Times* vice president Ivan Veit told Bradford that circulation had dropped by 12.8 percent weekdays and 3.5 percent on Sundays. Circulation continued to drop through that year.[18]

Moreover, as one historian of journalism observed, the assassination of President Kennedy on November 22, 1963, and the events that followed "changed the balance of power in the news business." Television networks threw out their regular programming and riveted Americans with saturation coverage, while "newspaper editors were put in the position of monitoring television and expanding on its coverage."[19]

Because Kennedy was so young, the *Times* did not have an obituary already prepared. The paper immediately put its immense resources into its coverage of the assassination, in Dallas, in Washington, and in New York. Seymour Topping, a veteran foreign correspondent who happened to be in the newsroom, recounted the drama there.

As soon as news of the shooting reached New York, before Kennedy's death was known, Topping wrote,

> Arthur Gelb, the deputy metropolitan editor collared me. "Will you do the foreign policy section of the obit?" he asked pleadingly. I hesitated. Sequestered in Moscow for three years, I had not been able to keep abreast of all aspects of Kennedy's management of foreign affairs. But I agreed and took my place on the front rewrite desk beside Homer Bigart, the distinguished and tough veteran of the Korean War, who was writing the obit's domestic policy review. Copy boys were bringing stacks of clippings. At 2:30 p.m. [Clifton] Daniel, his horn-rimmed glasses perched atop his silver hair, came to the rewrite desk and, pausing before Bigart and me, said: "He's dead." Between then and 6:30 p.m. Bigart and I wrote what made up a page of the *Times*. Afterward we walked together to Bleeck's saloon on Fortieth Street. We drank and talked about Kennedy until Homer went into the telephone booth to call his wife. . . . I elbowed up to the crowded bar to order another scotch and when I returned, I glanced through the window of the telephone booth and saw that Bigart, the indomitable war correspondent, was weeping. He was not alone.[20]

For days after Kennedy's death, Americans watched fascinating television coverage of Vice President Lyndon Johnson taking the oath of office, Jacqueline Kennedy in her pillbox hat seemingly ignoring the bloodstains on her suit, President Kennedy's funeral, and Jack Ruby shooting Lee Harvey Oswald. Even more than the Army-McCarthy hearings and the televised debates between Kennedy and Richard Nixon in their 1960 campaign, the Kennedy assassination and its aftermath showed readers that they could see the news happen in real time and not just read about it the next day. Newspapers could no longer control the arena as they once had.

As the *Times* itself reported a year after the great strike started, "New York television stations have been broadcasting more local news. New Yorkers have been reading more news magazines and television and theater guide magazines. Commuters have been reading more suburban newspapers."[21]

The Newspaper Die-Off

Even before the 1965 reprise of the 1962–63 walkout, it was clear that some of the city's daily papers could not survive. The first to go was the *Daily Mirror*. The Hearst Corporation pulled the plug on October 16, 1963, even though the tabloid still had the second-largest circulation in the country.

The *Herald Tribune* sought to save itself through a merger or a joint operating agreement with the *Times* under a provision of federal antitrust law that allowed struggling papers to combine their production and business operations while maintaining separate newsrooms. Negotiations continued for months, but the differences proved insurmountable. The *Times*, in a position of strength, made clear it did not want to acquire the *Trib* but also would not seek to eliminate it as a competitor. It had no incentive to undertake a joint operating agreement.

One long negotiating session unfolded on June 11, 1963, at the exclusive Links Club on Manhattan's Upper East Side (its website notes slyly that it is "easily accessible by most public transportation," as if any straphanger could join).[22] The *Trib*'s negotiator, Walter Thayer, presented a detailed plan to *Times* vice president Harding Bancroft. He proposed a joint venture in which each would have equity in the other so that each would be motivated to make the other successful. The *Trib* would become an afternoon paper and give up its Sunday edition, they would merge their European editions, and the *Times* would own the joint venture's building and equipment, while the *Trib* would pay rent.[23]

The *Times*'s publisher, Orvil Dryfoos, was amenable to an agreement, even though his business managers argued that the financial benefits the *Trib* was projecting were unrealistic. But Dryfoos, whose diseased heart had been fatally weakened by the pressures of the great strike, died on May 25 at the age of fifty. His successor, the thirty-seven-year-old Arthur Ochs "Punch" Sulzberger, scuttled the negotiations. As Richard Kluger wrote, "His family may have been sentimental about the idea; Punch Sulzberger was not." By the time of the June 11 meeting, Thayer was wasting his breath because Sulzberger had already decided.[24]

Left on its own, the *Herald Tribune* remained a lively competitor to the *Times* in its news pages, but its financial position eroded at an accelerating rate. In 1966 it merged with the afternoon *Journal-American* and the *World-Telegram and Sun* into an ill-conceived, ill-fated venture known as the *World Journal Tribune*.

Under their arrangement, the new organization would produce three papers: a morning edition, still to be operated as the *Herald Tribune*, even as its editorial staff moved into the newsroom of the *World Telegram*; an afternoon edition, produced by the *World Telegram*; and a Sunday edition, operated by the *Journal-American*.

The restructured papers were to begin publishing on April 25, but a Newspaper Guild strike at the *Times* postponed the operation. That dispute was settled in early July, but the craft unions still balked at the proposed labor arrangements at the *World Journal Tribune*. On August 15, Jock Whitney, with the assent of his partners in the new venture, gave up and announced that the *Trib* would not publish again. One of the country's most distinguished newspapers died an ignominious, if quiet, death.

"The shrunken staff of the New York Herald Tribune heard of the newspaper's demise yesterday with sadness but no great shock," wrote the *Times* reporter assigned to the story, Homer Bigart. "The staff had been largely depleted of its old pros during the 114-day shutdown of the new publishing enterprise, the World Journal Tribune. The newsmen had sensed an ultimate closing of the morning paper when the merger was announced last March and had started looking for jobs."

Bigart asked Red Smith, the *Trib*'s star sports columnist, if the death of his paper had really been necessary. "I can't believe it was," Smith replied. "I think it underlines the spectacular immaturity, the complete childishness, of labor-management relations in the newspaper business here."[25]

Smith landed on his feet. He and his column soon moved to the *Times*, as did some other *Trib* writers. The *World Journal Tribune,* colloquially known as the *Widget*, finally began publication in September, but it was a pallid product with no identifiable character. It died unmourned eight months later, leaving the city with only three daily papers: the *Times*, the *Daily News*, and the *Post*. All three are still published. *Newsday*, a well-regarded paper in the Long Island suburbs, made a run at the city market with the creation of *New York Newsday* in 1985. It lasted ten years.

Testifying before a US Senate subcommittee in 1967, Bertram Powers said that the atrophy of New York's newspapers was caused not by the unions' demands but by the indifference and incompetence of the publishers. The *Mirror*, for example, was a "poor, colorless imitation of the News," he said. The *Sun* "died of hardening of the arteries." The *World Journal Tribune* was doomed by poor planning, outdated equipment, and "management's inability to anticipate and meet the needs of its market."[26] He had a point.

A New Mrs. Bigart

The great strike of 1962–63 had one outcome for Bigart that set him apart from his newsroom colleagues: he emerged with a new wife, his second Alice, the wife he was talking to as he wept on the night of Kennedy's death.

On July 6, 1963, he married Alice Jane Weel, whom he had met when both were covering the Army-McCarthy hearings, he for the *Herald Tribune*, she as the producer of a nightly roundup on CBS Television. The best man was Sam Pope Brewer, a superb Middle East correspondent for the *Times* who is unfortunately remembered less for his accomplishments than for the fact that his wife left him for the infamous British spy Kim Philby.

During the strike, Weel had produced a half-hour midday program aimed at female viewers. A CBS news release announcing expanded news coverage during the strike said, "The ladies and other stay-at-homes have not been ignored." Weel's daily show, *Midday News with Women's Pages*, was "pegged toward the lighter and more genteel side of the day's events," including "the openings of art shows, dramatic premieres (on and off Broadway) and the latest showings in the world of fashion," along with "the latest in children's toys and books." Of course, it also aired some actual news. The program featured interviews with prominent women, such as Lillian Hellman and Sen. Margaret Chase Smith.[27]

Alice Weel was a much more sophisticated person than Bigart's first wife. A graduate of Bryn Mawr College, she went to the graduate school of journalism at Columbia University and got her first news job as New York correspondent of a London newspaper. CBS hired her because it was expanding its news coverage during World War II and could not find enough men.[28]

A television news producer's job bears little resemblance to that of a movie producer. In television, especially in those early days of cumbersome film and sound equipment, a show's producers were responsible for lining up interviews, arranging for the on-air correspondent and film crew to be in the right place at the right time, and managing logistics. If the producer was an accomplished writer and the on-air correspondent was not, so much the better. Weel was good enough at the job to be assigned to work with Don Hewitt, later the longtime producer of *60 Minutes*, and with the correspondents Harry Reasoner, Walter Cronkite, Eric Sevareid, and Mike Wallace—a CBS all-star team.

A TV chitchat column distributed nationally by King Features Syndicate shortly after her marriage to Bigart gave this description: "Pert Alice Weel is a down-to-earth, friendly lady with a warm laugh that makes it easy for her to win new friends and get along well with old ones. She possesses an engaging sense of humor about her work (often frenetic) and her life (often exciting.)"

About her new life as the wife of Homer Bigart, she said, "Because he works odd hours and I do too, we don't lead the normal 9-to-5 existence. For that reason we appreciate more the time we have together."[29]

TWELVE

CIVIL RIGHTS IN MANY FORMS

It was not easy for the country's mainstream newspapers to chronicle what became known as the civil rights movement, the quest by African Americans for equal opportunity and equal justice. The papers were White-owned institutions that catered to mostly White readers and White advertisers; their reporting and editing staffs were almost entirely White.

As late as 1968—after Jackie Robinson had broken baseball's color line, after President Truman integrated the armed forces, after the Supreme Court ordered the integration of public schools, after passage of the landmark Civil Rights Act of 1964, after the Selma-to-Montgomery march in 1965—a federal commission found that "the journalistic profession has been shockingly backward in seeking out, hiring, training, and promoting Negroes."

The National Advisory Commission on Civil Disorders, an eleven-member panel appointed by President Lyndon B. Johnson to investigate the causes of urban riots and chaired by former Illinois governor Otto Kerner, reported that "fewer than 5 percent of the people employed by the news business in editorial jobs in the United States today are Negroes. Fewer than 1 percent of editors and supervisors are Negroes, and most work for Negro-owned organizations. The lines of various news organizations to the militant blacks are, by admission of the newsmen themselves, almost nonexistent." Moreover, the commission found, "there is only one Negro newsman with a nationally syndicated column."[1]

Even in Washington, which had so many Black residents that it was known as "Chocolate City," the "great liberal *Washington Post* was scared to tell the truth" about race issues, Ben Bradlee recalled. "The editors were so much a part of the establishment that we didn't dare talk about race unless we were running some sappy story about a black achiever, or some safe story about a white bigot."[2]

Few if any White publishers or editors were more aware of that gap than Turner Catledge, the managing editor and then executive editor of the *New York Times*, who had grown up in segregated Mississippi. He wrote in a memoir,

Once the Supreme Court issued its 1954 school-desegregation decision, it was clear that race relations would be one of the great continuing stories during my years as editor. I once told [publisher Arthur Hays] Sulzberger that the unfolding race-relations drama was the biggest sociological story in American history, and I wanted to see it reported as such. Even before the Supreme Court decision, I wanted to see us write more about race relations, and also to employ Negro reporters.

Being a southerner, loving the South, and knowing all too well its sins against the Negroes, I think I had a special feeling for, and concern about, the unfolding racial drama.[3]

Catledge was not just "a southerner"; he was as southern as it was possible to be. He was raised in Mississippi's rural Neshoba County, the scene in 1964 of one of the era's most shocking events—the murder of three civil rights workers outside the town of Philadelphia. The newsroom of the *New York Times* may have been filled with Ivy Leaguers, but Catledge went to college at Mississippi A&M College (now Mississippi State University) because it was all his family could afford. For Catledge, as for Homer Bigart and legions of other young men from small towns, journalism was the elevator to higher economic and social standing.

Sulzberger, the publisher from 1935 to 1961, was not entirely unfamiliar with the South. His wife's family had long-standing ties to Tennessee and owned the daily newspaper in Chattanooga. With his support, Catledge deployed the *Times*'s matchless reporting resources to cover the long-running, fast-moving, and frequently violent story of school integration and the establishment of voting rights for African Americans across the former Confederate states and in the border states such as Maryland that had not joined the Confederacy but were segregated nonetheless.

The day after the Supreme Court's unanimous decision in *Brown v. Board of Education*, striking down as unconstitutional the "separate but equal" segregation of public schools, the *Times* published ten pages of background and interpretation. The following year, Catledge went to his hometown to assess the atmosphere and found that the collective reaction had "not been bad at all."[4] To get a wider view, he dispatched a team of ten reporters on a five-week tour of the South to evaluate progress, or lack of it, toward the integration of public schools and colleges. Their "Report on the South" was published on the front page on March 13, 1956. Many southern leaders, the report said, had concluded that integration was inevitable, but there was also hostility and a desire for "vengeance" throughout the region.

Over the next decade, the *Times* sent one top-flight reporter after another to the region. All were White males, and most of them were Southerners themselves, such as Roy Reed, John Herbers, Claude Sitton, and Fred Powledge. As events required, the *Times* supplemented their ranks with additional newsroom stars, including Joseph Lelyveld, an up-and-comer who would later become the executive editor; Peter Kihss, the former *Herald Tribune* star; and Homer Bigart. Kihss, for example, covered the struggle of a young Black woman named Autherine Lucy to enroll at the University of Alabama. On major stories, this crew might be supplemented by David Halberstam, who had worked in Nashville, or Gay Talese, who had attended the University of Alabama.

One reason the *Times* sent only White reporters on these assignments was that it had only a handful of Black reporters. Another was that Sulzberger and Catledge were reluctant to use Black reporters on civil rights coverage, especially in the South, where they could not stay in most hotels or eat in most restaurants. Catledge acknowledged that he and Sulzberger also harbored doubts about the ability of Black reporters to write objectively about civil rights issues—doubts that in themselves were discriminatory, as the leaders of the *Times* harbored no such reservations about the ability of White, southern reporters to write objectively about these issues.[5]

Sending reporters such as Kihss and Bigart to supplement coverage in the South was not as easy as it sounds because of the *Times*'s rigid territorial bureaucracy; they worked for the Metropolitan News Desk, not the National Desk. When Claude Sitton moved from the Atlanta bureau to become the National News editor in New York and wanted to supplement his staff for major events by borrowing Metropolitan News reporters, he had to negotiate the loan with Metropolitan Editor A. M. Rosenthal. "Sitton would naturally desire the services of one of Rosenthal's best men, such as Homer Bigart," Gay Talese observed, "but whether or not he got Bigart might depend on how Rosenthal felt toward Sitton on that particular day. If Rosenthal was feeling kindly, and if Homer Bigart himself liked the assignment and wanted to work on it, Sitton might get Bigart." Otherwise, Rosenthal might offer "the reporter he was most anxious to get out of sight."[6]

Not all civil rights news unfolded in the South. Newspapers in the big cities of the North and Northeast could no longer ignore the frustrations and aspirations of African Americans struggling against discrimination in housing, labor unions, and delivery of public services. Bigart reported on race issues in West Virginia, upstate New York, New Jersey, and Pennsylvania.

He wrote extensively about the campaign by New York's Black leaders to integrate the building trades, where all-White unions controlled the jobs. In the reporting of those stories, he had lunch with Malcolm X, whom he described as "very unthreatening."[7] In September 1957, he went to Levittown, Pennsylvania, to report on harassment and threats of violence against the first Black family to move in. He found William Edward Myers Jr., his wife, and their three children determined to stay. Crowds of rock-throwing, name-calling White people, organized as the "Levittown Betterment Committee" and aiming to "restore our entire white community," had failed to force the family out because the local Board of Commissioners supported the family. "We've had some weak moments," Myers told Bigart, "but we've never been near the point of packing up and clearing out."[8]

A week later, Bigart was in Little Rock, Arkansas, where White citizens were in an ugly uproar over a federal court order that nine Black students be admitted to Central High School. When Governor Orval Faubus dispatched the Arkansas National Guard to keep them out, President Eisenhower federalized the guard and sent US Army troops to enforce the court order. Soldiers of the 101st Airborne Division, bayonets fixed on their rifles, escorted the students into the building.

"An impressive show of Federal force cowed racist agitators at Central High School this morning, permitting the integration of nine Negro students without serious disorder," Bigart's account began. The troops "broke up small, sullen knots of civilians as soon as they formed." The demonstrators heckled the troops and called them Nazis, but there was no serious violence. "The vast majority of Little Rock's citizens went about their normal business. Downtown was quiet."[9]

That article provoked a testy letter to Catledge from William H. Fields, the managing editor of the *Atlanta Constitution*, the South's most influential paper. Underlining the words "racist agitators" and "small, sullen knots of civilians," Fields said the story "is a typical example of untruthful and inflammatory reporting common in northern newspapers."

Catledge drafted a detailed response in which he conceded that "there might have been one or two expressions in Bigart's story that could have been softened somewhat," but the editor said the descriptions, while harsh, were accurate. Instead of sending that letter, however, he set it aside in favor of a terse note in which he conceded nothing: "I do not think our stories in general, and this one in particular, can be characterized as 'untruthful and inflammatory.'"[10]

The commander of the federal force in Little Rock was Maj. Gen. Edwin A. Walker, whom Bigart had met at Anzio. Five years after Little Rock, Bigart found him again, in Dallas, retired from the army and trying to organize "a march of civilians on Mississippi to help Governor Ross R. Barnett resist any Federal troops in the integration crisis." In radio broadcasts, Walker was urging citizens to unite against the "Antichrist Supreme Court" and march in support of Barnett if federal troops moved in there.

Walker told Bigart that he had been on the wrong side when he enforced integration at Little Rock Central. "This time I am out of uniform and on the right side," he said.[11]

Even in the deepest South, Bigart found his all-American dummy act useful. Joe Lelyveld once conducted a long interview with a local minister in Philadelphia, Mississippi. At the end, the minister asked him, "There was a man down here, an older man. Said he was from the New York Times. Name of Bigaht. Know 'im?"

"Yes, sir," Lelyveld said.

"Couldn't have a normal conversation with that man. He didn't know anything. I had to explain *evvvvrything* to him."[12]

The deliberate mispronunciation of Bigart's name was hardly unusual in the South, where people hostile to northern reporters played on its similarity to "bigot" or pronounced it to rhyme with the N-word. Nor was he the only target; hostility to the "outside" press was widespread.

According to Herbers, reporters often adjusted their attire to suit the situation and the mood, hoping not to become targets. Some wore rumpled overalls and billed caps, trying to look like local citizens. Some wore suits and ties, so that people "may have trouble deciding whether you are an observer from Washington or president of the local Rotary Club." Herbers preferred "wash-and-wear pants and short-sleeve shirt, with or without tie," to look like an FBI agent. FBI agents were rarely attacked. "Little can be done for photographers," Herbers observed.[13]

For more than a decade, Bigart interspersed his coverage of New York and the region with trips across the South, as he had previously alternated domestic reporting with assignments overseas. The civil rights work was in many ways similar to foreign assignments: go to an unfamiliar and perhaps violent place and report on the conditions, the issues, and the people driving them. In his civil rights reporting, there was no trace of the disdainful or condescending attitudes toward Black people he had sometimes displayed in his reporting from Africa. On the contrary, his ingrained suspicion of authority figures and his sympathy for their victims led him to sensitive and perceptive coverage of a cause he found justified.

His sentiments showed most dramatically in June 1964, at the height of the "Freedom Summer" demonstrations, when he was part of the *Times* team covering the murders of three young civil rights activists: James Chaney, Andrew Goodman, and Michael Schwerner.

Arrested on trumped-up charges in Philadelphia, Mississippi—Turner Catledge's boyhood home—the three were soon released and ordered to get out of town. On the road to Meridian, a group of White men that included some law enforcement officials stopped them. They were never seen alive again. Their bodies were found forty-four days later entombed in an earthen dam on a farm outside Philadelphia.[14]

The FBI soon arrested Neshoba County sheriff Lawrence Rainey and his deputy on charges related to the murder. FBI agents staked out the county courthouse, which housed the sheriff's department, and took both men into custody when they showed up. Bigart was waiting with the agents as they began their stakeout at 8:30 a.m.

"The men they were after, the huge bear-shaped sheriff, Lawrence Rainey, 41 years old, and his deputy, Cecil Price, 26, had gone out on a 'whiskey raid,' hunting a moonshine still, and did not return until just before 9 o'clock," his front-page story said.

It had rained all night. "Sheriff Rainey's black boots were caked with mud. Deep South sheriffs are usually big men, often running to fat. This one weighs over 240 pounds and is developing a paunch," Bigart observed.

In the account he sent to the *Times*, he added that FBI agents were also "picking up a dozen other suspects, a potpourri of peckerwoods and rednecks that included a fundamentalist preacher, an itinerant bouncer for beer taverns, a Philadelphia policeman, and two alleged officials of the White Knights of the Ku Klux Klan." The copy editor who prepared that story for printing allowed the language to stand.

When the first edition appeared in the newsroom, the senior editors were outraged and promptly deleted the words "peckerwoods and rednecks" for the paper's later editions. The *Times*'s motto, which appears atop the front page every day, is "All the News That's Fit to Print." The words "peckerwoods and rednecks" did not qualify, as Bigart certainly knew when he wrote them.

Bigart's colleague John Herbers wrote of this episode:

> Bigart, one of the great reporters of this century, was in the waning years of his career and liked to play games with his New York Times copy editors who had ironclad rules—often maddening to reporters—on what was not fit to be printed in the Times. But the story was on deadline. Some sentry fell asleep at the switch and Homer's mischievous characterization got into the first edition, causing an uproar in the newsroom. The next edition carried blander, more Times-like language.[15]

That same summer, Bigart's reporting from Savannah prompted another letter of protest from another senior editor. Henry H. Schulte Jr., the executive editor of the *Savannah Morning News* and the *Savannah Evening Press*, wrote to Sulzberger to complain about "the obvious errors in Mr. Homer Bigart's story on Savannah and her racial problems," which had appeared on the front page of July 19. "I am distressed that a professional reporter of Mr. Bigart's stature would permit himself such errors, and I know that in the interests of fairness and accuracy, which The Times prides itself on, you will hear me out on the matter."

Bigart's offending article had been an upbeat account of progress, hardly critical of Savannah, and seemed an unlikely target for Schulte's irritation. "A year ago this charming old city was torn with racial unrest," it began. "Throngs of Negroes roamed the genteel streets and gaslit alleys of downtown Savannah, clamoring against segregation. Today the city is completely quiet." The only thing worrying the city fathers, the article said, was the fear that the presidential candidacy of Republican Barry Goldwater "would hearten the ardent segregationists, endow extremist groups with respectability, and upset the good relations that have been quietly worked out between the white and Negro communities."

That would seem to be a positive report, but Schulte picked at details. In particular, he objected to Bigart's assertion that "city officials, clergymen and Negro leaders say" that the coverage in Schulte's newspapers "has not been helpful to the cause of moderation." He noted that Bigart did not name any of the people who supposedly said that.

Sulzberger asked Catledge to respond, which he did on July 30. He apologized for not responding sooner, noting that he had been unable at first to contact Bigart because he was "on vacation in Honolulu."

Catledge said Bigart "readily agrees" that he had erred about the date on which an advertisement placed by local clergymen had appeared in the paper. However, he is "quite firm" about the role of the newspapers. "He talked to a considerable number of city officials, clergymen and Negro leaders and found them generally critical of the newspapers. They insisted, however, on not being quoted, presumably because they don't want to be in your bad books."[16]

Go to the Scene

As he had when covering wars, Bigart demonstrated that the best way to understand and report any event in the civil rights drama was to be there, no matter how dangerous the environment.

He went to Norfolk, Virginia, when the governor closed public schools rather than integrate them. When schools reopened, Bigart was in the cafeterias to see how Black and White students would interact. He went to Canton, Mississippi, where he found the city tense with apprehension about the impending arrival of student activists—Black and White—seeking to help local Black citizens register to vote.

In Americus, Georgia, Black demonstrators had infuriated White residents by sitting wherever they wanted in a movie theater instead of in the segregated seats in the balcony designated for them. Bigart found the town "deceptively sleepy by day" but "tense with terror after dark. White gangs, consisting mostly of teenagers, foray nightly into the Negro residential district." There they peppered houses with birdshot, firecrackers, and rocks, hoping to "frighten Negroes from any further testing of the new liberties they may enjoy under the Civil Rights Act."[17]

He was in Plaquemines Parish, Louisiana, the domain of the committed segregationist boss Leander Perez, to see what would happen the first time Black people tried to register to vote. Perez, Bigart noted, was such an extreme bigot and foe of integration that the Roman Catholic Church had excommunicated him. But on this occasion, Bigart found, Perez and other local White leaders made no attempt to stop aspiring Black voters because federal agents were there to enforce the Voting Rights Act.

The agents, Bigart reported, posted a notice on the door of the registration center behind the post office: "It is a Federal crime to intimidate, threaten or coerce or attempt to threaten, intimidate or coerce any person from performing his duties under the Voting Rights Act of 1965. Maximum penalty five years imprisonment or $5000 fine or both."

"For 44 minutes, the examiners waited," Bigart wrote, with his trademark attention to detail. "Nobody came." One agent wondered aloud if anyone would risk Perez's wrath. Then, "up the ramp strode a short, stocky Negro in sport shirt and dungarees." He registered without incident but refused to identify himself or say anything to reporters. Others who came after him, however, had plenty to say.

One was Andrew B. Franklin, a fifty-three-year-old commercial fisherman who had served in the US Marine Corps during World War II. His previous attempts to register, he said, had been foiled by the extremely difficult questions about the Constitution that Blacks—but not Whites—had been required to answer.

"That parish registrar once told me I had to know the whole Constitution," Franklin said. "I told him, 'How come I didn't have to know it when I fought for my country?'" There are not three lawyers in the United States who could recite the entire document, he said.[18]

An Embarrassing Low Point

In the spring of 1967, in the midst of the country's civil rights agitation and growing anti-war tumult, Bigart was reporting on the activities of such high-profile African American figures as Adam Clayton Powell Jr., James Meredith, and H. Rap Brown when he accepted—probably for the money—a commission from the *Saturday Review* to write an article for a package the magazine was planning about travel and the travel business. That article, "The Men Who Made the World Move," stands as an embarrassing low point in his illustrious career.

It was a gushing, wholly uncritical paean to tycoons of the travel and related industries, in particular Conrad Hilton, the hotel magnate; Laurance Rockefeller, the developer of resorts at Caneel Bay in the Virgin Islands and at Mauna Kea in Hawaii; Juan Trippe, founder of Pan American World Airways; and David Ogilvy, the "tweedy, urbane, pipe-smoking" advertising executive whose firm gave the world the Hathaway Shirts eye patch and Commander Whitehead of Schweppes.

Rockefeller's resorts, the article said, feature "peace, privacy, and tranquility." The article amounted to a free advertisement for Mauna Kea: "In Mauna Kea and Laurance's other resorts someone has finally invented hotels that are quiet, uncrowded and tasteful—and worth the extra effort it takes to reach their lovely isolation."[19]

There was much more in that syrupy vein. It appears that none of the interviewers who later talked to Bigart about his work asked him about the embarrassing travel article, nor is it mentioned in books about the *Times* by those who worked there.

After it was published, Bigart went right back to his day job at the *Times*, covering the trial of Dr. Carl Coppolino, a society doctor in Florida accused of murdering his wife. Coppolino's lawyer was the celebrated F. Lee Bailey, but the doctor was convicted anyway after a four-week trial.

Standoff in Pennsylvania

Far from Dixie, Bigart found one of the most tense, volatile racial confrontations in Chester, Pennsylvania, just south of Philadelphia. He described it with his usual precision and telling detail. His story was a useful corrective to the complacency of citizens in the northern states who told themselves that race was an issue in the South but not in their neighborhoods.

Bigart wrote,

> This grim industrial city is festering with racial tension. Negroes call it "the Birmingham of the North."
>
> Ugly clashes since last November have produced a climate so menacing that dialogue between white and Negro leaders has been silenced. Hundreds have been herded into jail; at least 20 have been injured.
>
> Last week the situation was so alarming that the Protestant Episcopal Bishop of Pennsylvania, Dr. Robert L. DeWitt, and the dean of the University of Pennsylvania School of Law, Dr. Jefferson Fordham, drove at midnight to Harrisburg, routed the Governor out of bed, and begged him to intervene.

By every metric, Bigart reported, life was stacked against the Black people among Chester's 63,400 residents. The public schools were segregated in fact, if not in law. The unemployment rate among Blacks was 14 percent, twice that of Whites. Almost 13 percent of the Black residents "live in abject squalor, with an income of less than $1000."

Despite all that, the Blacks "were docile until Stanley E. Branche came to Chester" and stirred them up. Branche is not much remembered now, but at the time he was well known among the ranks of Black leaders striving to rouse and organize Black Americans to demand economic justice and equal rights. Bigart described him as "a husky, light-skinned Negro," a paratrooper veteran of Korea who later went to music school, studied law enforcement, and became "an impassioned speaker." He recruited students from Swarthmore and Haverford Colleges, on the other side of Philadelphia, to join the marches and demonstrations he organized in Chester, where he had bought a house.[20]

The *Times* sent Bigart to Chester to cover a mass rally sponsored by Branche's Committee for Freedom Now, but Branche called it off because, he said, he feared an influx of "undesirable elements" from Philadelphia and New York that he could not control.

A few days later, Bigart was back at his desk in the New York newsroom, writing a long profile of J. Edgar Hoover, for whom President Johnson had waived the mandatory retirement age of seventy so he could stay on as FBI director. Then Bigart went across the Hudson River to the suburb of Madison, New Jersey, which was in an uproar over the question of whether a White barber was required to cut the hair of a Black man.

As he had in war zones, Bigart occasionally found humor or interesting local color amid the tensions of the civil rights struggle. Perhaps the best example is a story he wrote about the burning question dividing the little town of Raleigh, Mississippi: Was the annual long-distance tobacco-spitting contest worthy of coverage by the state's educational television network?

In that contest, Bigart noted deadpan, "there are two major events, one for accuracy and one for distance." The arena was a "32-foot spitway, a range of plywood covered with butcher paper."

The *Times* published that piece under the uncharacteristically puckish headline "Now, Class, Today We're Going to Learn Something about Tobacco-Spitting."[21] This amusing trifle was the equivalent of a piece Bigart had filed from wartime Italy about the dating preferences of members of the Women's Army Corps—a moment of levity that he found amid the conflict.

Appalachia's Grim Reality

When Bigart at the end of his career was honored by *[MORE]* magazine with its A. J. Liebling Award, the citation noted among other attributes his "tenacious pursuit of social injustice long before such reporting became fashionable."[22] The reference was to a subset of civil rights reporting of which Bigart became the premier exemplar: illuminating the chronic poverty and privation suffered by vast numbers of Americans—not just Black people but rural White people and Native Americans as well.

This was not war reporting or political reporting. War and politics were quantifiable and usually produced clear-cut outcomes. Territory was taken or not. One candidate won; the other lost. Here, Bigart was turning over rocks beneath American society and describing the ugly creatures that ran out, often to the displeasure of people who did not want to hear about it.

In early October 1963, Harrison Salisbury, by then the national news editor at the *Times*, wrote a memo to Clifton Daniel, then the managing editor:

> For the last two or three years there has been a small-scale war raging in the eastern mountains of Kentucky and Tennessee. At times it comes close to anarchy. The principal participants are the miners—surviving members of the United Mine Workers union.
>
> We have occasionally done a stray story on this situation but have never come to grips with the fact that the whole Cumberland region—one of the oldest and most picturesque and "American" parts of the country—is literally coming apart at the seams.

He said he wanted to send Bigart there for "two or three weeks to write some stories about what is really happening there, why it is happening and what can be done about it." Bigart, he said, was "eager to go out on the story."[23]

Rosenthal agreed to lend him to Salisbury for this project, and Bigart was soon on his way.

As was so often the case when Bigart was dispatched to some remote locale, he had been there before. The previous December, he had reported from the depressed coal mining area of Kentucky that poverty and despair were driving hungry men toward violence. That article was the first of several reports by Bigart that injected the word "Appalachia" into Washington's political vocabulary.

Some people in the backwoods were so cut off from modern America and its prosperity that they did not even know that they lived in an area the federal government categorized as "depressed," Bigart found. "But the miners in the coal towns are sharply aware that they are living miserably while most of the nation prospers. Many have become bitter. For them the class struggle is a reality." Some mines, a church, and a railroad bridge had been bombed. Martial law appeared imminent.[24]

When Salisbury sent Bigart back ten months later, he found little violence but pervasive depression, mental as well as economic. His report, datelined Whitesburg, Kentucky, appeared on the front page on October 20, 1963, under the headline "Kentucky Miners: A Grim Winter / Poverty, Squalor and Idleness Prevail in Mountain Area."

Strip mining had devastated "a once-magnificent landscape that now looks dour and malevolent," his report said, "but to the sociologist, the erosion of the character of the people is more fearsome than the despoiling of the mountains. The welfare system has eroded the self-respect of the mountain people. Gone is the frontier bravado, the sense of adventure, the self-reliance that once marked the Kentucky mountaineer. Three generations of living on handouts have resulted in a whipped, dispirited community."

In the absence of jobs, "crowds of listless, defeated men hang around the county courthouses of the region," looking for some sort of relief. Some resorted to faking illnesses or injuries to qualify for welfare. "One man found he could simulate blindness by diluting snuff and dripping it into his eyes. It fooled the welfare board, so he tried it with his wife, with equal success," only to be exposed when he tried it again with his daughter.

One of the people Bigart interviewed was Thomas E. Gish, the editor of the local newspaper, the *Mountain Eagle*, whose editorials opposing strip mining had prompted mining executives to brand him a communist. More than thirty years later, Gish's wife, Pat, still operating that paper, wrote in a journalism magazine that "what Bigart saw and reported became fodder for policy discussions in the Kennedy White House when the first of his articles appeared on a Sunday in October 1963. President Kennedy moved immediately to get help into the area, and those 21 counties later became a principal focus of President Johnson's War on Poverty."[25]

Pat Gish was hardly alone in crediting Bigart's reports with stimulating the Kennedy administration into action and helping Appalachia, but Bigart demurred. "I don't think my stories had any helpful impact," he said. "They shocked people, but the shock doesn't last."[26]

That was not false modesty. It was the conclusion he drew from what he saw when he returned to coal country in 1971. Well-intentioned programs designed to bolster the region were running aground because they failed to involve poor people in planning and implementation. "Attempts by Washington to give the rural poor of Appalachia a voice in antipoverty programs are being frustrated so effectively by politicians, doctors, merchants and other local people that some of the programs are in danger of collapse," he reported. Tom Gish, whose newspaper supported the rights of the underprivileged, "was dropped from the board of a regional planning group. Now, the poor are represented by a banker, a county attorney and a clergyman."[27]

The 1963 article from Whitesburg demonstrated that the *Times*'s editors were willing to give Bigart more leeway to draw conclusions and pass judgment than they had been earlier and more than they would give other reporters. Most of his colleagues would not have been able to assert, without attribution to some credible source, that "the welfare system has eroded the self-respect of the mountain people." Bigart had been chastised for editorializing in reports from the Middle East and Vietnam. But by the late 1960s, with the "peckerwood" furor in the past,

Bigart seemed to find a modus vivendi with his editors that allowed him to deploy his vast experience of the world to illuminate the news beyond bare facts.

He did that in a powerful five-part series, "Hunger in America," published in February 1969. The articles exposed grim reality in rural corners of Florida, South Carolina, Kentucky, Mississippi, and Texas about which most readers of the *New York Times* knew nothing.

The first article focused on a young White doctor in Beaufort County, South Carolina, Donald E. Gatch, who had exposed the prevalence of rickets, scurvy, kwashiorkor, and other afflictions caused by malnutrition among the poor, most of whom were Black. Even now, half a century later, it is distressing to read Bigart's graphic account of what he found as he toured the county with the doctor: listless children with bloated bellies and deformed limbs, babies whose hair was falling out, and people of all ages reinfesting themselves with intestinal worms because they had no indoor plumbing and were "stepping on feces that contained the eggs of parasites."

As a result of publicizing his findings, Dr. Gatch lost most of his White patients as the county's White establishment shunned him. Every other doctor in the county signed a statement deploring his "unsubstantiated allegations" and declaring that the "rare cases" of infant malnutrition that they encountered were the result of "parental inexperience, indifference or gross neglect." The doctor lost his access to the hospital in the county seat.

But there were also rays of hope. The doctor's reports gained credibility when researchers from three southern medical schools, including the University of South Carolina, examined the health and diets of 178 "Negro preschool children." Their study "showed that nearly three of every four had intestinal parasites, either ascaris (roundworm) or trichuris (whipworm), or both." Then Sen. Ernest F. Hollings, a former governor of South Carolina, "turned up in Bluffton and made the hunger tour. The Senator saw a near-starving baby, a rachitic child and another child said to be recovering from scurvy. Deeply impressed, Senator Hollings said he would demand an end to 'Federal roadblocks and red tape,'" which he said were frustrating local efforts to help the poor. The senator also was planning to take his case to a Senate committee that was seeking funding for field trips to pockets of hunger in a dozen states.[28]

In farm country around Immokalee, Florida, Bigart found appalling rates of disease and unspeakable sanitary conditions among migrant laborers. His report from there, published on February 17, noted that the Senate committee was scheduled to visit a month later.

In the migrant labor camps, the privation and squalor extended far beyond the insufficient diet; their huts lacked electricity, heat, and indoor toilets. The workers

lived, Bigart noted, in a "condition of poverty far removed from the showy afflu-
ence of nearby Gulf Coast resorts." Some camps had outdoor spigots for water, but
he found that "few migrants are hardy enough to take cold showers out of doors in
the dead of winter, even in Florida, and the latrines are unspeakably filthy, seats
and floor smeared with dried defecation. So the people use the woods."

He interviewed a woman who lived in a trailer with her two small sons, ages
two years and five months. She said she earned about twenty-five dollars a week;
the rent was fifteen dollars a week. The *Times* published a picture of her and the
boys on its front page.

In the Mississippi Delta around Yazoo City, Bigart found widespread malnutrition among Black people despite the state's participation in relief programs that
had been established as part of President Johnson's "Great Society" campaign. A
team of doctors there had reported that "the federal food programs were not only
inadequate, but were run by local authorities with flagrant political or racial bias."

With his usual flair for finding the striking quotation, Bigart recounted a doctor's musing that Black people in the Delta might have been better off in the age of
slavery. "In open slavery times human life was of some value," the doctor said. "If
master paid $100 for a man he'd see that his property was well taken care of, just
like a prize bull. But now the black people are no longer on the plantations. There
is no feeling of responsibility toward them, no need to help them."

The fourth stop on Bigart's hunger tour was Alazan-Apache Courts, the oldest
public housing project in San Antonio, "where some 6,000 Mexican-Americans
live in wretched poverty and frequent hunger." He found families living mainly
on tortillas and beans, but thanks to his guide, a Catholic priest named Ralph H.
Ruiz, he learned that "nothing infuriates a Mexican-American more than to have
some Anglo suggest to him that all his troubles would vanish if he would only stop
eating beans and tortillas and get on a 'balanced diet.'

"If you have one dollar," the priest said, "and you can buy either one pound of
meat or 10 pounds of pinto beans, what are you going to buy? You are going to fill
the stomachs of your kids with beans."

Across Texas and the Southwest, Bigart found Mexican Americans living in
a state of chronic privation, but their conditions were not the worst. "Hungrier
even than the Mexican Americans, but less obtrusive because they are smaller in
number and confined mainly to isolated wastelands, are the reservation Indians."
One doctor on a Navajo reservation had reported "27 cases of marasmus (calorie
starvation) and 17 cases of kwashiorkor (extreme protein deficiency) in the last
five years."

The Navajos could no longer survive as sheep and goat herders. They "were
suffering the traumas of converting from a pastoral living to a cash economy."

For the last report of the series, on February 20, Bigart went back to the Kentucky coal fields, where he found that "the hollows of Appalachia and their hidden nests of tarpaper shacks are breeding another generation stunted by hunger and programed for a lifetime of poverty." In that part of Kentucky, as well as in the other areas he had visited, "a visitor hears this constant complaint: the Federal food programs, whether food stamps or direct distribution of surplus commodities, do not provide enough sustenance each month to stave off hunger." The amount and quantities were inadequate, and distribution was hampered by prejudice, corruption, and incompetence among local officials.

Rep. William Fitts Ryan, a New York Democrat, had the articles in that series inserted into the *Congressional Record*. In introducing them, he said, "In a country as rich as ours it is a disgrace that any of our citizens should suffer from hunger and malnutrition."[29] But as the existence of those federal programs and the interest of the Senate demonstrated, official Washington was already well aware of the problem and had been groping for solutions since President Kennedy's tenure in the White House. The failure lay in devising workable remedies, as Bigart saw once again during a final visit to Appalachia in 1971, when Richard M. Nixon was president.

Throughout the region, "back in the hollows the conditions seem as wretched as ever." As a result of establishment hostility to the aid programs and corruption within them, "10 years after President Kennedy promised a new era for Appalachia, the million or so impoverished whites of the region largely remain rooted in penury and political impotence."[30] On that same swing through the region, Bigart found that increased Social Security payments, black lung benefits, and an expanded food stamp program "have enabled most of the poor to stave off hunger and subsist in cheerless deprivation." Yet thousands were still undernourished because they lacked the money to buy enough groceries, even with food stamps. Moreover, so many young people had fled to the cities that those left in the hills and hollows were the impoverished elderly, some "too proud" to ask for help.

The first paragraph of an article datelined Charleston, West Virginia, told the unhappy story: "Pockets of hunger remain in the hollows of Appalachia despite the Nixon Administration's pledge to put an end to hunger and malnutrition, and after nearly a decade of massive Federal aid to the distressed region."[31] In West Virginia, Bigart found, some schools did not even have school lunch programs. In those that did, some children were unable to partake because their parents lacked the money even to pay their nominal share—fifteen cents.

In Lee County, in far southwestern Virginia, he found parents who could not look forward to visits from children who had migrated to big cities because they did not have anything to feed them.

Grim Life on the Reservations

Bigart's account of poverty on the Navajo reservation stoked his interest in the plight of the Native Americans, probably the people in American society who receive the least attention from the mainstream press.

He had been alerted to the problems on the reservations in 1966, when Secretary of the Interior Stewart L. Udall forced the resignation of Philleo Nash, the commissioner of Indian Affairs. Nash, appointed by President Kennedy, was well-liked and respected, but according to Bigart, Udall found him "too slow in pushing industrial development on the reservations." To see for himself, Bigart embarked on a tour of several reservations in the Dakotas.

"Tucked away in obscure corners of 25 states are the poorest Americans," he found. "They are the 380,000 Indians who live in or near Federal reservations, where many still exist in squalor despite the antipoverty program," which had been promulgated with great expectations by the Johnson administration. At a reservation near the Canadian border, he reported that "hundreds of Chippewas got through the winter in hovels unfit for pigs." He found one family living in an abandoned railroad car, stuffing rags into the windows to hold off the cold. Among the Chippewas, even the members of the tribal council subsisted on welfare.

The reservations in the Dakotas, he reported, are "perhaps the most destitute." In other states, especially Montana, he found conditions modestly better. There, the Crows and the Northern Cheyennes are "relatively well off" because they "have been successful in retaining their Indian culture," but even so, almost all of those on reservations "are pathetically laggard in the march of the Great Society."[32]

Bigart was ahead of his time. As late as 2016, despite his work and a few other distinguished exceptions, a prominent news media journal found that the mainstream press largely ignored Native American issues, including their land's exploitation by energy companies and the crimes on the reservations that went unpunished.[33]

THIRTEEN

THE LONG ROADS END

Alice Weel was stricken by cancer while still in her forties and died in early January 1969. She and Homer Bigart had been married less than six years. Because of her final illness and death, the *Times* scrapped a plan to have him cover the trial of Sirhan Sirhan, who had fatally shot Robert F. Kennedy Jr. as he campaigned for the presidency the year before, but Bigart promptly went back to work, reporting the "Hunger in America" series. Then the trajectory of his life changed decisively.

One evening when he was a dinner guest at Betsy Wade's home, he was introduced to Eve Merriam, a well-known poet, who said she knew the perfect wife for him—Else Holmelund Minarik, the author of the popular *Little Bear* picture books for children. Illustrated by many artists, including the renowned Maurice Sendak, they sold millions of copies and were the basis of a television series on Nickelodeon. At the age of fifty and a widow for several years, she was living a life entirely different from Bigart's in comfortable semiretirement on a farm outside Nottingham, New Hampshire.

Arranging for Bigart and Minarik to meet was difficult given her location, but according to Wade, "we finally got our two tigers together at the Moon Palace," a Chinese restaurant near Columbia University.[1] He was apparently smitten right away, telling a dumbfounded colleague that "I showed her mine and she showed me hers." Before the colleague could respond, he added, "Our bankbooks."[2]

They were married on October 3, 1970.

A month later, he went to Georgia for Lieutenant Calley's court-martial. He spent the rest of that year and most of 1972 on the big, complicated stories in which he had come to specialize: the death of Haitian dictator François Duvalier, the court-martial of Capt. Ernest Medina, poverty and privation in Appalachia, and the desegregation of schools in Mobile, Alabama. He spent more than two months in Harrisburg, Pennsylvania, reporting on the highly politicized trial of "the Harrisburg seven": Philip Berrigan, an anti-war Catholic priest; Sister

Elizabeth McAlister; and five other defendants. They were accused of conspiring to kidnap White House national security adviser Henry A. Kissinger, blow up the heating tunnels around the US Capitol, and vandalize draft board offices. After a trial in which, Bigart wrote, "the Government's strategy backfired" and jurors were "flummoxed" by the judge's incoherent instructions, the defendants were convicted only of smuggling letters into and out of a federal prison.[3]

Bigart went to Oklahoma to write about welfare recipients trying to make a living by growing wine, to the consternation of teetotaling local preachers. He reported on the efforts of White people joining with Blacks to rebuild churches that had been torched in Texarkana, Texas. He recounted a nasty divide among the people of El Paso over a union's efforts to organize at a Farah slacks factory. In Maine he described the plight of clam diggers wiped out by a "red tide." And in Maryland, he covered his last big trial—the prosecution of Arthur Bremer, the twenty-one-year-old busboy who shot George Wallace as he was campaigning for president in that state, leaving him permanently paralyzed. Bremer was sentenced to sixty-three years in prison but was released after thirty-five.[4]

Bigart devoted his usual energy and brought his usual perceptive eye to those big stories, but he had reached a point where he wanted to spend more time with Else and less by himself in hotel rooms. She often traveled with him on his assignments, cooking meals where she could, and on weekends they usually left New York for the long drive to the farm in New Hampshire.[5] The result was that Bigart was seldom in the newsroom. By autumn, he was planning to retire.

"I didn't want to live another year anyplace with a population over 2,000," he said.[6]

In the months before his retirement, his absence from the newsroom was of little concern to his editors. Now assigned to the National Desk, he was on the road frequently. If he was writing about the Berrigan trial in Pennsylvania or a labor organizing dispute in El Paso, he was not at his desk in New York anyway, and if he had not been assigned to any particular story, why did he need to come in to the office and sit there doing nothing? This arrangement was not unique to Bigart; any National Desk staff reporter who lived in New York would have been out of town often and in the newsroom irregularly. But Bigart was also writing from home, a special situation that caught the attention of Abe Rosenthal, the executive editor.

On October 2, 1972, the day before Bigart officially notified the paper of his intent to retire after the presidential election that November, Rosenthal wrote a testy note to National Editor David Jones:

> I would appreciate it if you would take on a personnel question and clear it up and settle it. I found out, rather to my astonishment, that Homer Bigart seems to have

some kind of deal under which he no longer comes into the office at all and writes his stuff from Vermont or wherever he lives. I did not know this was taking place and it is not supportable. However, I understand that Mr. Bigart is going to retire or is thinking of retiring in October. If this is true and he wishes to retire in the next month or so, there is no use upsetting this arrangement that was made without my knowledge. But if it is not true and he intends to stay on longer, I want him to be treated the same way that others are. He can go out on national assignments but when they don't have one he is expected to return to the office. He is also expected to write in this office. He cannot be an absentee.

Jones responded that while it was true Bigart hadn't been in the office much, he wasn't away more than other national staff reporters. In fact, he had been quite productive that summer, writing a stream of "in-depth stories that required a considerable amount of work;" five had run on page 1. Rosenthal backed down, telling Jones that he didn't fully understand that Bigart now worked mostly for the National News staff, not for the Metropolitan News staff, and therefore could be expected to be absent frequently. He made no further mention of any "deal."

Rosenthal's irritation had been directed at Jones, not at Bigart, whom Rosenthal admired. After Bigart made it official that he would be leaving, Rosenthal wrote him a "Dear Homer" letter:

What the hell is there to say except that you are one of the greatest reporters who ever lived, and now you are retiring. There is no easily defined emotion as far as I'm concerned because I'm all mixed up. I know very well there will never be another Bigart, and that makes me sad. I also know you are leaving when a man should leave, when he's still full of juice, and that makes me glad.

I've thought of all kinds of things to do to say goodbye, but somehow I don't think that you are the retirement-party type. I'm not even sure you would show up for one if we gave one. But it really would give some of your friends here a great deal of pleasure if we did have a chance, a dozen or so of us, to get together for one stag night and have a lot to drink and a lot to eat and a lot to talk. So a couple of days after you get this letter, you'll get a call asking if by any chance you can find your way to New York for a night.[7]

By the time he received that letter, Bigart had left New York for good and was living contentedly on Else's farm. His final article before he retired was a routine report from Philadelphia on November 7 saying that President Nixon had carried Pennsylvania in a landslide over his Democratic challenger, George McGovern. His byline appeared one last time on December 2, 1973, on the *Times*'s obituary of David Ben-Gurion, Israel's first prime minister, but Bigart had written it long before.

He agreed to return to New York for Rosenthal's proposed party. When a secretary called to set a date, she later wrote in a memo to Rosenthal, Bigart told her that

> he had just been in a rather severe automobile accident on Monday, 11/27—a collision. He said both he and his wife [Else] and the occupants of the other car were taken to the hospital but that all were home now and in satisfactory condition. He very definitely wanted to postpone the party as a) he had no transportation and b) didn't feel like traveling, we left it that if he was feeling better as time passed, he would call us and we would set it up. But the party is most likely postponed for a long time if not to be forgotten altogether.[8]

That was prescient. The gathering Rosenthal envisioned took place only after Bigart died in 1991—and not at the *Times* building but at David Halberstam's apartment.

In his retirement, Bigart had lived quietly with Else in New Hampshire, mostly staying out of the public eye. A former colleague who visited him in 1989 found his attention occupied by a "slobbering dachshund," though he said he preferred the cat, "being as she's almost mute." Outside, the wind rustled outside through trees Bigart had planted himself. "New York seems distant, and he hopes never to see another skyscraper," the colleague wrote. He was no longer able to snowshoe, but Else drove to town each morning to fetch the stack of newspapers he still devoured.[9]

Grumpier than ever in his final years, Bigart described that town, West Nottingham, as "a miserable slum."[10]

In retirement, as always, Bigart found relaxation in alcohol. Al Burt, a columnist for the *Miami Herald*, wrote that he also had visited Bigart at the farm, "joining him in a Polish vodka before breakfast from the freezer." Homer and Else often spent much of the winter in the Florida Keys, Burt added. "Once, he and his wife spent the night with us en route; what a good memory I have of us sitting up late at night drinking Spanish brandy."[11]

At the posthumous retirement party hosted by Halberstam, most of the guests were former colleagues at the *Times*, but Karen Rothmyer, who had interviewed Bigart for her book about Pulitzer Prize winners, was also invited. She recounted an "evening full of jokes and laughter and sharply etched memories of a man who was respected and loved."

The master of ceremonies was Harrison Salisbury. Bigart "was what he was because he was the best," he told the guests. "He was always the last man to finish his story and his story was always better than anyone else's because he put so much time into it."

As she listened to the stories, Rothmyer wrote, she recalled how difficult it had been to track him down to interview him:

> Bigart was not to be found in the [library] card catalogue, the newspaper index, or the pages of "Who's Who." Some people thought he was dead, but the closest I could come was an obituary of his first wife. When I finally tracked him down, living in retirement with his third wife in a New Hampshire farmhouse, I began to understand how Bigart could have been so famous among his peers and yet left almost no public trace. A stranger to the lecture circuit and the book tour, a reporter who had never felt comfortable anywhere other than in the world of newspapers, Bigart was more interested in telling stories than in trying to remember what had happened to his prize citations.

When she heard that Bigart had died, Rothmyer wrote,

> I felt a sense of loss that went beyond regret at the passing of a great reporter. Bigart belonged to an era of newspapering that has already receded into myth. He was a link with a time in journalism when reporters were paid by the word, when the idea was to stay as far away as possible from the office, and when the best thing about the job was hanging out with the other working stiffs, preferably in an establishment offering free food and liquid refreshment. The memorial evening, as pleasant and nostalgic as it was, showed how far journalism has traveled since Bigart's day: There were as many pinstripes as you'd find on Wall Street, and the waiters were offering sparkling water along with the canapés.[12]

In fact, Bigart had not been entirely invisible after his retirement. He occasionally wrote book reviews for the *New Republic* and the *Saturday Review*. Two of the reviews dealt with important books about the Vietnam War and showed that he had not lost his incisive touch.

First, he took on *Winners and Losers: Battles, Retreats, Gains, Losses, and Ruins from the Vietnam War*, an impressionistic denunciation of the war by his *Times* colleague Gloria Emerson, who had reported from Vietnam in the early 1970s. Like Bigart, she had won a George Polk Award, and her book won a National Book Award, but he didn't think much of it. He described her tone as relentlessly angry because the country isn't angry enough at itself or sufficiently remorseful; the nation wants to forget the war, but she doesn't. "Her summons to nationwide repentance, however unrealistic, is tremulously sincere," his review said. "She wants everybody down on his knees right now, before there is another war."

He went after her in unequivocal terms for her decision, recounted in her book, to accompany a group of Vietnamese teenagers on a mission to firebomb an American vehicle and kill its occupants. Fortunately for her, this mission failed when a student's aim was bad, and he missed the open window. "There is a question of ethics involved here," Bigart wrote. "In the muddle and confusion of an undeclared war, just how far should an American correspondent go in his search for truth?" His answer: Not that far.[13]

Then he reviewed *Big Story: How the American Press and Television Reported and Interpreted the Crisis of Tet 1968 in Vietnam and Washington*, a massive, detailed report by Peter Braestrup, another former *Times* correspondent and later my colleague in Saigon when I was reporting from there for the *Washington Post*. Braestrup's thesis was that the American press corps, having developed a dim view of the war and of the US role in it, beginning with Bigart's time there in 1962, misconstrued the Tet Offensive of 1968 as a defeat. In reality, Braestrup argued, the Tet Offensive was a massive setback for the Vietcong because so many of their troops and cadres died in an uprising that ultimately failed.

History has largely validated Braestrup's view: the Vietcong were in fact depleted by the offensive to the point that they were no longer an effective fighting force, and North Vietnam had to send its own regular army troops to the south to keep the war going. But wars are not fought only on the battlefield; they are also fought on the political front at home. And there, the Tet Offensive was a breaking point for Americans who had been told for years that their South Vietnamese partners were making steady progress. When Walter Cronkite—by then known as the "most trusted man in America" as the anchor of the *CBS Evening News*—went to Vietnam to see for himself and pronounced the war an unwinnable stalemate, his report cemented the Vietcong's political triumph. Reports about Tet by Cronkite and others, including one that a few Vietcong fighters had even penetrated the US Embassy, accelerated the growing anti-war movement and contributed to the notion that the press was somehow responsible for the eventual communist victory.

Bigart said in his review that Braestrup "tries very hard to be fair" and had made a clear distinction between the professional reporters who worked diligently to pin down the truth and the "hippies" and neophytes writing for fringe organizations. Still, even among the most able reporters, "he finds errors of fact, or of omission, lazy analyses, ill-formed analyses, and worst of all, a chronic tendency to pessimism." As Bigart observed,

> Here one is tempted to speak up for the pessimists. Wasn't a strong dose of gloom the precise antidote for the rosy illusions promoted by the Kennedy and Johnson administrations to sell their escalating involvement in an unnecessary war? Suppose

the few correspondents who were in Saigon before the American troop commitment had exposed more starkly the weaknesses of the Saigon regime and its feeble prospects—even with massive American aid—of prevailing against an indigenous Communist-led nationalist revolution. But of course no newsman in Saigon in 1962 ever dreamed that his government would be lunatic enough to send half a million troops to Southeast Asia.[14]

It was, in a way, a retrospective defense of Bigart's own reporting. He had been the first American reporter to describe both "the weaknesses of the Saigon regime and its feeble prospects" and the US Embassy's efforts to disguise the truth more than five years before the Tet Offensive.

When Bigart died, nineteen years had passed since he had retired and left New York, but his former colleagues had not forgotten him, as the party at Halberstam's apartment demonstrated. Tom Wicker, the *Times*'s Washington columnist, wrote a tribute that described him as "one of the best reporters ever to pound a typewriter." He recalled Bigart's "brilliant and illuminating dispatches from both the European and Pacific theaters of World War II, the Korean War, the Vietnam War, the Israeli struggle for independence and others of the many conflicts that marked his time."[15]

Perhaps the most eloquent tribute came from the writer Richard Reeves, who had been a reporter at the *Herald Tribune* at the time of its death and then joined the *Times*. One day he was sitting at Bigart's desk, chatting with another reporter, when Bigart appeared and evicted him with a jerk of his thumb, saying nothing. "He didn't speak to me for a year," Reeves recalled. That did not diminish Reeves's admiration for him.

"First of all, Bigart was good," Reeves wrote.

He played the bumbler, beginning his questioning at a sealed-off airplane crash scene by pointing to the tail of the plane and asking, "What do they call that part?" He stammered, rather badly, reinforcing an impression that he was a simple fellow who all the world should help. He was anything but simple, anything but gullible. He was the first reporter to predict disaster for the United States in Vietnam. . . . And he wrote like an angel obsessed, ever looking for the exact word, the better image. The series of stories he wrote on the lives of miners in eastern Kentucky was the first link in a chain of events that led to the federal government's war on poverty. The president then, John F. Kennedy, knew all the statistics but it was Bigart's words that moved him to action just before he was killed in November 1963.

Second of all, Bigart never wanted to be anything but a reporter. Power, money, fame, and ideology were specimens on a slide. There was sham to be exposed.

Moreover, Reeves said, "his wit was vicious, stammer and all, leading to all sorts of Bigart stories, most of them true, all of them enduring," including, of course, those stories about Marguerite Higgins.

"I don't know whether Homer Bigart, who never graduated from college, was famous or even particularly well-known outside the business," Reeves concluded. "But he gave us all the style and the spine to get it 'right.' I pray we'll see his like again."[16]

EPILOGUE:
WHAT WOULD HOMER DO?

f the British were coming today, Paul Revere would not ride. He would tweet or send multiple texts. The information would still be important, and people would still want to receive it, but the delivery method would bear no resemblance to those of the past. In this century, the computer and the mobile phone have revolutionized the news business.

The day of the enterprising thirteen-year-old on a bicycle flipping papers onto front porches is almost over, as is the era of the busy newsstand displaying competing daily papers. On one recent morning, newsstands along Forty-Second Street in New York were selling candy and snacks but no newspapers. "They won't give them to us," one proprietor said, "because they lose money on them."

Why would publishers invest in giant printing presses and fleets of delivery trucks when news can be sent to unlimited numbers of readers with a few keystrokes? Even some news outlets that began as traditional papers no longer have printed editions. The *New York Times*, the *Washington Post*, and some other long-established daily papers still distribute their product in print, but online subscriptions far outnumber sales of the printed version. Some newspapers that are still publishing printed editions have sold their buildings and closed their newsrooms; their entire staffs work remotely. Others have eliminated print editions on some days of each week. Many of today's major news organizations, such as *Axios* and Bloomberg, were created in the internet era and have never printed any articles.

On October 13, 2021, the *Washington Post* published a story about a US Marine Corps officer who had been charged with dereliction of duty and whose lawyers were negotiating a plea bargain with prosecutors. The article contained this sentence: "The possibility of a plea deal was first reported by Coffee or Die Magazine." That online outlet, established in 2018 by Black Rifle Coffee Company in Utah, says it "covers stories both about and for the military, first responder, veteran, and coffee enthusiast communities."[1]

This evolution of the way news is disseminated has a parallel in the way news is developed. In this era of social media, almost anyone with access to the internet can produce blogs, newsletters, podcasts, and posts on Twitter. This may be liberating and democratic, but it is also dangerous because no one exerts quality control over much of this material. That is the reason so many Americans still believe that Donald Trump won the presidential election in 2020 and helps explain why so many Americans refused to be vaccinated against COVID-19.

A corollary of this evolution is that it is misleading and lazy to discuss "the news media" as if the news business were a unitary operation about which it is possible to generalize.

In Homer Bigart's youth, before the advent of radio and television, the "news media"—a term no one used—meant newspapers and a few magazines. There were good newspapers and bad ones, big ones and small ones, dailies and weeklies, but they were all newspapers. Now there is no one term or phrase that signifies an enterprise or an industry that includes journalism in all its print and electronic forms. The news as reported by the *New York Times* is not the same as the news reported by Breitbart.com or the *Washington Free Beacon*. The news as reported by Greg Kelly on Newsmax is not the same as the news reported by Lester Holt on NBC. A prominent person in politics, business, sports, or the arts who criticizes the news media scores no rhetorical points because there is no such entity.

During the Lebanese Civil War in the late 1970s, I was in the bar of the Commodore Hotel, the press hangout in Beirut, when a new correspondent appeared—a writer for the *National Enquirer*, the gossip tabloid. He wasted a lot of breath trying to convince the rest of us that he was a "real" reporter looking for the same serious news as we were. He never did break into the circle of colleagues welcome at that bar. Today his reception might be different, as can be seen at the White House, where representatives of marginal or fringe organizations such as One America Network carry the same press credentials as reporters for the *Wall Street Journal*.

Government officials, military officers, business executives, and politicians may prefer to talk to the public through news organs that they consider responsible and serious, but they have no control over what consumers of news choose to read or watch. That is why even the most responsible officials sometimes talk to news outlets of which they are inwardly contemptuous. They see it as the only way to reach those audiences who make it a point not to read or listen to what Sarah Palin called the "lamestream media."[2]

In the summer of 2019, the *New York Times* published a twelve-page special section called "A Future without the Front Page." Noting the mass disappearance and shrinkage of newspapers across the country, mostly because of plummeting advertising revenue, the *Times* asked, "What happens when the presses stop rolling? Who will tell the stories of touchdowns scored, heroes honored and neighbors lost? And who will hold mayors, police officers and school boards accountable?"[3]

The section focused on the final edition of the *Warroad Pioneer*, a weekly paper in a small town in Minnesota that had published its last edition after 121 years. It could have been about any of the hundreds of small papers that have thrown in the towel over the past two decades or about any of the surviving daily papers that have been eviscerated by hedge funds that scooped them up as their costs rose and their revenue declined. Nor is it only small papers that have disappeared; Detroit, Salt Lake City, and New Orleans are among the major cities that no longer have daily printed newspapers. The *Arkansas Democrat-Gazette*, in Little Rock, stopped printing on weekdays and gave its subscribers iPads to keep reading.[4]

The disappearance of local papers does more than cut off channels of information for the citizenry. It deprives editors at remaining regional newspapers such as the *Des Moines Register* or the *Louisville Courier-Journal* of information about outlying communities in their circulation areas. And it eliminates vital training grounds for young journalists looking to break into the news business. One prominent columnist used to say that the best place for an aspiring young reporter to start was a respected daily paper in a midsize state capital that had a major university and a high crime rate. How many such papers are there now?

What has not changed in this new era of news is the demand for the product—the news itself. The Athenians were eager for news of the Battle of Marathon. President Abraham Lincoln spent long evenings at the telegraph office awaiting reports on Civil War battles. People still want and need to know what is happening at the school board, at city hall, at the state capitol, in Congress. They want to know who won the local high school's football game and what is on sale this week at the supermarket.

Remember the Studebaker?

During Homer Bigart's career, it was possible to walk down any street in the country and see cars bearing the brand names DeSoto, Hudson, Packard, Pontiac, LaSalle, Studebaker, Mercury, Oldsmobile, Nash, and Plymouth. All are long gone. The closures of their factories were severe economic blows to the cities they were in. But the automobile is still with us and will remain with us indefinitely. It may be powered by different fuel and may drive itself, but it will exist because it is essential to our national life.

A similar transformation is unfolding in the news business. No single dominant format or type of organization has emerged to replace the traditional newspaper, but conduits for delivering information to the public will remain. All-news radio has existed for decades. CNN, the pioneer of all-news-all-the-time television, was created in 1980. In the current chaotic news landscape, it is hard to predict which organizations and formats will emerge as industry standards.

One model that that could prove workable has been developed in New Bedford, Massachusetts. That city's daily newspaper, the *Standard-Times*, which traces its origins to 1850, has thinned, and its staff has dwindled as its owner, the struggling Gannett chain, has cut back. Its coverage of local issues and events has declined correspondingly, to the point where Mayor Jon Mitchell complained to a *New York Times* reporter, "We don't have a functioning newspaper anymore, and I say that with empathy for the folks who work there. It used to be that I couldn't sneeze without having to explain myself. Now I have to beg people to show up at my press conferences. Please, ask me questions!"

Prompted by his belief that effective, honest local government requires input from informed citizens, he offered his support to a group of journalists, including some former staff members of the *Standard-Times*, who have created an online-only outlet called the *New Bedford Light*. The publisher is Stephen Taylor, a veteran of the *Boston Globe*, which his family once owned. The *Light* went online in June 2021 under the editorial direction of Barbara Roessner, a former managing editor of the *Hartford Courant*.[5]

"Welcome to The New Bedford Light, your new home for community-based local news," Roessner says in "A Message from the Editor." "As you can see, we are not a typical breaking news outlet. We hope to be something different, something more.

"Our goal is to go deep on big issues, often driven by data, and to reflect the incredible diversity of our city through its vibrant local culture. We seek to provide information and insight that stimulates healthy debate and bolsters civic life; we want to celebrate the experience and creative expression of *all* New Bedford's people."[6]

In practice, that means the *Light* will not devote resources to some of what used to be standard fare in local papers, such as high school sports, nor does it focus on daily events such as crime. Instead, it focuses on extensive, explanatory coverage of one major issue at a time, such as the effects of COVID-19 on New Bedford or the boom in its housing market.

The *Light* is free to readers, whom it invites to send contributions not only of money but also of news tips, ideas for stories, and articles to be considered for publication. It does not accept advertising. The money comes from donations, grants from foundations, and sponsorships by local businesses. "As an independent, nonprofit news outlet we are reliant on reader support to help fund the kind of in-depth journalism that keeps the public informed and holds the powerful accountable. Thank you for your support," the *Light* says on its website.

A similar project has been initiated in Baltimore. In October 2021, Stewart Bainum, a hotel magnate who tried unsuccessfully to purchase the venerable *Sun*, announced the creation of a nonprofit, online-only journal called the *Baltimore Banner*. He hired a senior editor from the *Los Angeles Times* to run its news operation. He said he planned to hire fifty reporters and had committed $50 million of his own money to the venture. He said he expected subscriptions, donations, and grants from foundations to provide operating revenue. Bainum's outlet draws its name from the Star-Spangled Banner, which was flying over Fort McHenry at Baltimore Harbor when the dawn's early light brought the news "that the flag was still there."

The *Banner*'s chief executive, Imtiaz Patel, a *Wall Street Journal* veteran, said he had consulted leaders of other digital start-ups, such as Denver's *Colorado Sun*, and of established nonprofit online outlets, such as *ProPublica*, to design a business model. The Lenfest Institute for Journalism, which owns the *Philadelphia Inquirer*, is also supporting the *Banner*.[7] That institution says on its website, "Journalism requires new business models, powerful innovations and diverse audiences. The Lenfest Institute for Journalism is working throughout local news ecosystems, in Philadelphia and beyond, to crack the code on a sustainable future for this vital resource."[8]

Meanwhile, the changing technology of distributing the news is paralleled by the changing technology of acquiring it and delivering it to editors. News reporters of Homer Bigart's day often sent their dispatches by cable or read their typed articles to dictationists at the home office who transcribed them. When a fax machine was available, they used that. If they returned to the news business now, they would need to learn how to use Twitter, Instagram, text messaging, and other new avenues of communication.

Once they did so, they would find the new technology liberating. During the war in Bosnia in the 1990s, a reporter was cut off from the traditional methods of transmitting her copy, such as cable or telex. But she was able to attach her article to an email that she could send on her mobile phone. Reporters covering Russia's war in Chechnya in the 1990s used satellite phones powered by car batteries. Nobody files by cable or Telex anymore. In the same way, reporters or editors no longer spend time rummaging through yellowed clippings in search of information from past editions; that material is digitized, available with a few clicks.

But reporters and editors today understand that the technology is a tool, not the point of their work. The job itself remains the same: find out what happened, who did it and why, and what the consequences are, and then tell people about it. They understand also that much of what newspapers print and television news programs broadcast is not news at all in the traditional sense. Personality profiles, portraits of interesting places, and evaluations of trends—items that may not have any time element and are often written at length in the first person—have been a staple of the business since the advent of the "new journalism" pioneered by Tom Wolfe, Hunter S. Thompson, Jimmy Breslin, and Gay Talese in the 1960s and 1970s.

While it is unlikely that Homer Bigart ever thought of himself as a practitioner of this "new journalism," he would have had no trouble deploying its techniques because he did it himself in some his liveliest, most durable work. From Anzio, Korea, Mississippi, Honduras, Brooklyn, and a thousand places in between, he showed that he could inject the personal into the factual to get closer to the truth. His work was the new journalism before that term had been coined.

NOTES

Note to the Reader

Sources that appear in the selected bibliography are cited in their short form here, while sources that do not appear in the bibliography are cited in their long form.

Introduction

1. Federal Communications Commission, "Television," 72, accessed April 3, 2022, https://transition.fcc.gov/osp/inc-report/INoC-3-TV.pdf.

2. Rosenthal Papers.

3. Malcolm W. Browne, "The Fighting Words of Homer Bigart: A War Correspondent Is Never a Cheerleader," *New York Times Book Review*, April 11, 1993.

4. Rooney, *My War*, 92.

5. Beech, *Tokyo and Points East*, 39.

6. *New York Herald Tribune*, July 12, 1950.

7. Homer Bigart obituary, *New York Times*, April 17, 1991.

8. Betsy Wade obituary, *New York Times*, December 3, 2020.

9. Wade, *Forward Positions*, xxiv.

10. Kluger, *The Paper*, 309.

11. Memorandum of January 1, 1961, *New York Times* Personnel Records, New York Public Library.

12. Wade, *Forward Positions*, xxiv.

1. From Small Town to Gotham

1. Rothmyer interview.

2. Rothmyer interview.

3. Oral history interview.

4. Douglas Martin, "Listen, We've Got Another Homer Bigart Story," *New York Times*, November 25, 1989.

5. Martin.

6. Kluger Papers.

7. Oral History interview.

8. NYPL Foreign Desk Records; and *New York Times*, Personnel Records, New York Public Library.

9. Kluger Papers.

10. Oral History interview.

11. Joel Sayre, "Newspaper Town," *New York*, December 1974, 76–79.

12. "Inside the Times," *New York Times*, September 28, 2020.

13. *New York Times*, November 26, 2019.

14. Mott, *American Journalism*, 632.

15. Michael Reynolds, *Hemingway: The Paris Years* (New York: W. W. Norton, 1999), 92.

16. Mott, *American Journalism*, 615.

17. Mott, 615.

18. Sayre, "Newspaper Town."

19. "Walter Winchell: The Power of Gossip," *American Masters*, Ben Loeterman Productions and THIRTEEN (WNET), PBS, season 34, episode 5, aired October 20, 2020.

20. "Commissioner Ford Frick Biography," *Baseball Almanac*, accessed December 2, 2021, https://www.baseball-almanac.com/articles/ford_frick_biography.shtml.

21. Jill Lepore, "In Every Dark Hour," *New Yorker*, February 3, 2020.

22. "History of Sports Broadcasting," BEONAIR Network of Media Schools, accessed December 2, 2021, https://beonair.com/history-of-sports-broadcasting.

23. Walker, *City Editor*, 1.

24. Walker, 2–3.

25. Walker, 40.

26. Kluger, *The Paper*, 252–53.

27. Rothmyer interview.

28. Wade, *Forward Positions*, xix.

29. Kluger Papers.

30. Oral History interview.

31. Kluger, *The Paper*, 270, 279.

32. Kluger, 364.

33. Rothmyer interview.

34. Kluger Papers.

35. Oral History interview.

36. Oral History interview.

37. *New York Herald Tribune*, January 23, 1936.

38. *New York Herald Tribune*, January 18, 1935.

39. *New York Herald Tribune*, July 10, 1939.

40. Kluger, *The Paper*, 365.

41. Kluger, *The Paper*, 266.

42. William K. Zinsser, "The Daily Miracle: Life with the Oddballs and Mavericks at the Herald Tribune," *American Scholar*, December 1, 2007, https://theamericanscholar .org/the-daily-miracle/.

43. Zinsser.

44. L. L. Engelking obituary, *New York Times*, October 20, 1980.

45. *New York Herald Tribune*, July 6, 1941.

46. *New York Herald Tribune*, May 19, 1940.

47. *New York Herald Tribune*, March 17, 1940.

48. *New York Herald Tribune*, August 18, 1941.

49. *New York Herald Tribune*, November 20, 1942.

50. *New York Herald Tribune*, August 23, 1941.

2. Homer Bigart Goes to War

1. *New York Herald Tribune*, November 5, 1939.

2. *New York Herald Tribune*, September 25, 1940.

3. *New York Herald Tribune*, November 7, 1942.

4. *New York Herald Tribune*, November 8, 1942.

5. *New York Herald Tribune*, January 21, 1943.

6. Rooney, *My War*, 65–68.

7. Rothmyer interview.

8. Wade, *Forward Positions*, xi–xii.

9. *New York Herald Tribune*, March 21, 1943.

10. *New York Herald Tribune*, May 21, 1943.

11. Art Leatherwoood, "Handbook of Texas," Texas State Historical Association, accessed December 2, 2021, https://www.tshaonline.org/handbook/entries/eaker-ira-clarence.

12. Rebecca Grant, "Eaker's Way," *Air Force Magazine*, December 1, 2005.

13. Hamilton, *Writing 69th*, 40.

14. Douglas Brinkley, *Cronkite* (New York: HarperCollins, 2012), 95.

15. *New York Herald Tribune*, February 9, 1943.

16. Cronkite, *Reporter's Life*, 98.

17. Rothmyer interview.

18. Hamilton, *Writing 69th*, 30.

19. Cronkite, *Reporter's Life*, 98; and Hamilton, *Writing 69th*, 53.

20. Reprinted in Hamilton, 117–20.

21. Rooney, *My War*, 133.

22. Cronkite, *Reporter's Life*, 99.

23. *New York Herald Tribune*, February 27, 1943.

24. Cronkite, *Reporter's Life*, 99.

25. *New York Times*, February 27, 1943.

26. *New York Herald Tribune*, March 7, 1943.

27. Salisbury, *Journey for Our Times*, 198.

28. Oral History interview.

29. Hamilton, *Writing 69th*, 139.

3. The Italian Campaign

1. Oral History interview.
2. Rothmyer interview.
3. In the US edition, the title was sanitized to *Bearings: A Foreign Correspondent's Life behind the Lines* (New York: Viking, 1978).
4. *New York Herald Tribune*, July 29, 1943, delayed in transmission.
5. *New York Herald Tribune*, August 8, 1943.
6. *New York Herald Tribune*, August 10, 1943.
7. *New York Herald Tribune*, August 17, 1943.
8. *New York Herald Tribune*, October 11, 1943.
9. *New York Herald Tribune*, October 14, 1943.
10. *New York Herald Tribune*, October 16, 1943.
11. *New York Herald Tribune*, October 28, 1943.
12. *New York Herald Tribune*, November 20, 1943.
13. Robert Citino, "Last Ride at Anzio: The German Counterattacks, February 1944," National WWII Museum, July 12, 2018, www.nationalww2museum.org/war/articles/last-ride-anzio-german-counterattacks-february-1944.
14. *New York Herald Tribune*, January 24, 1944.
15. *New York Herald Tribune*, February 1, 1944.
16. *New York Herald Tribune*, February 4, 1944.
17. *New York Herald Tribune*, February 19, 1944.
18. *New York Herald Tribune*, March 15, 1944.
19. Moseley, *Reporting War*, 225–26.
20. *New York Herald Tribune*, May 20, 1944.
21. *New York Herald Tribune*, March 27, 1944.
22. *New York Herald Tribune*, May 17, 1944.
23. Kluger, *The Paper*, 370.
24. *New York Herald Tribune*, July 3, 1944.
25. *New York Herald Tribune*, July 5, 1944.
26. *New York Herald Tribune*, August 22, 1944.
27. *New York Herald Tribune*, September 7, 1944.

4. The Pacific and the Bomb

1. Rothmyer interview.
2. Kluger interview.
3. *New York Herald Tribune*, November 15, 1944.
4. *New York Herald Tribune*, November 22, 1944.
5. *New York Herald Tribune*, January 14, 1945.
6. *New York Herald Tribune*, December 2, 1944.
7. *New York Herald Tribune*, February 19, 1945.
8. *New York Herald Tribune*, January 14, 1945.
9. *New York Herald Tribune*, January 23, 1945.

10. *New York Herald Tribune*, January 17, 1945.

11. *New York Herald Tribune*, January 25, 1945.

12. *New York Herald Tribune*, January 26, 1945.

13. *New York Herald Tribune*, January 29, 1945.

14. *New York Herald Tribune*, February 25, 1945.

15. *New York Herald Tribune*, February 8, 1945.

16. *New York Herald Tribune*, March 9, 1945.

17. *New York Herald Tribune*, March 13, 1945.

18. "Battle of Okinawa," History.com, last updated March 30, 2021, www.history.com/topics/world-war-ii/battle-of-okinawa#section_8.

19. *New York Herald Tribune*, April 2, 1945.

20. "Battle of Okinawa," National WWII Museum, accessed December 4, 2021, www.nationalww2museum.org/war/topics/battle-of-okinawa.

21. New York State Military Museum and Veterans Research Center, "The National Guard in War: An Historical Analysis of the 27th Infantry Division (New York National Guard) in World War II: Chapter Five—Saipan," accessed December 4, 2021, https://museum.dmna.ny.gov/unit-history/conflict/world-war-2-1939-1945/27th-infantry-division-world-war-two/national-guard-war-historical-analysis-2th-infantry-division-new-york-national-guard-world-war-ii/national-guard-war-historical-analysis-27th-infantry-division-new-york-national-guard-world-war-ii-chapter-five-saipan.

22. *New York Herald Tribune*, May 4, 1945.

23. Excerpted in *New York Herald Tribune*, June 17, 1945.

24. *New York Herald Tribune*, June 17, 1945.

25. *New York Herald Tribune*, June 18, 1945.

26. *New York Herald Tribune*, August 15, 1945.

27. *New York Herald Tribune*, September 2, 1945.

28. *New York Herald Tribune*, August 28, 1945.

29. Knightley, *First Casualty*, 300.

30. New York Herald Tribune, September 5, 1945.

31. Alex Wellerstein, email to author, July 16, 2020.

32. Rothmyer interview.

33. *New York Herald Tribune*, September 10, 1945.

34. *New York Herald Tribune*, September 13, 1945.

35. *New York Herald Tribune*, August 31, 1945.

36. *New York Herald Tribune*, May 8, 1945.

5. Cold War, Tough Calls

1. Hohenberg, *Foreign Correspondence*, 246.

2. *New York Herald Tribune*, June 17, 1946.

3. Barnes, "Foreign Reporting," in Herzberg, *Late City Edition*, 90.

4. Kluger interview.

5. *New York Herald Tribune*, February 21, 1949.

6. *New York Herald Tribune*, February 24, 1949.

7. Michael Schudson, *Discovering the News: A Social History of American Newspapers* (New York: Basic Books, 1978), 4.

8. Text in Dilip Hiro, *Dictionary of the Middle East* (New York: St. Martin's Press, 1966), 47–48.

9. League of Nations, "Mandate for Palestine," August 12, 1922, at Economic Cooperation Foundation's The Israeli-Palestinian Conflict: An Interactive Database, https://ecf.org.il/media_items/291.

10. *New York Herald Tribune*, December 30, 1946.

11. *New York Herald Tribune*, February 10, 1947.

12. *New York Herald Tribune*, May 17, 1947.

13. *New York Herald Tribune*, October 25, 1947.

14. Ed Lengel, "The Greek Civil War, 1944–1949," National WWII Museum, accessed December 4, 2021, https://www.nationalww2museum.org/war/articles/greek-civil-war-1944-1949.

15. Harry Truman, "President Harry S. Truman's Address before a Joint Session of Congress, March 12, 1947," Yale Law School Lillian Goldman Law Library, the Avalon Project, https://avalon.law.yale.edu/20th_century/trudoc.asp.

16. *New York Herald Tribune*, January 9, 1948.

17. *New York Herald Tribune*, January 25, 1948.

18. *New York Herald Tribune*, January 28, 1948.

19. *New York Herald Tribune*, February 19, 1948.

20. *New York Herald Tribune*, February 28, 1948.

21. Marton, *Polk Conspiracy*, 128.

22. Marton, 43; and Kluger, *The Paper*, 339.

23. National Archives, Athens post files, 1948.

24. *New York Herald Tribune*, April 8, 1948.

25. Marton, *Polk Conspiracy*, 134.

26. *New York Times*, October 28, 1990, section 7.

27. He was referring to a *New York Herald Tribune* article by Bigart published on February 1, 1948.

28. Rothmyer interview.

29. Bigart letter dated July 11, 1948.

30. Rothmyer interview.

31. Benjamin C. Bradlee, "Standards and Ethics," in *The* Washington Post *Deskbook on Style*, ed. Thomas W. Lippman (New York: McGraw-Hill, 1989), 4.

32. Marton, *Polk Conspiracy*, 195.

33. *Editor & Publisher*, March 19, 1949, 66.

34. Wade, *Forward Positions*, photo caption after page 182.

35. Marton, *Polk Conspiracy*, 197–212.

36. *Encyclopaedia Britannica*, s.v. "Markos Vafiades," accessed December 4, 2021, www.britannica.com/biography/Markos-Vafiades.

6. Two Wars in Korea

1. Halberstam, *Coldest Winter*, 102.

2. Mott, *American Journalism*, 848.

3. Bradlee, *Good Life*, 197.

4. Kluger, *The Paper*, 441.

5. Moseley, *Reporting War*, 266.

6. May, *Witness to War*, 124.

7. May, 125.

8. Higgins, *War in Korea*, 2.

9. Beech, *Tokyo and Points East*, 168.

10. Edwards, *Women of the World*, 201.

11. James A. Michener, introduction to Beech, *Tokyo and Points East*, 11–15.

12. Bigart letter to Richard Kluger, January 27, 1982, Kluger Papers.

13. Beech, *Tokyo and Points East*, 170.

14. Higgins, *War in Korea*, 65.

15. *LIFE*, October 2, 1950, 54.

16. Beech, *Tokyo and Points East*, 172.

17. Bigart letter to Kluger, January 27, 1982, Kluger Papers.

18. Beech, *Tokyo and Points East*, 172.

19. Beech, 178.

20. Prochnau, *Once upon a Distant War*, 341.

21. Kluger, *The Paper*, 444.

22. Higgins, *War in Korea*, 27.

23. Melvin Voorhees, *Korean Tales* (New York: Simon & Schuster, 1952), online edition, unpaginated, accessed December 5, 2021, https://archive.org/stream/koreantales 009201mbp/koreantales009201mbp_djvu.txt.

24. May, *Witness to War*, 154.

25. *New York Herald Tribune*, July 12, 1950.

26. A. J. Liebling, "The Wayward Press," *New Yorker,* August 12, 1950, 48.

27. *New York Herald Tribune*, July 23, 1950.

28. *New York Herald Tribune*, July 13, 1950.

29. *New York Herald Tribune*, August 22, 1950.

30. Goulden, *Korea*, 174.

31. *New York Herald Tribune*, July 31, 1950.

32. Joe Alsop column, "Matter of Fact," *New York Herald Tribune*, November 28, 1951.

33. *New York Herald Tribune*, September 18, 1950.

34. Kluger, *The Paper*, 448; and Bigart letter to Kluger, 1982, Kluger Papers.

35. Rothmyer interview.

36. Beech, *Tokyo and Points East*, 182–83.

37. Prochnau, *Once upon a Distant War*, 341.

38. *New York Herald Tribune*, September 4, 1950.

39. Bigart letter to Gladys, September 10, 1950.

40. *New York Herald Tribune*, December 6, 1950.

41. "Why We Got Licked," *LOOK*, January 16, 1951.

42. Associated Press dispatch, January 18, 1951; printed in many newspapers.

43. Voorhees, *Korean Tales*.

44. "Homer's Odyssey," *Newsweek*, January 22, 1951, 52.

45. "Marguerite Higgins Hits 'Red Beach,'" The Pulitzer Prizes, accessed December 5, 2021, https://www.pulitzer.org/article/marguerite-higgins-hits-red-beach.

7. The Red Menace at Home and Abroad

1. Aronson, *Press and the Cold War*, 78.

2. Kluger, *The Paper*, chap. 14.

3. *New York Herald Tribune*, April 15, 1949.

4. *New York Herald Tribune*, April 17, 1949.

5. *Washington Post*, February 4, 1999.

6. *New York Herald Tribune*, January 10, 1950.

7. *New York Herald Tribune*, January 13, 1950.

8. *New York Herald Tribune*, August 24, 1949.

9. Dean Acheson, *Present at the Creation: My Years in the State Department* (New York: W. W. Norton, 1969), 359–60; and *New York Times*, January 30, 1950.

10. *New York Herald Tribune*, August 14, 1952.

11. *New York Herald Tribune*, February 26, 1953.

12. *New York Herald Tribune*, February 18, 1949.

13. *New York Herald Tribune*, June 10, 1951.

14. *New York Herald Tribune*, June 24, 1951.

15. Community College Review, "Katharine Gibbs School–New York City," accessed December 6, 2021, www.communitycollegereview.com/katharine-gibbs-school-new-york-city-profile.

16. *New York Herald Tribune*, August 12, 1951.

17. Bigart letter of September 17, 1951.

18. Bigart letter of September 26, 1951.

19. Bigart letter of August 11, 1951.

20. Bigart letter of September 17, 1951.

21. Kluger, *The Paper*, 477.

22. Zwicker obituary, *New York Times*, August 12, 1991.

23. Kluger Papers.

24. *New York Herald Tribune*, March 20, 1954.

25. *New York Herald Tribune*, April 23, 1954.

26. *New York Herald Tribune*, April 27, 1954.

27. *New York Herald Tribune*, April 30, 1954.

28. *New York Herald Tribune*, May 5, 1954.

29. *New York Herald Tribune*, June 9, 1954.

30. U.S. Senate, "The Censure Case of Joseph McCarthy of Wisconsin (1954)," Powers & Procedures: Censure, accessed December 6, 2021, www.senate.gov/about/powers -procedures/censure/133Joseph_McCarthy.htm.

31. Kluger interview.

32. *Washington Post*, June 24, 1986.

33. Bigart letter of June 28, 1954.

34. *New York Herald Tribune*, June 26, 1954.

35. *New York Herald Tribune*, June 21, 1954.

36. *New York Herald Tribune*, July 3, 1954.

8. Leaving the Sinking Ship

1. Reid Family Papers.

2. Kluger, *The Paper*, 433.

3. Talese, *Kingdom and the Power*, 198.

4. Catledge, *My Life and the* Times, 171; Talese, *Kingdom and the Power*, 198; and Halberstam, *Powers That Be*, 219.

5. Kluger, *The Paper*, 725.

6. Halberstam, *Powers That Be*, 219.

7. Catledge, *My Life and the* Times, 136.

8. Halberstam, *Powers That Be*, 219.

9. Kluger interview.

10. Oral History interview.

11. Catledge Papers.

12. Oral History interview.

13. Oral History interview.

14. Oral History interview.

15. Obituary of Homer Bigart, *New York Times*, April 17, 1991.

16. Oral History interview.

17. Oral History interview.

18. Oral History interview.

19. Wade, *Forward Positions*, 161.

20. Bigart letter of May 29, 1956.

21. Wade, *Forward Positions*, 161.

22. Russell Baker, *The Good Times* (New York: William Morrow, 1989), 272–74.

23. Oral History interview.

24. Wade, *Forward Positions*, 161.

25. Daniel Gordis, *Israel: A Concise History of a Nation Reborn* (New York: Ecco, 2016), 328.

26. NYPL Foreign Desk Records.

27. *New York Times*, June 24, 1956.

28. NYPL Foreign Desk Records.

29. NYPL Foreign Desk Records.

30. Oral History interview.

31. Gelb, *City Room*, 249.

32. *New York Times*, October 29, 1956.

33. Thomas W. Lippman, *Crude Oil, Crude Money: Aristotle Onassis, Saudi Arabia, and the CIA* (Santa Barbara: Praeger, 2019), 207; and History.com, "Suez Crisis," last updated April 27, 2021, www.history.com/topics/cold-war/suez-crisis.

34. *New York Times*, November 3, 1956.

35. NYPL Foreign Desk Records.

36. *New York Times*, February 2, 1957.

37. NYPL Foreign Desk Records.

38. NYPL Foreign Desk Records.

39. Bigart archive, Wayne County Historical Society, Honesdale PA.

40. Oral History interview.

41. *New York Times*, June 8, 1961.

42. *New York Times*, June 4, 1961.

43. *New York Times*, September 8, 1963.

44. *New York Times Book Review*, September 8, 1963.

45. NYPL Foreign Desk Records, letter of December 21, 1961.

46. Wade, *Forward Positions*, 230.

47. Wade, 230.

48. *New York Times*, November 23, 1961.

49. Wade, *Forward Positions*, 230.

50. Catledge Papers.

51. *New York Times*, August 10, 1966.

9. Cuba, Congo, and Cannibals

1. Phillips obituary, *New York Times*, October 30, 1985.

2. *New York Times*, February 24, 1957.

3. *New York Times*, June 9, 1957.

4. *American Legion Magazine*, March 1961, 18.

5. Hugh Thomas, "The U.S. and Castro, 1959–1962," *American Heritage*, October–November 1978.

6. NYPL Foreign Desk Records.

7. Oral History interview.

8. NYPL Foreign Desk Records.

9. Oral History interview.

10. *Foreign Relations of the United States, 1858–1960*, vol. 6, *Cuba* (Washington, DC: Government Printing Office, 1991), document no. 686, pp. 38–42.

11. *New York Times*, February 27, 1958.

12. Teel, *Reporting the Cuban Revolution*, 123.

13. *New York Times*, March 3, 1958.

14. Catledge Papers.

15. *New York Times*, April 9, 1958.

16. *New York Times*, April 15, 1958.

17. *New York Times*, April 19, 1959; and Teel, *Reporting the Cuban Revolution*, 3–4.

18. Teel, 186.

19. Catledge, *My Life and the* Times, 267.

20. *New York Times*, December 24, 1959.

21. *New York Times Magazine*, June 26, 1960.

22. *New York Times*, December 24, 1959.

23. Catledge Papers, letter of January 7, 1960.

24. "West Africa: Cocoa and Cannibalism," *Times Talk*, February 1960, found in Ruth Adler, ed., *The Working Press: Special to* The New York Times (New York: Putnam, 1966), 139–42.

25. NYPL Foreign Desk Records.

26. NYPL Foreign Desk Records.

27. NYPL Foreign Desk Records.

28. NYPL Foreign Desk Records.

29. *New York Times*, April 3, 1960.

30. NYPL Foreign Desk Records.

31. NYPL Foreign Desk Records.

32. *New York Times*, January 3, 1960.

33. *New York Times*, January 25, 1960.

34. NYPL Foreign Desk Records.

35. For a full account of the Cold War in Africa, see Piero Gleijses, *Conflicting Missions: Havana, Washington, and Africa, 1959–1976* (Chapel Hill: University of North Carolina Press, 2002).

10. Reality Check in Vietnam

1. Karnow, *Vietnam*, 254.

2. *New York Times*, March 22, 1961.

3. *New York Times*, December 31, 1961.

4. Malcolm W. Browne, "The Fighting Words of Homer Bigart: A War Correspondent Is Never a Cheerleader," *New York Times Book Review*, April 11, 1993.

5. Oral History interview.

6. Oral History interview.

7. Browne, "Fighting Words," note 4.

8. NYPL Foreign Desk Records.

9. NYPL Foreign Desk Records.

10. NYPL Foreign Desk Records.

11. *New York Times*, January 8, 1962.

12. *New York Times*, January 11, 1962.

13. *New York Times*, January 18, 1962.

14. *New York Times*, February 2, 1962.

15. *New York Times*, February 25, 1962.

16. *New York Times*, February 10, 1962.

17. *New York Times*, March 25, 1962.

18. Frederick Nolting, "Telegram from the Embassy in Vietnam to the Department of State, Saigon, February 6, 1962," in *Foreign Relations of the United States, 1961–1963*, vol. 2, *Vietnam, 1962* (Washington, DC: Government Printing Office, 1990), document 48, https://history.state.gov/historicaldocuments/frus1961-63v02/d48.

19. Dean Rusk, "Telegram from the Department of State to the Embassy in Vietnam, Washington, February 21, 1962," in Glennon, Baehler, and Sampson, document 75, https://history.state.gov/historicaldocuments/frus1961-63v02/d75.

20. John F. Kennedy, "The President's News Conference, February 14, 1962," The American Presidency Project by Gerhard Peters and John T. Wooley, https://www.presidency.ucsb.edu/documents/the-presidents-news-conference-175.

21. James D. Rosenthal, interview by Charles Stuart Kennedy, May 24, 1996, Academy for Diplomatic Studies and Training Oral History Project, Library of Congress, tile.loc.gov/storage-services/service/mss/mfdip/2004/2004ros02/2004ros02.pdf.

22. Wade, *Forward Positions*, 85.

23. *New York Times*, February 9, 1962.

24. *New York Times*, March 9, 1962.

25. NYPL Foreign Desk Records.

26. Oral History interview.

27. Wade, *Forward Positions*, xxii.

28. NYPL Foreign Desk Records.

29. "Heave Ho, Vietnamese Style," *Times Talk*, April 1962.

30. Wade, *Forward Positions*, 195–98.

31. Catledge Papers.

32. Oral History interview.

33. Catledge Papers.

34. NYPL Foreign Desk Records.

35. Frances FitzGerald, *Fire in the Lake: The Vietnamese and the Americans in Vietnam* (New York: Vintage Books, 1972), 165.

36. Dean Rusk, "Telegram from the Department of State to the Embassy in Vietnam, Washington, April 4, 1962," in *Foreign Relations of the United States, Vietnam, 1962*, document 145, https://history.state.gov/historicaldocuments/frus1961-63v02/d145.

37. *New York Times*, April 24, 1962.

38. Mecklin, *Mission in Torment*, 103–5.

39. Catledge Papers.

40. Bigart letter of May 27, 1962.

41. Bigart letter of May 27, 1962.

42. "Heave Ho, Vietnamese Style," *Times Talk*, April 1962.

43. NYPL Foreign Desk Records.

44. *New York Times*, May 14, 1962.

45. Salisbury, *Without Fear or Favor*, 38–39.

46. Wade, *Forward Positions*, 209.

47. Sheehan Papers.

48. Halberstam, *Making of a Quagmire*, 1.

49. *New York Times*, June 11, 1970.

50. "My Lai Massacre," History.com, accessed December 6, 2021, https://www.history.com/topics/vietnam-war/my-lai-massacre-1.

51. *New York Times*, March 30, 1971.

52. *New York Times*, December 16, 1970.

53. *New York Times*, December 5, 1970.

54. *New York Times*, March 31, 1971.

55. Joyce K. Thornton, "Calley, William Laws, Jr.," accessed December 6, 2021, https://www.encyclopedia.com/humanities/encyclopedias-almanacs-transcripts-and-maps/calley-william-laws-jr.

11. The Great Strike and a New Alice

1. A. H. Raskin, "The Strike: A Step-by-Step Account," *New York Times*, April 1, 1963.

2. Talese, *Kingdom and the Power*, 303–4.

3. Scott Sherman, "The Long Good-Bye," *Vanity Fair*, November 30, 2012, www.vanityfair.com/culture/2012/11/1963-newspaper-strike-bertram-powers.

4. *Editor & Publisher*, October 11, 1962.

5. Davies, *Postwar Decline*, 11.

6. Kluger, *The Paper*, 649.

7. Raskin, "The Strike."

8. Kluger Papers.

9. Kluger, *The Paper*, 652.

10. *Editor & Publisher*, December 15, 1962.

11. Sherman, "Long Good-Bye."

12. *Editor & Publisher*, January 12, 1962.

13. These details can be found in Raskin, "The Strike"; Sherman, "Long Good-Bye"; and Kluger, *The Paper*.

14. CBS News Release, December 28, 1962, box 28, Bliss Papers, American University Library, Washington, DC.

15. Gelb, *City Room*, 407–10.

16. Homer Bigart, "An Historic Mission," in *The Pope's Journey to the United States*, ed. A. M. Rosenthal and Arthur Gelb (New York: Bantam Books, 1965), 1–8.

17. Kluger, *The Paper*, 716.

18. Amory H. Bradford Papers, New York Times Company Records, 1946–75, box 3, New York Public Library.

19. Davies, *Postwar Decline*, 126.

20. Topping, *On the Front Lines*, 221.

21. *New York Times*, December 8, 1963.

22. The Links Club, "Guests," accessed December 7, 2021, https://www.thelinksclub .org/guests.

23. Bradford Papers, box 2.

24. Kluger, *The Paper*, 660.

25. *New York Times*, August 16, 1966.

26. Text of Powers's testimony in Kluger Papers.

27. CBS news release, Bliss Papers, box 28.

28. Hosley and Yamada, *Hard News*, 48–49.

29. *Greenfield (IN) Daily Reporter*, September 9, 1960.

12. Civil Rights in Many Forms

1. National Advisory Commission on Civil Disorders, *Report of the National Advisory Commission on Civil Disorders* (Rockville, MD: National Institute of Justice, 1967), www .ojp.gov/ncjrs/virtual-library/abstracts/national-advisory-commission-civil-disorders -report.

2. Bradlee, *Good Life*, 113.

3. Catledge, *My Life and the* Times, 219.

4. Salisbury, *Without Fear or Favor*, 357.

5. Catledge, *My Life and the* Times, 219.

6. Talese, *Kingdom and the Power*, 391.

7. Oral History interview.

8. *New York Times*, September 19, 1957.

9. *New York Times*, September 26, 1957.

10. Letter of October 1, 1957, Catledge Papers.

11. *New York Times*, September 29, 1962.

12. Roberts and Klibanoff, *Race Beat*, 372.

13. "Racial Conflict, North and South," *Times Talk*, August 1964.

14. Mississippi Civil Rights Project, "The Murder of Chaney, Goodman, and Schwerner," accessed December 7, 2021, https://mscivilrightsproject.org/neshoba/event -neshoba/the-murder-of-chaney-goodman-and-schwerner/.

15. John Herbers, "Judgmental Reporting," *Nieman Reports* 48, no. 4 (Winter 1994): 3, https://niemanreports.org/wp-content/uploads/2014/04/Winter-1994_150.pdf.

16. Catledge Papers.

17. *New York Times*, July 9, 1964.

18. *New York Times*, August 11, 1965.

19. *Saturday Review*, April 22, 1967, 54.

20. *New York Times*, May 3, 1964.

21. *New York Times*, June 20, 1972.

22. Wade, *Forward Positions*, xviii.

23. Memo of October 8, 1963, Catledge Papers.

24. *New York Times*, December 6, 1962.

25. Pat Gish, "In the Midst of Poverty, People's Stories Are Hard to Tell," *Nieman Reports*, June 15, 1999, https://niemanreports.org/articles/in-the-midst-of-poverty-peoples -stories-are-hard-to-tell/.

26. Oral History interview.

27. *New York Times*, June 18, 1971.

28. First article of series, *New York Times*, February 16, 1969.

29. Hon. William F. Ryan, "Extensions of Remarks: Hunger in America, February 17, 1969," *Congressional Record*, vol. 115, pt. 3 (Washington, DC: Government Federal Printing Office, 1969), 3812–14, https://www.congress.gov/91/crecb/1969/02/18/GPO -CRECB-1969-pt3-5-3.pdf.

30. *New York Times*, June 15, 1971.

31. *New York Times*, June 18, 1971.

32. *New York Times*, March 13, 1966.

33. Jon Marcus, "Bringing American Studies to a National Audience," *Nieman Reports*, February 11, 2016, https://niemanreports.org/articles/bringing-native-american-stories-to-a -national-audience/.

13. The Long Roads End

1. Wade, *Forward Positions*, 231.

2. Bigart obituary, *New York Times*, April 17, 1991.

3. *New York Times*, April 9, 1972.

4. *Baltimore Sun*, November 10, 2007.

5. Wade, *Forward Positions*, 231.

6. Oral History interview.

7. Rosenthal Papers.

8. Rosenthal Papers.

9. *New York Times*, November 25, 1980.

10. Oral History interview.

11. Undated essay, Al Burt Papers, Special Area Studies Collections, George A. Smathers Libraries, University of Florida, Gainesville.

12. Karen Rothmyer, "The Quiet Exit of Homer Bigart," *American Journalism Review*, November 1991, https://ajrarchive.org/Article.asp?id=1543.

13. *New Republic*, January 22, 1977.

14. *New Republic*, May 27, 1978.

15. *New York Times*, April 20, 1991.

16. Richard Reeves syndicated column, as printed in the *Appleton (WI) Post-Crescent*, April 20, 1991.

Epilogue

1. "About Us," *Coffee or Die Magazine*, accessed December 7, 2021, https://coffeeordie .com/about/.

2. Andy Barr, "Palin Trashes 'Lamestream Media,'" *Politico*, November 18, 2009, www.politico.com/story/2009/11/palin-trashes-lamestream-media-029693.

3. *New York Times*, August 4, 2019.

4. *Washington Post*, November 9, 2021.

5. *New York Times*, June 21, 2021.

6. Barbara Roessner, "A Message from the Editor," *New Bedford Light*, accessed December 7, 2021, https://newbedfordlight.org/a-message-from-the-editor-barbara-roessner/.

7. *Washington Post*, October 26, 2021.

8. "About," The Lenfest Institute, accessed December 7, 2021, www.lenfestinstitute.org/about/.

SELECTED BIBLIOGRAPHY

Note to the Reader

The sources that appear in this bibliography are cited in their short form in the endnotes, while sources that do not appear in this bibliography are cited in their long form.

Archival Sources

Homer Bigart wrote no memoir and kept no diary, nor is there any previous biography about him. There are, however, extensive documentary resources about his life and career. The following principal archives of documents and letters are cited in the reference notes.

Bigart, Homer. Archive. Wayne County Historical Society, Honesdale, PA.

———. Letters to his family. Wisconsin State Historical Society, Madison. Cited by date.

Catledge, Turner. Papers. Mississippi State University Library, Starkville. Cited as Catledge Papers.

Kluger, Richard. Papers. Boxes 2, 6, and 9. Sterling Memorial Library, Yale University, New Haven, CT. Cited as Kluger Papers.

New York Times. Foreign Desk records, boxes 5 and 6. New York Public Library. Cited as NYPL Foreign Desk Records.

Reid Family. Papers. Whitelaw Reid correspondence, part III, box 5, folder 7. Library of Congress, Washington, DC. Cited as Reid Family Papers.

Rosenthal, A. M. Papers. Series 1, box 5, folder 5.6. New York Public Library. Cited as Rosenthal Papers.

Sheehan, Neil. Papers. Professional files, box 224, folder 11. Library of Congress, Washington, DC. Cited as Sheehan Papers.

Homer Bigart gave three extended interviews that are cited in the reference notes.

Clark, Mary Marshall. *New York Times* interviews for the Columbia University oral history program, August 11, 1987. Cited as Oral history interview. Transcripts of most of these interviews are available at the New York Public Library, but Bigart's is not. The author obtained a partial transcript from private sources.

Kluger, Richard. Transcript in his papers, Yale University. Cited as Kluger interview.

Rothmyer, Karen. Transcript in her book *Winning Pulitzers* (Columbia University Press, 1991), 66–68. Cited as Rothmyer interview.

Published Sources

Aronson, James. *The Press and the Cold War*. New York: Monthly Review Press, 1970.

Barnes, Joseph A. "Foreign Reporting." In *Late City Edition*, edited by Joseph G. Herzberg, 83–92. Hamden, CT: Archon Books, 1969.

Beech, Keyes. *Tokyo and Points East*. Garden City, NY: Doubleday, 1954.

Bradlee, Ben. *A Good Life: Newspapering and Other Adventures*. New York: Simon & Schuster, 1995.

Braestrup, Peter. *Big Story: How the American Press and Television Reported and Interpreted the Crisis of Tet 1968 in Vietnam and Washington*. Boulder, CO: Westview Press, 1977.

Catledge, Turner. *My Life and the* Times. New York: Harper & Row, 1971.

Cronkite, Walter. *A Reporter's Life*. New York: Ballantine Books, 1997.

Davies, David R. *The Postwar Decline of American Newspapers, 1945–1965*. Westport, CT: Praeger Publishers, 2006.

Edwards, Julia. *Women of the World: The Great Foreign Correspondents*. Boston: Houghton Mifflin, 1948.

Gelb, Arthur. *City Room*. New York: G. P. Putnam's Sons, 2003.

Goulden, Joseph C. *Korea: The Untold Story of the War*. New York: Times Books, 1982.

Halberstam, David. *The Coldest Winter: America and the Korean War*. New York: Hyperion, 2007.

———. *The Making of a Quagmire: America and Vietnam during the Kennedy Era*. New York: Rowman & Littlefield, 1965.

———. *The Powers That Be*. New York: Alfred A. Knopf, 1979.

Hamilton, Jim. *The Writing 69th*. Privately printed, 1999.

Higgins, Marguerite. *War in Korea: Marguerite Higgins Reports from the Front Lines*. Uncommon Valor Reprint Series. Garden City, NY: Doubleday, 1951.

Hohenberg, John. *Foreign Correspondence: The Great Reporters and Their Times*. 2nd ed. Syracuse, NY: Syracuse University Press, 1995.

Hosley, David H., and Gayle K. Yamada. *Hard News: Women in Broadcast Journalism*. Westport, CT: Praeger, 1987.

Karnow, Stanley. *Vietnam: A History*. New York: Viking Press, 1983.

Kluger, Richard. *The Paper: The Life and Death of the* New York Herald Tribune. New York: Alfred A. Knopf, 1986.

Knightley, Phillip. *The First Casualty: From the Crimea to Vietnam; The War Correspondent as Hero, Propagandist, and Myth Maker*. New York: Harcourt Brace Jovanovich, 1975.

Marton, Kati. *The Polk Conspiracy: Murder and Cover-Up in the Case of CBS News Correspondent George Polk.* New York: Times Books, 1990.

May, Antoinette. *Witness to War: A Biography of Marguerite Higgins.* New York: Beaufort Books, 1983.

Mecklin, John. *Mission in Torment: An Intimate Account of the U.S. Role in Vietnam.* Garden City, NY: Doubleday, 1965.

Moseley, Ray. *Reporting War: How Journalists Risked Capture, Torture and Death to Cover World War II.* New Haven, CT: Yale University Press, 2017.

Mott, Frank Luther. *American Journalism: A History, 1690–1930.* New York: Macmillan, 1962.

Prochnau, William. *Once upon a Distant War.* New York: Times Books, 1995.

Roberts, Gene, and Hank Klibanoff. *The Race Beat: The Press, the Civil Rights Struggle, and the Awakening of a Nation.* New York: Alfred A. Knopf, 2006.

Rooney, Andy. *My War.* New York: Public Affairs, 2000.

Rothmyer, Karen. *Winning Pulitzers: The Stories behind Some of the Best News Coverage of Our Time.* New York: Columbia University Press, 1991.

Salisbury, Harrison. *A Journey for Our Times: A Memoir.* New York: Carroll & Graf, 1983.

———. *Without Fear or Favor: An Uncompromising Look at the* New York Times. New York: Ballantine Books, 1981.

Talese, Gay. *The Kingdom and the Power.* Cleveland: World Publishing, 1969.

Teel, Leonard Ray. *Reporting the Cuban Revolution: How Castro Manipulated American Journalists.* Baton Rouge: Louisiana State University Press, 2015.

Topping, Seymour. *On the Front Lines of the Cold War: An American Correspondent's Journal from the Chinese Civil War to the Cuban Missile Crisis and Vietnam.* Baton Rouge: Louisiana State University Press, 2010.

Wade, Betsy, ed. *Forward Positions: The War Correspondence of Homer Bigart.* Fayetteville: University of Arkansas Press, 1992.

Walker, Stanley. *City Editor.* Baltimore: Johns Hopkins University Press, 1999.

INDEX

Note: Illustrations are indicated by page numbers in *italics*.

ABOUT THE AUTHOR

Thomas W. Lippman is a Washington-based author and journalist who has specialized in Middle Eastern affairs and US foreign policy for more than four decades. He was a reporter and editor at major newspapers for forty years and is a former Middle East bureau chief and Vietnam correspondent of the *Washington Post*. The author of nine books, including most recently *Crude Oil, Crude Money: Aristotle Onassis, Saudi Arabia, and the CIA* (Praeger, 2019), Lippman won the 2009 Benjamin Franklin Award for biography from the Independent Book Publishers Association for his profile of another unsung hero, Col. Bill Eddy (USMC).